North of America

```
PS      Doyle, James, 1937-
217
.C34    North of America
D68
1983
```

DATE			
FEB	1992	JUN	'86

KVCC KALAMAZOO VALLEY COMMUNITY COLLEGE LIBRARY

59973

KER & TAYLOR CO.

Contents

	INTRODUCTION	1
I	COLONIAL AND EARLY REPUBLICAN IMAGES	9
II	FRENCH CANADA	21
III	"A YANKEE IN CANADA"	32
IV	THE CANADIAN PAST: THE IDYLL OF ACADIA	40
V	THE CANADIAN PAST: THE ROMANCE OF NEW FRANCE	47
VI	FRANCE AND ENGLAND IN NORTH AMERICA	57
VII	ENGLISH CANADA: TRAVELLERS, PATRIOTS, AND FUGITIVES	72
VIII	THE NORTHEASTERN FRONTIER	85
IX	POST-CIVIL-WAR LITERARY TRAVELLERS	96
X	SPORTSMEN AND TOURISTS	113

XI	CHARLES HAIGHT FARNHAM AND WALT WHITMAN	121
XII	THE NORTHWESTERN FRONTIER	130
	CONCLUSION	147
	NOTES	153
	LIST OF WORKS CITED	165
	INDEX	177

ACKNOWLEDGMENTS

Parts of chapters of this book have appeared, in slightly different versions, in various periodicals, as follows: chapter 7, *The Journal of Canadian Culture*; chapter 11, *The University of Toronto Quarterly*; chapter 12, *Essays on Canadian Writing* and *Great Plains Quarterly*. I am grateful to the editors of these periodicals for permission to reprint the relevant material.

I have received invaluable assistance from the staff of the special-collections department of the University of British Columbia library, which possesses much of the rare published materials—particularly travel books and fiction—quoted or referred to in this study. I acknowledge also the kind help of librarians at the New York Public Library and the University of Minnesota, both of which have distinguished collections of dime novels.

I am grateful to Wilfrid Laurier University for awarding me a research fellowship in 1980, which enabled me to complete some of the research and writing for this book.

This book has been published with the help of a grant from the Canadian Federation for the Humanities using funds provided by the Social Sciences and Humanities Research Council of Canada. Additional grants were made available from the Ontario Arts Council and The Canada Council.

INTRODUCTION

In the imaginative literature of the United States, as in other expressions of the thought and experience of that complex nation, Canada has perennially figured as a vague, peripheral, and ambiguous concept. Those relatively few authors who have travelled northward, whether actually or imaginatively, have reported a kaleidoscopic variety of images involving strangeness and familiarity, hostility and friendliness, primitive wilderness and modern civilization. To the inhabitants of the colonies that ultimately comprised the United States, Canada was a remote stronghold of French popery and Indian barbarism. To many post-Revolution authors, such as the Georgia humourist William Tappan Thompson in his *Major Jones's Sketches of Travel* (1848), Canada was the last retreat of decadent British imperialism in the New World; in Henry Wadsworth Longfellow's *Evangeline* (1847), part of the northern regions appears as an idyllic vision of pre-lapsarian peace and contentment. Henry Thoreau, after visiting Quebec City and environs in 1850, wondered in "A Yankee in Canada" whether he had found a grim, sub-arctic region of exploration and adventure, or some fantasy world of mediaeval romance. On the other hand, Thoreau's contemporary Richard Henry Dana recorded in his journal an excursion to the same region in 1853, where he found a well-ordered, modern society. The New England historian Francis Parkman, in his multi-volumed *France and England in North America* (1865-92), struggled to explain the ambiguities and contradictions of New France; and William Dean Howells, writing of Quebec province in 1871, frankly acknowledged his inability to comprehend the region. "It is not America," he observed in his novel *Their Wedding Journey*; "if it is not France, what is it?"[1]

If nineteenth-century American literary artists were baffled by the northern geographical and social extensions of the continent, twentieth-century American students of cultural history have shown little interest in the subject of their country's literary image of Canada. Seminal works such as Henry Nash Smith's *Virgin Land* (1950), R. W. B. Lewis's *The American Adam* (1955), Leo Marx's *The Machine in the Garden* (1964), and Howard Mumford Jones's *O Strange New World* (1964) have described the evolution of American literary conceptions of the encounter between a European, Enlightenment-formed sensibility and a virtually untouched, ostensibly infinite continent; but none of these studies has examined, or even mentioned, the American response to Canada. Literary scholars have occasionally given individual consideration to the work of authors such as Francis Parkman or William Dean Howells, who wrote about Canada, but there have been no sustained attempts at a synthesis of the American literary image of the country. A doctoral dissertation by Joseph-Delphis Gauthier, *Le Canada français et le roman américain (1826-1948)* (Laval, 1948), has considered the subject in terms of the ethnic, generic, and chronological limitations indicated in the title; but the author is much more interested in "le Canada français" than in "le roman américain," with the result that his commentary consists almost entirely of demonstrating the inaccuracies of the American literary image of French Canada.

This neglect of the subject of the American imaginative representation of Canada is obviously related to the comparative paucity and insignificance of the images of the northern country in the American literary tradition. With the possible exception of Parkman's epic work of historiography, there are no American literary masterpieces dealing with Canada; there is nothing to compare, for instance, with Herman Melville's evocation of the sea, or Henry James's depiction of Europe. When major writers like James, Whitman, Howells, or Thoreau turn their attention briefly to Canada, the results are frequently disappointing in comparison to their best-known works. The American literary interest in Canada is most evident in the travel narrative and the adventure novel, genres that have frequently attracted the second-rate writer or the minor efforts of the first-rate one. Nevertheless, Canada is a small but indisputable part of the mosaic of American literary images, and the conception of the country as it appears in both casual popular writing and more rigorously artistic efforts deserves scrutiny.

The variety and uncertainty of American literary responses to Canada can be related to the turmoil of social, political, and cultural forces that constitutes the early history of the North American continent. Both "the

United States" and "Canada" are labels that have referred, at various times, to widely divergent sets of political and geographical facts; these facts, furthermore, especially in the first two hundred years of European exploration and settlement, were constantly changing with rapidity and violence. The writers who have tried to give literary embodiment to this perennial state of change have themselves been subjected to various influences. It is not surprising, for instance, to find a divergence of opinion between the Boston Brahmin Dana and the anarchistic transcendentalist Thoreau, or between the ante-bellum southern humourist Thompson and the post-war midwestern realist Howells. Individual authors, furthermore, often had preconceived notions of the continent and specialized purposes in writing to which their impressions of Canada were related, often with little regard for empirical reality. Republican authors are liable to distort or overlook the virtues of a colonial society in their zeal to demonstrate the superiority of their own political convictions. Charles Dudley Warner, on the basis of a hasty glance at Cape Breton Island in 1874, dismissed the whole of the new Dominion as "a foggy land... which is neither a republic nor a monarchy, but merely a languid expectation of something undefined."[2] And there is the extreme case of Longfellow, who never visited Nova Scotia, perhaps in order not to disturb his imaginative conception of Acadia.

In partial justification of Longfellow and other American writers, however, it can be argued that the imaginative author has less obligation to empirical reality than to his own subjective visions, or to the conventions of the literary tradition in which he is working. Longfellow was attempting to create a poetic myth of Arcadia, not a factual discourse on Acadia; Charles Dudley Warner's *Baddeck* is an attempt to imitate the comic-travelogue genre developed by Mark Twain and other American writers; and one purpose of *Major Jones's Sketches of Travel* is to defend southern aristocratic plantation society. In any work purporting to deal with a foreign society and culture, the real subject can almost always be discerned as the author's own national—or even personal—experience, rather than that of the country he is examining. Thus Francis Parkman's study of pre-conquest Canada resolves into an attempt to demonstrate how the libertarian impulses of New England eventually prevailed over the absolutist customs and institutions of New France.

This egocentricity of American culture can, however, be related to a more comprehensive context than mere self-absorption. The intelligent and imaginative American who writes about Canada—or about any foreign country—is most likely to be preoccupied by a theme that pervades his national literature: the meaning of the New World. For the citizen of the United States, the "New World" and "America" are liable to be interchangeable terms. It is not that he is unconscious of the nationalistic aspirations of Canada or the countries of Latin America, but his own national experience is at the centre of his perceptions of the western hemisphere. This bias of perception, which all cultures experience to some degree, is reinforced in the United States by a long tradition of belief that America represents a climactic stage in human history. This belief informs the visions of the City on the Hill and the New Jerusalem, which can be found in the writings of the Pilgrims of Plymouth and the Puritans of Massachusetts Bay, and it has by no means been excluded from the literature of the twentieth century.

But the conception of America as a new land of promise, offering infinite opportunity and a new beginning for mankind, is most extensively reflected in the literature of the nineteenth century. Once the political independence of the new republic was established, American writers set to work on the related tasks of representing imaginatively their country's collective aspirations and asserting its cultural as well as its political uniqueness. When Ralph Waldo Emerson exhorted his countrymen in his essay "Nature" (1836) to throw off the influence of the past and of Europe and make their cultural declaration of independence, he was giving rhetorical expression to impulses that had been experienced by the Puritans and Pilgrims, by eighteenth-century revolutionaries, and by many would-be artists in early nineteenth-century America who hoped to contribute to the development of a national culture. The themes of the New World, Modernism, the New Eden, Utopia, and many other terms and images, all more or less synonymous with America, pervade the literature of the nineteenth-century United States. All potential objects of inspiration sooner or later were gathered into the immensely rich tradition that emerged as if in response to Emerson's appeal; and far off on the periphery of America's consciousness but resolutely gathered into this tradition, far off in the remote and formidable north, was Canada.

The Canada that appears in nineteenth-century American literature is not always the country its own inhabitants know. But neither is it always the Canada of popular cliché, the country of frozen wastes and cheerful French woodsmen, although these and similar stereotypes occur frequently enough. In the most artistically significant versions, the image of the northern country is a vague, enigmatic variation on the geographical and historical experience of the United States, not quite impressive enough to constitute a serious challenge to the assumptions and values of the republic but prominent enough to be seriously contemplated and at times vigorously refuted. Immediately after the Revolution a few American writers turned their attention northward to consider the implications of the Canadian rejection of independence, and for the next century and more the northern provinces were to provoke reconsideration, in the minds of a few Americans at least, of questions relating to the vital centre of American political experience. Nineteenth-century Americans often assumed that Canadians would be a pioneering people like themselves, engaged in a struggle to subjugate the continent in accordance with prevalent notions about progress and the relationship between man and nature. But besides having rejected American ideas of political independence, some Canadians were quite different from Americans in their insistence on retaining decadent European habits of conduct, language, and belief, and in their apparent indifference to the gospel of progress. To further complicate matters, there were important differences between the American and the Canadian pasts. The nineteenth-century United States was creating an indigenous body of legend involving Pilgrim fathers, revolutionary heroes, and frontier adventurers, who were all being moulded into the representation of an aggressive and individualistic notion of liberty. The Canadian chronicle, however, presented a confusing panorama of French colonial despots, aristocratic societies, French and English conflict, and finally a rather placid and unheroic chronicle of migration and settlement, emphasizing communal rather than individual activity. The setting for these events, furthermore, was not always consistent with American imaginative conceptions of the New World. Instead of being located on the edge of an infinitely expanding and readily accessible frontier, Canadian settlements usually gave onto a cold and hostile wilderness where survival, let alone subjugation of nature, seemed scarcely possible.

The earliest American literary responses to Canada emerged in the form of the travel narrative, that immensely popular nineteenth-century literary genre that appealed to the people of the United States for its democratic accessibility as a medium of expression for even the most casual and uncreative of tourists. Early republican travellers largely confined their excursions to what guidebooks came to call the "northern" or "fashionable" tour, which usually included Montreal, Quebec, the farming region on the St. Lawrence, and, for the more adventurous, the Montmorenci and Saguenay regions. Inevitably, they were struck by the air of foreignness about these places, and particularly by the indifference of local inhabitants to what Americans took to be self-evident assumptions about the direction of history in the New World. Many of the authors of early travel narratives were surprisingly tolerant of the omnipresent images of British colonialism and militarism in Montreal and Quebec, for the hierarchical, authoritarian societies were not uncongenial to the conservative sensibilities of prosperous and cultured travellers from Boston and New York. The French-Canadians, on the other hand, were almost always objects of suspicion, and their leisurely, rural way of life and their supposedly decadent religious institutions were objects of contempt.

This antagonism to French Canada was evident, also, in the literary exploitation of the past. Nineteenth-century Americans, even as they claimed to be committed to modernism and the future, were fascinated by the past, as is demonstrated by the immense popularity of historical romances as well as more formal and supposedly factual works of historiography. In the efforts of fictionists like James Fenimore Cooper and his many disciples and imitators, and historians such as George Bancroft and Francis Parkman, there was emerging an indigenous mythology emphasizing the self-reliant, rugged individualism associated with the early stages of white settlement and political experience in the regions that ultimately comprised the United States. In this context, the Canadian past—as represented particularly by the undemocratic and militaristic society of New France—seemed opposed to what Americans took to be the inevitable course of history in the New World. Although heroes such as Champlain or Montcalm might be seen as prototypes of the American individualist, the decline and fall of New France was seen as a justification of Anglo-American political and social experiences and beliefs.

But American attitudes towards Canada continued to shift and change throughout the nineteenth century as a result of a great number of factors, including the inclinations of individual authors, social and aesthetic influences on literary activity, and the constant evolution of political and sociological circumstances on both sides of the border. After the American Civil War, for instance, some American writers expressed scepticism and pessimism about the course of United States history, and sympathy for alternative possibilities such as Canada potentially represented. Many of the old prejudices, against Roman Catholicism and British imperialism, or against the idea of the formidable northern wilderness, remained; but there was some feeling that such disadvantages might be preferable to the corruption and cynicism towards which life in the United States seemed to be moving. At least as early as Longfellow's *Evangeline*, there had been a strain of fantasy and idealization in the American literary image of Canada; but in the last decades of the century this idealization took on more concrete and realistic forms.

At the same time, however, there were American authors who continued to expound the nationalist rhetoric defending the essential validity and inevitability of republicanism in the New World. This continuation or renewal of faith in America was particularly associated with the post-war westward movement, and expressed in the vigorous expositions of "Manifest Destiny" among politicians, journalists, and popular authors, who envisaged the ultimate domination of Anglo-Saxon American republicanism over the whole western hemisphere. As the Canadian western frontier opened in the 1880s, particularly after the completion of the transcontinental Canadian Pacific Railway, and American immigrants poured over the border into Manitoba, Saskatchewan, and Alberta, the American literary image of Canada more and more emphasized the geographical and sociological unity of the continent as a whole. "Manitoba is western in its spirit and its sympathies," wrote Charles Dudley Warner in his "Comments on Canada" (1890),[3] as he admired the American spirit of enterprise and frontier adventure in the city of Winnipeg; and his belief in Canada's westward, continental destiny and its unity of aim and experience with the United States was echoed in such works as W. H. H. Murray's *Daylight Land* (1888), Julian Ralph's *On Canada's Frontier* (1892), and with special emphasis in Samuel E. Moffett's dogmatic *The Americanization of Canada* (1907).

Not all American literary chroniclers of the westward movement were gratified by the prospect of continental unity, however. Emerson Hough, author of the popular historical novel of westward migration *The Covered Wagon* (1922), argued, in an idiosyncratic book-length essay, *The Sowing* (1909), that an independent Canada might stand a chance of avoiding the many mistakes committed by Americans in the settlement of their western regions. And on a more literarily distinguished level, Hamlin Garland in *The Trail of the Goldseekers* (1899) lamented, as he trekked through the British Columbia wilderness, the loss of the "wild places" in North America, as American urban and technological civilization pushed constantly westward and northward.[4]

But the whole story of the nineteenth-century American literary image of Canada is not briefly or easily told. Like the United States literary tradition as a whole, the image of Canada involves a variety of trends and counter-trends, varying levels of artistic achievement, and, above all, the unique contributions of many individual creative imaginations. The comprehensive scrutiny of this image, furthermore, must take into account a multiplicity of contexts, including many of the social and political factors that interact with literary creativity, as well as the amorphous entity known as "popular culture," to which many of the writings relevant to this subject unquestionably belong. Finally, it is necessary to keep in mind the comparatively minor significance of the image of Canada in the large context of American creative preoccupations. As Gerald M. Craig has expressed it, "Americans, caught up in their own vibrant life, are not noted for their readiness to devote sustained attention to any other society for its own sake."[5] Nevertheless, the quantity of American literary works concerned with Canada in the nineteenth century is perhaps larger than many readers might suspect. And the artistic and ideological complexity of this image is worth careful attention. The exploration of a minor element in the development of the literary theme of the New World may serve to illuminate questions relating to both the United States and Canada, whose peoples have never ceased to be fascinated by their respective national experiences.

I

COLONIAL AND EARLY REPUBLICAN IMAGES

From the earliest years of New England colonization, the English-speaking inhabitants of the regions that became the United States were made recurrently aware of the wilderness and settlements to the north. Throughout the seventeenth century, the Puritans of New England apprehensively watched French military, colonial, and religious expansion on the St. Lawrence and westward into the regions of the Mississippi; in the eighteenth century, a series of skirmishes, Indian raids, and formally declared wars kept Canada in the forefront of the colonial American consciousness. The "French and Indian wars" inspired a good many New England literary works, the most prominent of which were the "captivity narratives" written by prisoners carried off to Canada by Iroquois and French war parties. These autobiographical fragments, written by Puritan parsons, farmers, and housewives, reflect a uniformity of style and attitude by virtue of the shared cultural loyalties of the authors, but their conceptions of Canada and of the captivity experience vary somewhat according to individual background.[1] *The Redeemed Captive Returning to Zion* (written in 1707), by the Reverend John Williams of Deerfield, is in many ways a typical Puritan theological treatise, in which the author records his discernment of the divine will in the trials and temptations of captivity. There is often an earthy directness in his reports of encounters with French Jesuits and his understated descriptions of the sufferings of himself and his fellow captives, but the focus of the narrative as a whole is inward, towards his own spiritual state, rather than outward, towards the landscape and society of Canada. In contrast to Williams's narrative, other prisoners' tales are more informative as to external detail. The *Memoirs of Odd Adventures, Strange*

Deliverances, etc., in the Captivity of John Gyles, Esq. (1736) and *The Narrative of the Captivity of Nehemiah How* (written in 1747) are two examples of vivid and plain-spoken autobiographical writing by New England Puritan laymen, who concentrate on observations of the Canadian wilderness and its French and Indian inhabitants.

But almost all the New England captives recorded their sense of the paradox of Canada, a paradox that in various forms pervades American writing about the northern country. In expectation, and on initial encounter, Canada is seen as a cold and barren wilderness, inhabited by French "papists" and pagan savages; but in sustained experience the country appears to the Anglo-American as a subjugable forest frontier much like his own country, and the inhabitants—at least the French— appear to be congenial and sympathetic pioneers much like himself. "The French were very kind to me," confesses the Reverend John Williams; and John Gyles eventually becomes quite fond of the *habitant* couple to whom he is enslaved.[2]

Other pre-Revolution Americans who left literary records of Canada report somewhat less sympathetic impressions. A Boston soldier named John Maylem wrote *Gallic Perfidy: A Poem* (1758) about the massacre at Fort William Henry, where hundreds of the author's cohorts succumbed to "fell Canadian rage." Robert Stobo, a Virginia officer taken hostage to Quebec after George Washington surrendered to the French at Fort Necessity in 1754, complained of his suffering in Canadian dungeons and of the treachery of "Britain's faithless enemies."[3] But the rhetoric of soldiers might be expected to be more militant than that of pious civilian captives; and Stobo's narrative is filled with self-dramatizations and lurid details drawn from eighteenth-century fiction. Stobo might, in fact, be considered the first colonial American to make conscious literary use of Canadian settings and themes; but he was purporting to be writing true history. The first substantial Anglo-American exploitation of Canada in traditional literary genres is the work of a playwright and poet named George Cockings.

The English-born Cockings (d. 1802) served as a petty official in Boston under the British colonial government until 1776, when he returned to his native country. While in New England he composed two substantial works, both published in America. *War; an Heroic Poem, from the Taking of Minorca, by the French; to the Reduction of the Havannah, by the Earle of Albermarle* (1762), dealt, among other things, with the captures of Louisbourg and Quebec; the second book was called *The Conquest of Canada; or, The Siege of Quebec. An Historical Tragedy of Five Acts* (1773). Both *War* and *The Conquest of Canada* are rather stilted literary exercises, inspired respectively by Milton's *Paradise Lost* and Addison's *Cato*. In the interminable rhyming couplets of the eight-book epic, the author emphasizes the world-wide scope of the triumphant British military achievements; in the blank-verse drama, he represents Wolfe as a tragic hero, and implies parallels between the French-English conflict in Canada and the great wars of classical antiquity and more recent European history. In both works, Cockings's aims are to relate the French-English conflict in North America to the European tradition of tragedy, epic, and myth, and to demonstrate that even the remote northern wilderness of the New World can yield characters and events comparable to those that inspired Shakespeare, Milton, or the ancient Greek poets. The idea of Canada as an element in a New World epic is a recurrent nineteenth-century American literary notion that is finally brought to fruition not by a poet or dramatist but by the historian Francis Parkman.

In the meantime, in the late colonial and early republican periods in America, the literary exploitation of Canada—and of the New World as a whole—was being developed mainly by less deliberate artists, by the captives, soldiers, and travellers who kept prosaic or awkwardly poetic records of their personal experiences. The New England Puritans and other early American colonists were more occupied with religious, political, and material concerns than with developing a tradition of *belles-lettres*, but, after the Revolution, Americans became more aware of the possibilities of developing a New World tradition of imaginative literature, especially one that reflected the new political and social ideals and the unique geographical circumstances of the United States. Genuinely significant literary achievements were slow in coming, however, as European-influenced poets struggled to force their impressions of the new continent into the stilted neo-Classical forms currently popular in England. Thus, with a few exceptions, the liveliest impressions of Canada continued through the first post-Revolution generation to be recorded in the journals and diaries of the writers whose purposes were not necessarily artistic.

> On the morning of the 6th Nov. we marched in straggling parties, through a flat and rich country ... decorated by many low houses, all white washed, which appeared to be the warm abodes of a contented people. Every now and then a chapel came in sight; but more frequently the rude, yet pious imitations of the sufferings of our Savior, and the image of the virgin. These things created surprise, at least in my mind, for where I expected

there could be little other than barbarity, we found civilized men, in a comfortable state, enjoying all the benefits arising from the institutions of civil society.[4]

Thus in the autumn of 1775 a young soldier named John Joseph Henry described his first impressions upon emerging with the ragged and exhausted remnants of the army led by Benedict Arnold from the Maine-Canadian wilderness into the St. Lawrence valley. The sense of incongruity between the settlements and the wilderness remains for some time a stock response of early literary observers in the New World: it is one of the recurrent impressions, for instance, recorded by Alexis de Tocqueville in his travel notes and his *Democracy in America*. But the young American soldier's surprise at finding "civilized men, in a comfortable state" in this northern frontier is particularly emphatic. Like the authors of captivity narratives, Henry reveals cultural preconceptions emphasizing the barbarity of the northern forest and the foreign Roman Catholic culture of Canada, and he is astonished to find the Canadians to be a pioneering people with experiences and customs much like Americans.

Yet the sense of affinity is far from complete. Henry hastens to explain that his remarks are intended only as

> a description of our sensations, entertained in our minds by the conveniences we now enjoyed, in opposition to our late privations. We had just arrived from a dreary and inhospitable wild, half-starved and thinly clothed, in a land of plenty, where we had full rations and warm quarters; consequently our present feelings, contrasted with former sufferings, might have appreciated in too high a degree the happiness of the Canadian—What is now said, ought not to be taken in anywise as an allusion to the political rights, but be confined solely to the apparent prosperity and economy of families.

"The French Canadians," more bluntly declares one of Henry's companions, a soldier named Abner Stocking, "were too ignorant to put a just estimate on the value of freedom."[5] To these young Americans imbued with the ideals of political independence and republicanism, the inhabitants of Canada are alienated from the revolutionary colonists by their reactionary politics as well as by their language and religion, even though their social and domestic arrangements appear comfortably familiar. The alleged decadence of French-Canadian religion, politics, and language remains throughout the nineteenth century one of the main sources of American negative responses to Canada, even among those writers who recognize affinities between the Canadian and American pioneering experiences.

The northern campaign of 1775 inspired at least one notable piece of American writing that was more consciously literary than the diaries of Arnold's soldiers. Hugh Henry Brackenridge, later the author of the novel *Modern Chivalry*, was an Episcopalian clergyman and schoolmaster living in Philadelphia when the news of the defeat at Quebec reached the American settlements. Brackenridge immediately set to work on a blank-verse tragedy entitled *The Death of General Montgomery in the Storming of the City of Quebec* (published in 1777). The author had never seen Quebec, so his representations of the northern colony and wilderness are brief and generalized; but the play is significant, like the work of George Cockings, as an attempt to adapt the setting and events to traditional literary conventions. With his mind running on the mediaeval romances that are to form part of the inspiration for *Modern Chivalry*, Brackenridge has Montgomery say to his aide:

> It seems to me, MacPherson, that we tread
> The ground of some romantic fairy land,
> Where knights in armour, and high combatants
> Have met in war. This is the plain where Wolfe,
> Victorious Wolfe, fought with brave Montcalm;
> And even yet, the dreary, snow-clad tomb,
> Of many a hero, slaughter'd on that day,
> Recalls the memory of the bloody strife.[6]

The imaginary Canada of Brackenridge's play, like the similar fantasyland of Cockings's play and poem, is distinguished from the experienced Canada of the captivity narratives and soldiers' diaries by its unity and simplicity. The "romantic fairy land" of Quebec has no incongruities between nature and settlements, no foreignness of language and culture to bemuse or alienate the Anglo-American observer. The only disconcerting element in *The Death of General Montgomery* is the tragic historical fact that is the play's main theme: Montgomery is killed, the Americans are defeated, and Canada remains a bastion of decadent British colonialism.

Thus, even before the end of the Revolution, many of the main elements in the American image of Canada had emerged. The formidable northern wilderness, the congenial but decadent French-speaking settlers, the epic and sometimes tragic scope of events leading to the fall of

Quebec and the American Revolution: these were some of the prominent impressions—experienced or imagined—recorded by Americans on various levels of literary achievement.

Among writers of the revolutionary period, a few Loyalists ought to be briefly mentioned, for even though most of them chose to go into exile rather than live under republicanism, they were by birth or long residence American, and their literary output is at least peripherally relevant to United States culture. Hector St. John de Crèvecoeur, the famous "American farmer," is perhaps the most notable of these writers. His interest in Canada was quite limited—he returned to his native France when the American Revolution broke out—but his arguments in favour of the *status quo* in America include an idyllic picture of the French-Canadian *habitants* that contrasts with the ambivalent attitudes of earlier writers and prefigures the nineteenth-century sentimentalization by such writers as Longfellow:

> No society of men could exhibit greater simplicity, more honesty, happier manners, less litigiousness; nowhere could you perceive more peace and tranquility.... England has found them the best of subjects. If the influence of religion was more visible here than in any other of the English colonies, its influence was salutary;... for what else do we expect to gain by the precepts of religion but less ferocious manners and a more upright conduct?

Even before the Conquest, Crèvecoeur continues, the French-Canadians "were happier than the citizens of Boston perpetually brawling about liberty without knowing what it was."[7]

A similar but more detailed image of French Canada is presented by another author of Loyalist sympathies, a New-Jersey-born Episcopal clergyman named John Cousens Ogden (1751–1800). Ogden was not a Loyalist in the usual sense of the term, for although he was an opponent of American independence, he somehow managed to avoid either voluntary exile or forcible ejection, and retained his pastorate at Litchfield, Connecticut, until his death. His book, *A Tour through Upper and Lower Canada.... Containing a View of the Present State of Religion, Learning, Commerce, Agriculture, Colonization, Customs and Manners, among the English, French, and Indian Settlements* (1799), like Crèvecoeur's brief sketch, is an idyllic picture of Canadian society under the benevolent paternalism of British rule.

"An happy harmony prevails among all orders of the inhabitants,"

Ogden writes of Montreal. "An urbanity, hospitality, and interesting gentility of manners pervade most classes of people." The French-Canadian "peasantry," he continues, are characterized by "a decent, respectful, affability of manners." Considering the fact that he is a Protestant clergyman, Ogden is remarkably tolerant of Roman Catholicism, but this is evidently because he sees the religious institution, like the British colonial government, as promoting social stability by keeping the *habitants* content in subservience. "Religion appears truly venerable, not only in its temples and other edifices, but in the hospitality, politeness, and genteel deportment of most of its professors."[8]

Of the more recently settled Upper Canada, Ogden says:

> People of every language and nation have come hither and formed prospering colonies. Heaven has blessed their labors, industry, and enterprize. Few have experienced greater success. The nation of England has fostered them with great care.[9]

Although Ogden presumably did visit Quebec, Montreal, and several settlements in Upper Canada, his narrative conveys few impressions of actual experience. It is full of such abstractions as "harmony," "order," "prosperity," and "happiness," but he seldom illustrates these abstractions with reference to specific individuals and situations. Nor does he mention such problems as French-English nationalistic or religious rivalry: indeed, he would have the reader believe that French and English, Protestant and Catholic live side by side in perfect accord in Canada.

No other early post-Revolution American writers present such an idyllic image of Canada; even the exiled Loyalists, although they express considerable resentment against the new American government, are more realistic about primitive social conditions in the northern wilderness. The English-born poet Joseph Stansbury (1743–1809), who had settled in Philadelphia in 1767, fled during the Revolution to Nova Scotia, which he regarded with abhorrence, as he makes clear in his lament, "To Cordelia":

> Believe me, Love, this vagrant life
> O'er Nova Scotia's wilds to roam,
> While far from children, friends, or wife,
> Or place that I can call a home
> Delights not me;—another way
> My treasures, pleasures, wishes lay.[10]

Another Loyalist refugee, the Massachusetts-born Episcopal clergyman Jacob Bailey (1731-1808), at first regarded Nova Scotia as "the retreat of freedom and security from the rage of tyranny and the cruelty of oppression," but he gradually became discouraged by the wildness and social primitivism of the Annapolis Valley, where "there is not a building equal to the houses of the middling farmers of New England."[11]

As Stansbury's and Bailey's writings indicate, even before the end of the revolutionary period the American perception of Canada was expanding from its initial focus on a geographically circumscribed, predominantly French-speaking region. As travellers or Loyalist immigrants moved into the maritime provinces and Upper Canada, they began to perceive the outlines of the modern bicultural and geographically far-flung society, and to note its parallels and contrasts with the United States. In the immediate post-Revolution years, these American responses to Canada were liable to be sympathetic rather than otherwise; after the failure of attempts to enlist Canadians in the revolutionary cause, militant republicans turned indifferently away from the northern colonies to concentrate on the internal concerns of their own country. At least until the war of 1812, the few post-Revolution American literary responses to Canada were the work of Loyalists, Loyalist sympathizers, Federalists, and others of conservative, anglophile political inclinations, or individuals with interests other than political.

In the latter category, Benjamin Mortimer (1767-1834) was a Moravian missionary from New York, sent in 1798 with his more famous colleague, John Heckewelder, to minister to a small community of Christian Indians at Fairfield, on the Thames River in Upper Canada. Mortimer's journal of the overland trek to Fairfield is probably the earliest American traveller's depiction of the western frontier of Upper Canada, which in 1798 was largely forest wilderness, just beginning to be settled, mainly by "late Loyalists" from the United States. As a missionary, Mortimer's main interest was in the state of religion among the white settlers and the Indians, but he also took note of the economic and social circumstances of the region. "Most of the inhabitants of Canada are emigrants from the United States," Mortimer noted, "but no sooner did we enter the country, than we perceived that some difference exists between their national characters."[12] The Canadian settlers are less prosperous and apparently less ambitious than their counterparts who have remained in the United States, seeming quite satisfied with the small, remote land grants given them by the British government. Mortimer also notes the retarded state of commerce in the province:

> There are no stores or shops in the whole province of Upper
> Canada, except in the towns of Newark and York, and in the
> neighborhood of Detroit. The most common articles, to be had
> in every village in the eastern parts of the United States, can
> hardly be procured here for any money. Br. Heckewelder for
> instance was in want of tobacco, and could get none. He began
> at length to day to smoke dried leaves of trees.[13]

The most advanced social and economic circumstances Mortimer finds in Upper Canada are those of the Six Nations Indians near the village of Brantford. These refugees from the American Revolution, who in the United States would be living in poverty, enjoy, under the British government and their colourful leader, Joseph Brant, the amenities of modern civilization, including permanent housing, a school system, and religious instruction. In fact, Mortimer notes, religious and secular education seems better looked after among the Indians than the whites: "'the Indians in Moravian town and Brandt's town have churches and schools,'" he quotes one white settler. "'The white people have neither. Our children will become heathen, and theirs Christians.'"[14]

Mortimer thus finds in Upper Canada a society with various parallels and contrasts to that of the United States, not as advanced economically, yet revealing in unexpected ways a greater degree of social and spiritual refinement. Mortimer's impressions of the northern provinces were not entirely shared by his companion and leader, John Heckewelder. The eminent missionary apparently kept no record of the 1798 expedition, but he did keep brief notes of an earlier journey, to Fairfield and Montreal, in 1793. At the village of Queenston, Heckewelder noted, "we were visited at our camp by many people of this neighborhood, some of which were very sensible that they had changed better for worse, in coming from the United States to these parts."[15] At Montreal, he found some indication of mercantile progress comparable to that of the United States, but he found the French-Canadians ignorant and apathetic, and he was repelled by descriptions of the harsh winters of the region. In 1805, a Boston lawyer and congressman of conservative political inclinations named Timothy Bigelow made a tour to Montreal, Kingston, and Niagara Falls. Like Heckewelder, he was favourably impressed by the English inhabitants, particularly the merchant class, but he found the French "ignorant, superstitious, prejudiced, mean-spirited, and slovenly... hardly to be distinguished in their complexion from the Indians."[16]

But even Heckewelder and Bigelow, with their reservations about the

French and about opportunities for settlers in Canada, acknowledged the northern country as a possible alternative to the republicanism of the United States. While many republican authors were asserting the rightness and inevitability of their country's political and social organizations, a few of their countrymen were discovering that Canada offered other possibilities of equal or greater validity. Some of these writers, like Crèvecoeur and Ogden, for instance, were interested in using a selective, stylized image of Canada as a means of criticizing the United States. Canada is used as an instrument for anti-republican satire in a prose fantasy, *Memoir of the Northern Kingdom* (1808), written by an Episcopal clergyman of Boston, William Jenks (1778-1866). Purporting to be published in 1901 and written "A.D. 1872, by the Late Rev. Williamson Jahnsenykes, LL.D., and Hon. Member of the Royal American Board of Literature," the *Memoir* describes the ultimate disintegration of the American union. While New England and Virginia decline economically and founder politically, the "Northern Kingdom," with its metropolis of "Quebeck," flourishes under the benevolent paternalism of the British crown.

> Like London, Quebeck was now the mart not only of trade, but of literature; the "Royal American Board" of which, under the fostering patronage of a discerning Prince, became highly instrumental in the promotion of science.[17]

Eventually, New England forms a union with the Northern Kingdom; Virginia is annexed by France; and republicanism, degenerating to a licence for riot and self-indulgence, makes a last stand among the ignorant frontiersmen of Illinois.

The War of 1812 aroused further American interest in Canada, although not as much as might be expected, for even though several important battles were fought in Canada, American literary reactions to the war often had more to do with attitudes towards England and internal United States political controversies than with the question of the possible conquest of the northern provinces. But several authors of autobiographical journals, poems, novels, and even stage plays did turn their attention to the specifically Canadian aspects of the war. Some of these works involve the predictable bombast of militant nationalism, but others reflect the widespread anti-war sentiment of the time. Still others, particularly the journals of American soldiers and prisoners in Canada, are comparatively detached, objective, and sometimes even favourable in their impressions of the northern country and its inhabitants.

The brief, anonymous *Journal of an American Prisoner at Fort Malden and Quebec in the War of 1812* (conjecturally attributed to James Reynolds, surgeon's mate of an American lake vessel) expresses admiration for the "fine farms and several handsome towns" near Quebec, and praises the English inhabitants as "decent, friendly, and humane."[18] Another prisoner, William K. Beall of Kentucky, assistant quartermaster-general in the army of General William Hull, recorded his favourable impressions of Canada in more lyrical prose. "Insulated" from the "comfortable home, the endearing smiles, and the enlivening converse" of his family and friends, Beall is rather resentful towards the British, whom he represents as tyrannizing the Canadian colonials by excess taxation and enforced military service. But the landscape and settlements are nonetheless appealing to the eye:

> The view of Amherstburgh, a small town below Fort Malden, though indifferently built, and the adjoining country, appeared beautiful. The green meadows and wheatfields were waving before the wind in a lovely and superior imitation of Lake Erie, and everything appeared to wear the cheering smiles of peace and plenty.[19]

A satirical literary response appeared very early in the war in *The Wars of the Gulls* (1812), a brief, semi-allegorical fictional account of the outbreak of hostilities. The author, a New York pamphleteer named Jacob Bigelow, ridiculed the war hawks' notions of continental conquest by having the commander of "The Gulls" (the United States) make plans for a "viceroy of Labrador" and "military governor over the fragments of Quebec." Most of Canada, says the author contemptuously, is easily accessible to invading armies at any time, "for the ice never breaks up."[20] Another satirical view of the war is *The Adventures of Uncle Sam, in Search after His Lost Honor* (1816), by "Frederick Augustus Fidfaddy, Esq." This comic history and commentary uses Biblical and historiographical parody as well as allegory to expose the follies of the American politicians and generals. Most of the major battles are described, but no insistent attitude is adopted towards Canada or Canadians, the author's main concern being with the relevance of the war to his own country.

The chauvinistic literary supporters of the war represented Canada and Canadians as pathetic victims of British tyranny who welcomed the liberating intervention of Americans. In Samuel Woodworth's fictionalized history, *The Champions of Freedom* (1816), the oppressed Canadian colonists are eager to join the American invaders; in Mordecai Noah's spectacular stage play, *She Would Be a Soldier; or, The Plains of Chippewa* (1819), the settlers of Upper Canada are rustic Jacksonian democrats, intrinsically superior to their arrogant British governors. Richard Emmons (b. 1788), a Kentucky physician and would-be poet, was responsible for the most pretentious literary response to the war, a four-volume, forty-canto "epick" in rhyming couplets. *The Fredoniad: or, Independence Preserved* (1827). This interminable piece of bombast reviews the whole history of the war and more, revealing in allegorical episodes the infernal origins of Britain's plan to crush "Columbia," and describing the celestial vantage point of "Fredonia," the "guardian genius of Columbian Earth."[21] In the cluttered descriptions of various battles, Canada scarcely figures except as a series of place names.

As these few illustrations suggest, American literary interest in Canada in the eighteenth and early-nineteenth centuries was sporadic and peripheral to the main preoccupations of the inhabitants of the colonies and the young republic. The most frequent inspiration for early American interest in Canada was war: French and Indian raids, the Revolution, the War of 1812. But attitudes were not always hostile: many of the captives, soldiers, travellers, and litterateurs who recorded their experiences or visions of Canada were remarkably open-minded in their responses to the northern frontier and the pioneering society that seemed similar yet subtly different in comparison to their own. The idea of Canada as an alternative social and political response to the New World situation was growing in the American mind. But this idea emerged slowly and tentatively, as would-be literary artists wielded the stilted conventions of poetry and drama borrowed uncritically from Europe, or as less pretentious chroniclers set down the unreflective records of their experiences. By the end of the War of 1812, however, creative writing in the United States was in an upsurge of activity, climaxed by the so-called "renaissance" of the 1840s and 1850s. In the midst of this activity, the image of Canada became clearer, less tentative and eclectic, and, to a considerable extent, more concentrated on limited aspects of the northern country—such as the exotic society of French Canada.

II

FRENCH CANADA

In the decades of peace and relative prosperity that followed the War of 1812, Americans in increasing numbers discovered the pleasures and challenges of foreign travel. The considerable time and expense involved in even the least ambitious excursion meant that recreational travel was largely the prerogative of affluent and educated individuals, who were often likely to write and publish their travel memoirs. The travel narrative was an extremely popular literary form in the nineteenth century, particularly in the United States. This popularity stemmed partly from the fact that the travelogue provided stay-at-homes with the opportunity for vicarious enjoyment, and partly because its usually unpretentious form and style seemed democratically accessible, in both the reading and the writing, to almost anyone. Canada did not exercise as much appeal to American travellers and readers of travel narratives as Europe, but the northern provinces were by no means neglected. Lake steamers, stage coaches, and, later, railroads made all settled parts of Upper and Lower Canada accessible. The most popular attraction, however, was usually the older, more exotic society of Lower Canada.

Like earlier travellers, the more thoughtful tourists had ambivalent feelings about Canada. A veteran of the 1812 war named Joseph Sansom, in a volume published in 1817 as *Sketches of Lower Canada* (reprinted in an 1820 English edition as *Travels in Lower Canada*), was torn between his sense of affinity with Canadians as fellow North Americans and his impatience with their economic backwardness and political subservience. Seen as a part of the archetypal New-World experience of creating a new civilization out of the wilderness, the northern settlements are inferior to those of the United States:

> [I]t is only on the banks of its rivers that Canada pretends to any population, or improvement, whatever; whereas with us the cheering
> —Tract and blest abode of man
> is scattered... over the whole surface of the soil, by hardy adventurers.... And we have inland-towns little inferior in population to the capital of Canada. (p. 14)[1]

But in other respects, Canada is unified with its southern neighbour in opposition to Europe:

> [T]here are no beggars in Canada, any more than in the United States. The stranger is nowhere importuned for money, or disgusted by the shameless display of natural or acquired deformity with which European roads and cities universally abound. (p. 33)

Sansom believes that the political ties with Britain are the principal cause of Canada's inferiority to the United States, and he predicts that the northern provinces will eventually be absorbed into the republic by a combined process of assimilation and military conquest:

> I left Quebec with a confirmed opinion, that... its citadel, reputed the strongest fortification in America,... might possibly, in future wars between the two countries... fall a prey to American enterprise and intrepidity....
> I say not the same of Upper Canada, whose population is, or will be, essentially American; and whose attachment to the government of Great Britain must inevitably yield to the habits and opinions of their continental neighbours. (pp. 41-42)

Sansom has mixed feelings about the French-speaking inhabitants of Canada. On the one hand, he admires their honesty and garrulous friendliness, which qualities he illustrates by contrasting two individuals he met on his travels, a candid young French-Canadian and a haughty English-speaking colonist. On the other hand, he insists that the French-Canadians as a whole are much degenerated from their hardy *voyageur* and *coureur-de-bois* ancestors, and inferior to their ethnic counterparts in Europe:

> [T]he passion for military glory [is] almost extinct, as well as that thoughtless gaiety which distinguishes the French in Europe....
>
> Even in person and countenance they are perceptibly altered from their European ancestors. The Canadian peasant is not so tall as the native Frenchman; neither is he so well-shaped, or so comely in feature as his progenitors. (p. 75)

By the end of the first quarter of the nineteenth century, the degeneracy of French-Canadians was such an accepted article of faith in the United States that even the prestigious *North American Review* could incorporate into a review of a book about Canada a casual reference to "the natural indolence of the French inhabitants, arising perhaps, from a disregard of what we call comforts, from education and habits, and from their religious tenets."[2] Many travellers to Lower Canada echoed these sentiments. "Despotism seems to have stamped a feature of low submission upon the plodding, unambitious peasantry," said a tourist named Philip Stansbury in 1822, "whose minds are, moreover, awed into superstition by the displayed crucifix of their Catholic priests."[3] The French-Canadians, remarked another traveller in 1823, "appear to be very temperate, honest, industrious, and hospitable, but remarkably ignorant, and zealously devoted to their priests."[4]

Even tourist guidebooks expressed this widespread contempt for the *habitants*. *The Northern Traveller*, which was first published in 1825 and reprinted many times in the next decade, informed its readers that

> The French Canadians, notwithstanding the common prejudices against them, appear on acquaintance to be an intelligent people. They certainly are amiable, cheerful, and gay, and their backwardness in improvements is attributable to the system under which they live. They are generally brought up in great ignorance, and they are taught to dislike and avoid not only Protestant principles, but Protestants themselves.[5]

Thus the French of Lower Canada were widely despised by Americans for racial, political, and religious reasons. Often seen as physically and mentally inferior or "naturally" indolent, the *habitants* were further despised for their submission to British imperialism and the Roman Catholic Church. The church was particularly regarded with suspicion by Americans, for its association with decadent, despotic mediaeval traditions that seemed antagonistic to the liberal, individualistic customs and beliefs upon which United States society was purportedly based. American attitudes towards Roman Catholic cultures became more tolerant, but in the early nineteenth century both French Canada and Latin America were subjected to a good deal of religious calumny from United States writers.

The attacks on the church in Canada were carried on in guidebooks, periodicals, travelogues, sensationalist fiction, and purportedly true histories or biographies such as the notorious *Awful Disclosures of Maria Monk* (1836). This scurrilous and totally fictitious exposé of the Hotel Dieu Nunnery in Montreal was the work of two New York residents, an Anglo-Irish Episcopal priest named George Bourne and a professional writer named Theodore Dwight. Dwight, the author of the guidebook *The Northern Traveller*, came from a family background impressive for both its literary associations and its militant Protestantism: he was the great-grandson of Jonathan Edwards, the nephew of Timothy Dwight (the distinguished Congregationalist minister and author of the Miltonic imitation "Greenfield Hill"), and the son and namesake of a member of the neo-classical literary group known as the "Connecticut Wits." Bourne was also the author of a guidebook, *The Picture of Quebec* (1830), which praised the various societies for the propagation of Protestantism and English culture in Quebec City, and of an anti-Catholic novel entitled *Lorette. The History of Louise, Daughter of a Canadian Nun: Exhibiting the Interior of Female Convents* (1833).

Both *Lorette* and *Awful Disclosures* were obviously fabricated from the stereotypes of popular Gothic novels. In *Lorette*, the *habitants* are portrayed as degenerates who indulge in every kind of vice with the assurance of receiving absolution from their priests. The action moves from an infertile, perpetually snow-bound landscape of rural Lower Canada, featuring gloomy forests, lonely granges, and sinister monasteries, to the grottoed interior of a convent where the innocent heroine is held prisoner while repeated assaults are made on her chastity by vicious priests abetted by ugly and dissolute nuns. *Awful Disclosures* features the same kind of Gothic trappings: lecherous priests, mad nuns, subterranean passages and dungeons beneath the streets of Montreal, infant corpses buried in quick-lime under convent floors, and an innocent heroine who narrates her ordeal with a combination of gruesome explicitness and titillating suggestion.

The story of Maria Monk was widely read and accepted as fact by American readers, and caused a short-lived but violent wave of anti-Catholic and anti-Canadian feeling in various cities of the United States.

When the crusading New York journalist William Leete Stone published his carefully researched and calmly contemptuous exposé of the fraud, *Maria Monk and the Nunnery of the Hotel Dieu* (1836), the more intelligent element of the American population quickly lost interest in the sordid business; but on a popular level the anti-Catholic Gothic legend of French Canada persisted.[6] It is featured, for instance, in at least two early predecessors of the dime novel, Benjamin Barker's *Cecilia, or The White Nun of the Wilderness*, an execrably printed fifty-five-page pamphlet published in Boston in 1845, and Justin Jones's *Jessie Manton, or The Novice of Sacre-Coeur*, also published in Boston, in 1848.

But the religion of the French-Canadians was only one element in the American prejudice against them. Their alleged indolence and ignorance were attributed generally to their adherence to decadent European customs, to their situation far from the supposed centres of civilization, and to their historical status as a conquered and dispirited people. Even when a *Canadien* was transplanted to the supposedly more free and progressive environment of the American republic, he retained, according to some American writers, his characteristic torpor. In *Astoria* (1836), a narrative history of John Jacob Astor's ill-fated attempt to develop an independent American fur trade on the west coast, Washington Irving described the French-Canadian *voyageurs* who had been enlisted as boat-men for the expedition:

> The Canadians proved as patient of toil and hardship on the land as on the water; indeed, nothing could surpass the patience and good-humour of these men upon the march. They were the cheerful drudges of the party, loading and unloading the horses, pitching the tents, making the fires, cooking; in short, performing all those household and menial offices which the Indians usually assign to the squaws; and like the squaws, they left all the hunting and fighting to others. A Canadian has but little affection for the exercise of the rifle.[7]

Irving may have been merely echoing the opinions of his sources, but whether the origin is with the historian or with the documents relating to the Astoria expedition, the outlines of a familiar stereotype are recognizable. This stereotype is reminiscent of the typical nineteenth-century American image of the Negro or the Latin American, those "lesser breeds" who, according to prevalent conceptions of nationality and race, were unfitted for the grand enterprise of taming the frontier, and were relegated to the status of hewers of wood and drawers of water. Irving specifically associates the Canadians with the Indians, who throughout *Astoria* are represented as a brutish, violent, and doomed race at the bottom of the social and anthropological scale, which is headed by the American entrepreneurs and their intrepid underlings, the Kentucky frontier scouts. The French-Canadians, furthermore, are associated not simply with the Indians, but with the Indian women: they are seen as passive, almost irrelevant appendages to the great American frontier experience.

In another of his true-life stories of the prairies, *The Adventures of Captain Bonneville* (1837), Irving further compared the French-Canadian and native American frontiersmen, and concluded by quoting "a trader of long experience": " 'I consider one American,' he said, 'equal to three Canadians in point of sagacity, aptness at resources, self-dependence and fearlessness of spirit.' "[8] In this book, Irving's judgments on the basis of ethnic origin seem somewhat inconsistent, for the title character, an intrepid frontiersman equal or superior to the Americans, is of French descent. Bonneville, however, comes from a family that emigrated directly from France to the United States. The alleged inferiority of the French-Canadians is thus evidently related to their association with the collapse of the French empire in the New World: the *voyageurs* are the vestiges of a defeated people and of a departed imperial glory, whereas Bonneville, as the descendant of recent immigrants, is associated with the rising glory of the American republic.

A slightly different mode of evaluating the frontier hierarchy is used by Edgar Allan Poe in his unfinished novel "The Journal of Julius Rodman" (1840), which is partly based on *The Adventures of Captain Bonneville*. The members of Poe's imaginary westward expedition include five "Creoles of Canadian descent," who are

> good boatmen, and excellent companions, as far as singing French songs went, and drinking, at which they were preeminent.... They were always in good humor, and always ready to work; but as hunters I did not think them worth much, and as fighting men I soon discovered they were not to be depended upon.[9]

Poe goes on, like Irving, to compare the Canadians unfavourably with six Kentuckians, who are tall, powerful, experienced hunters, and dead shots with the rifle. The Canadians are once again placed low on the frontier social scale; Poe barely grants them precedence over the Negro slave Toby, the brutishly servile and indefatigably good-natured clown of the story. Poe does, however, make a distinction between the *voyageurs* and one of the leaders of the party, who is also a "Creole of Canadian descent," but who is distinguished from the *voyageurs* by his superior education and breeding. The basis for Poe's distinction between individuals thus seems to be not primarily ethnic or national, but social and intellectual.

A more detailed picture of the French-Canadian on the American plains and his relationship to other denizens of the region is given in *The Oregon Trail* (1847) by the eminent historian Francis Parkman. While seeking direct experience of the primitive Indian character as part of the research for his projected epic history of early French settlement in the New World, Parkman came into contact with various white frontiersmen, most of whom the fastidious Boston Brahmin historian despised for their uncouth familiarity, while grudgingly admiring their skills in hunting and tracking. Two individuals in his expedition particularly attracted his interest, a muleteer named Deslauriers and a hunter and guide named Henry Chatillon. Deslauriers is described in terms comparable to those used by Irving and Poe as

> ...a Canadian, with all the characteristics of the true Jean Baptiste. Neither fatigue, exposure, nor hard labor could ever impair his cheerfulness and gayety, or his politeness to his *bourgeois*; and when night came, he would sit down by the fire, smoke his pipe, and tell stories with the utmost contentment.[10]

Henry Chatillon is presented in quite different terms, however:

> His age was about thirty; he was six feet high, and very powerfully and gracefully moulded. The prairies had been his school; he could neither read nor write, but he had a natural refinement and delicacy of mind, such as is rare even in women. His manly face was a mirror of uprightness, simplicity, and kindness of heart; he had, moreover, a keen perception of character, and a tact that would preserve him from flagrant error in any society. Henry had not the restless energy of an Anglo-American. He was content to take things as he found them; and his chief fault arose from an excess of easy generosity, not conducive to thriving in the world.... His bravery was as much celebrated in the mountains as his skill in hunting.... He was a proof of what

unaided nature will sometimes do. I have never, in the city or in
the wilderness, met a better man than my true-hearted friend,
Henry Chatillon.[11]

Parkman's distinction between the two types of French frontiersman is explained by his account of their respective origins. Deslauriers is identified as a recent immigrant from Canada, while Chatillon is a native citizen of the United States, "born in a little French town near St. Louis."[12] Parkman thus classifies his characters not according to ethnic or social distinctions, but according to an implicit contrast between the United States and Canada. The free air of the republic may produce a lot of "restless energy," but it can still produce a superior breed of human being than Canada, with its long tradition of colonial dependence.

The colonial status of British North America and its inhabitants was one of the main concerns of nineteenth-century Americans who contemplated the subject, whether they observed Canadians in the western prairies or at home in their native province. Most travellers to Canada noted the submission of the French inhabitants to British imperial rule and either criticized the French for their political indolence or condemned the British for their tyranny. Some writers did both, with the result that the French-Canadians were seen simultaneously as victims and as accomplices in their own degradation. This ambivalent attitude is reflected in a noteworthy work of mid-century, *Major Jones's Sketches of Travel: Comprising the Scenes, Incidents, and Adventures, in His Tour from Georgia to Canada* (1848), by William Tappan Thompson.

Thompson (1812–82), a Georgia journalist born in southern Ohio of a Virginia father, was the author of three volumes written in backwoods dialect, modeled on the popular works of the "down-east" comic writer Seba Smith. These three books consist of ostensible letters to Thompson from Major Joseph Jones, a good-natured, naïve but perceptive and sceptical "Cracker" cotton planter, whose homely comments extol or satirize contemporary American customs and institutions. Solidly states'-rights and pro-slavery in his political orientation, Major Jones insists that his concept of America derives from the intentions of the founding fathers and revolutionary heroes, especially Washington and Jefferson. In his travels through the northern states, the account of which takes up about three-quarters of the book, Major Jones finds that the ideals of Jeffersonian democracy are being eroded by the abolitionist movement and by a generally hectic and self-seeking way of life, although at the same time he praises northern industrial and commercial initiative, and urges his fellow southerners to follow suit and become economically self-sufficient. In Canada, Major Jones finds a quieter and sometimes a more pleasant way of life: servants, for instance, are more honest and courteous than their Irish or "free nigger" counterparts in the States. But he also finds economic conditions far worse than those of either the American North or South:

> None of these towns along here on the Canady side ain't no grate shakes, and all of 'em makes a monstrous bad contrast with the smart bisness-lookin towns on the American side, showin plain enuff that our institutions is best calculated to promote the prosperity of the peeple. (p. 175)[13]

The main reason for Canada's retarded state of development, Thompson insists, is British imperialism. According to Major Jones, Canada is a conquered country forcibly occupied by a foreign military power, which adds insult to injury by giving its subject-people the mockery of a representative government. In Montreal the major visits "the Parlyment House, whar the Canady peeple make sich laws as ther masters over the water don't care about troublin themselves with."

> From the Parlyment House we went to the barracks whar the sogers was. Ther was a everlastin lot of 'em—in fact they was all over the city, and ther red cotes and shinin bayonets was to be seen at evry corner, in evry street and evry ally. They may be sed to be the *strikin* feater of Canady—and one can't help but wonder what upon yeath England can want of territory what takes sich a terrible lot of money and sogers to keep it. (p. 181)

Like so many of his countrymen, Major Jones finds the French-Canadians picturesque in appearance and courteous in demeanour, and their religion an object of good-natured contempt. But his ultimate conception of their status in North America is concisely summarized in a meditation on the monument to Wolfe and Montcalm in Quebec City:

> It was a hard piece of bisness, that contest, in which France lost her General and her cause; and though the English may try til dooms-day to make the French Canadians forgit the injustice they have suffered, by givin their Catholic churches all sorts of priviliges, and by bildin monuments, like they have in the Palace Gardin' with Wolf's name on one side and Montcalm's on the other, tryin to make the honors of that day *easy* between

'em,—they never can make loyal, contented subjects out of 'em as long as Cape Diamond stands whar it does. (pp. 182-83)

But not all mid-nineteenth-century Americans despised British imperialism or saw the French-Canadians as pathetic victims or degenerate colonials. More conservative, anglophile attitudes were still very much alive in the United States, as is demonstrated by the Canadian journal of Richard Henry Dana, Jr., who visited Montreal, Quebec, and the Saguenay region in the summer of 1853. The scion of one of the first families of New England, Dana was steeped in the tradition of Federalist politics and a class consciousness based on educational and economic distinctions. The author of *Two Years before the Mast* had considerable sympathy for the less privileged members of society through his first-hand experience of the exploitation of American sailors and his legal defenses of escaped slaves; but he was also a firm believer in the importance of social order. In *Two Years before the Mast* he denounces the incompetence and cruelty of merchant-marine officers—but he also emphasizes the illegality of mutiny. His opposition to the fugitive-slave law involved challenging the law in court—but not the open defiance of it. In Lower Canada, the main feature of society that attracted his attention was the semblance of stability: refined, aristocratic administrators running the province's affairs with evident efficiency, well-trained troops maintaining a display of martial readiness, a powerful church exercising spiritual discipline over cheerful and subservient *habitants,* and no outward appearance of social injustice to disturb a moral sensibility that apparently could be affected by only the most obvious evil.

With an unmistakable consciousness of his social position, Dana restricts his contacts in Canada almost entirely to such representatives of the administrative and ecclesiastical hierarchy as Lord Elgin (the British governor-general), the Roman Catholic archbishop of Quebec, and members of the officers' mess at the Citadel. Occasionally, he remembers to play the rôle of American democrat among British aristocrats: "It is a great advantage," he writes of his dinner with Lord Elgin, "to be an American among people of rank. If you are only polite & not obtrusive & act naturally, you may do as you please" (p. 580).[14] But elsewhere he confides frankly, "I cannot but record the pleasure I receive from the voices of educated Englishmen of good society" (p. 589). He does not ignore the French-Canadians, but his attitude towards them is extremely condescending. On a brief walk in the countryside near Quebec City, he talks to a number of farmers and villagers, and reports:

> I am delighted with the manners of the French Canadians of the middle and lower class,—the rural population. There is a native & indestructible politeness and grace about them which charms me.... I believe them to be a moral, religious, honest & kind people. (pp. 590-91)

Dana's image of Canada recalls that of John Cousens Ogden, who in 1799 admired the French-Canadians for their submissive, peasant-like qualities, and admired the British administration for its commitment to tradition and order. But the prevalent American tendency by mid-century was to see Canada in a less favourable light: to condemn the political system of the provinces for its lack of liberalism, or to despise the inhabitants for their submission to tyranny or for their alleged indolence. These negative responses are attributable to prevalent political and social presuppositions; but they can also be related to the inherent limitations of much of the American interest in Canada. Most travellers, novelists, and polemicists had only a passing curiosity about Canada, or were interested in one specialized or localized aspect of the country. Not until well on in the century did the northern provinces attract the detailed attention of an American writer of comprehensive interests and substantial literary abilities, a writer capable of going beyond superficial detail or specialized prejudices to provide a probing, if idiosyncratic, study of the subject. The study was eventually titled, with misleading simplicity, "A Yankee in Canada"; the writer was Henry David Thoreau.

III

"A YANKEE IN CANADA"

In "A Yankee in Canada" (written in 1850, but not published in its entirety until 1866), Thoreau denounces British imperialism and militarism and expresses his sympathy with the French-Canadians; but he also has several complaints to make about the northern colonists. The American attitude to the *habitants* often tended to be indecisive, but Thoreau's ambivalence toward the French of Canada is particularly acute. Throughout the narrative the author continually moves from positive to negative, setting praise and blame side by side, now extolling the simplicity of the Canadian way of life, now dismissing it contemptuously and perhaps surprising himself by coming out with extravagant praise for his own country, until finally dismissing the whole subject by bringing the narrative of his Canadian travels to an abrupt end, almost with the frustrated but relieved air of having abandoned an unsolvable conundrum. This constant indecision, suggesting an uncharacteristic inability to penetrate beyond ambiguities to the essence of a cultural experience, perhaps explains why "A Yankee" has been ranked low among Thoreau's works.[1] But if the work is not in the same category as *Walden*, there is a good deal to be said for "A Yankee in Canada" as a particularly illuminating example of the early-nineteenth-century American response to Canada.

For most nineteenth-century Americans the problems raised by Canada were bound up with the central question of the meaning of the New World as a whole, but few observers approached this subject with the same imaginative and intellectual enthusiasm as Thoreau. In the fall of 1850, when he took advantage of the Fitchburg Railway's ten-day tourist excursion from Boston to Montreal, he was in the early stages of thinking and research for an ambitious history, which he did not live to complete, of the North American Indian and the early arrival and settlement of Europeans in the New World. For Thoreau, the early history of North America, with its primeval forest or prairie setting and its semi-legendary heroes and events, offered some valuable objects of contemplation for the idealistic individual seeking relief from the degeneracy of urbanized, industrialized modern America, and for the intellectual inquirer seeking the causes of this degeneracy. Thoreau's travels, whether pursued imaginatively through his reading or, less frequently, involving actual removal to some easily accessible frontier such as the Maine woods, Cape Cod, or Canada, were inspired by his search for certain primitive ideals relating to his conception of the true America inherent in the vision of an unspoiled aboriginal continent. These ideals, furthermore, were often focused on an individual who served as a symbolic culture figure, synthesizing such ideas as primitive virtue, heroic individualism, and intuitive rapport with nature. In *The Maine Woods* Thoreau's representative man turns out to be Joe Polis, a Penobscot Indian guide whose simplicity of character and affinity with nature have not been entirely spoiled by his contacts with the white man's civilization. In *Cape Cod*, the ancient Wellfleet oysterman, in spite of his comical piety and cantankerousness, is Thoreau's representative of the American colonial and revolutionary period. In Canada, however, the search for a representative man is apparently unsuccessful. Although he meets and talks with many inhabitants of the northern province, Thoreau fails to find an individual who is an adequate personification of the various ideas and images Canada evokes.

But if Thoreau was disappointed with nineteenth-century Canada, it may be partly because his expectations associated with the country were unusually high. Perhaps he did not literally expect to find a world of *coureurs de bois* and *voyageurs*, but the idea of Canada's great northern wilderness seems to have stirred him to extravagant flights of poetic fancy. In a meditation on reading in *A Week on the Concord and Merrimack Rivers* (1849), he refers to the literature of early North American exploration:

> We naturally remembered Alexander Henry's Adventures here, as a sort of classic among books of American travel. It contains scenery and rough sketching of men and incidents enough to inspire poets for many years, and to my fancy it is as full of sounding names as any page of history,—Lake Winnipeg, Hudson's Bay, Ottaway, and portages innumerable; Chipeways,

Gens de Terres, Les Pilleurs, The Weepers; with reminiscences of Hearne's journey, and the like; an immense and shaggy and sincere country summer and winter, adorned with chains of lakes and rivers, covered with snows with hemlocks and fir trees. There is a naturalness, an unpretending and cold life in this traveller, as in a Canadian winter, what life was preserved through low temperatures and frontier dangers by furs within a stout heart.[2]

The object of Thoreau's northern excursion of 1850 was the settled region of Canada East, not the solitudes of Lake Winnipeg and Hudson Bay described by the eighteenth-century trader Henry in his *Travels and Adventures in Canada and the Indian Territories*. But the frequent meditations on the wilderness in "A Yankee in Canada" suggest that Thoreau's expectations of the northern province involved elements that were at least analogous to the imaginative ideals represented by Henry's northwest.

Thoreau's early writing contains another important intimation of what he might have expected to find in Canada. In his journal for July 14, 1845, while he was living in his house on the shore of Walden Pond, he wrote: "Who should come to my lodge just now but a true Homeric boor, one of those Paphlagonian men? Alek Therien he called himself; a Canadian now, a woodchopper, a post-maker...."[3] The woodchopper is the representative man in all Thoreau's writings who receives the highest praise. "A more simple and natural man it would be hard to find," Thoreau concluded in *Walden*. The admiration for Therien is by no means unqualified, for at times the author "did not know whether he was as wise as Shakespeare or as simply ignorant as a child."[4] But on the whole, Thoreau was inclined to see the woodchopper's ignorance as primitive naturalness. As he appears in *Walden*, he is the epitome of native intelligence and virtue, a man who lacks and has no need for literary culture beyond a vague familiarity with the names of poets and a few fragments of poetry, and who is able to experience a direct and unaffected response to nature.

Surprisingly, in his lengthy consideration of French-Canadian manners and customs in "A Yankee in Canada," Thoreau makes no comparative reference to Therien. Nor, conversely, in *Walden* or in the various journal entries concerning Therien written after 1850 does he suggest how the woodchopper compares with his countrymen in their native element. But it is difficult to imagine that Thoreau would not think of Therien during his visit to Canada; and if, as the tone of "A Yankee in

Canada" suggests, he found the French-Canadians disappointing, it may have been partly because his experience with Therien had given him an exaggerated notion of their virtues.

Thoreau's dissatisfaction with French Canada involves most of the criticisms made by other post-revolutionary American travellers to Canada. Like the invading soldiers of 1775, he is pleasantly surprised by the neat and well-appointed farms and villages along the St. Lawrence, but he is annoyed by the failure of the *habitants* to display the resourcefulness and self-reliance usually associated with the English-speaking settler in North America. Like the Maria Monk writers and others, he is suspicious of Roman Catholicism, especially for its tendency to perpetuate European decadence. Above all, he is hostile to British imperialism, which in his view represents European decadence, and which fosters the lassitude and lack of self-respect frequently displayed by the French-Canadians as a conquered people.

At the same time, however, Thoreau perpetually qualifies and even contradicts his observations, so that his attempt to calculate the moral balance of French Canada threatens to become an infinite series of debits and credits. In the course of a pedestrian excursion from Quebec City to Ste. Anne de Beaupré, he contemplates the differences between the English and French approaches to the early exploration and settlement of North America. The French, he reflects, were far more interested in travel and adventure than the English, and while they were sending fur-trading and exploratory expeditions out from their precarious St. Lawrence settlements down the waterways and into the western hinterland of the continent, the English were busy establishing a solid agrarian and mercantile society on the eastern seaboard.

> In no part of the seventeenth century could the French be said to have had a foothold in Canada; they held only by the fur of the wild animals which they were exterminating.... The New England youth, on the other hand, were never *coureurs de bois* nor *voyageurs*, but backwoodsmen and sailors rather. Of all nations the English undoubtedly have proved hitherto that they had the most business here. (p. 84)[5]

But this contrast between the romance of New France and the chronicle of New England evokes for Thoreau a particularly difficult conundrum. As he points out in *Walden*, New England mercantilism and agrarianism have brought Americans to the dismal point where they are ridden on by the railroad or encumbered by their barns and crops; but the process of social evolution that gives rise to railroads and farms still seems to be a more justifiable fulfilment of human purpose than the self-indulgent and ultimately aimless search for excitement and quick profit indulged in by the early French. "Yet," says Thoreau,

> ...I am not sure but I have most sympathy with that spirit of adventure which distinguished the French and Spaniards of those days, and made them especially the explorers of the American Continent,—which so early carried the former to the Great Lakes and the Mississippi on the north, and the latter to the same river on the south. It was long before our frontiers reached their settlements in the West. So far as inland discovery was concerned, the adventurous spirit of the English was that of sailors who land but for a day, and their enterprise the enterprise of traders. (p. 84)

The modern consequence of the failure of the French to commit themselves to the development of the continent, and their subsequent defeat at the hands of the more aggressive English, is that their French-Canadian descendants reside in isolation and ignorance on the small and poorly cultivated strips of farmland along the St. Lawrence, or in the antiquated parochial societies of Montreal and Quebec. But this isolationism and lack of ambition is not necessarily a fault:

> They are an almost exclusively agricultural, and so far independent population, each family producing nearly all the necessaries of life for itself. If the Canadian wants energy, perchance he possesses those virtues, social and others, which the Yankee lacks, in which case he cannot be regarded as a poor man. (p. 84)

The same sort of ambivalence characterizes Thoreau's attitude to the French-Canadians' religion. In his walk to Ste. Anne he comments wryly on the ubiquitous roadside chapels and crosses: "I could not look at an honest weathercock... without mistrusting that there was some covert reference in it to St. Peter" (p. 56). And earlier, at the cathedral in Montreal, he notes the unthinking, beast-like performance of the religious rituals:

> These Roman Catholics, priests and all, impress me as a people who have fallen far behind the significance of their symbols. It is

> as if an ox had strayed into a church and were trying to bethink himself. (p. 15)

"Nevertheless," Thoreau continues, "they are capable of reverence; but we Yankees are a people in whom this sentiment has nearly died out, and in this respect we cannot bethink ourselves even as oxen" (pp. 15-16).

In a comparable way, Thoreau is at first disconcerted by the redolence of mediaeval Europe, so seemingly inappropriate to the North American setting, invoked by Roman Catholicism:

> To a traveler from the Old World, Canada East may appear like a new country, and its inhabitants like colonists, but to me coming from New England... it appeared as old as Normandy itself, and realized much that I had heard of Europe and the Middle Ages.... To be told by a habitan, when I asked the name of a village in sight, that it is *St. Féréol* or *St. Anne*, the *Guardian Angel* or the *Holy Joseph's*.... As soon as you leave the States, these saintly names begin. (p. 70)

But like the French-Canadians' devotion to simple and parochial cultural values, these vestiges of mediaevalism are not necessarily sinister, because if they indicate an obsession with the past and with remote centres of culture they also invoke visions of a world of romance:

> I began to dream of Provence and the Troubadours, and of places and things which have no existence on the earth. They veiled the Indian and the primitive forest, and the woods toward Hudson's Bay were only as the forests of France and Germany. I could not at once bring myself to believe that the inhabitants who pronounced daily those beautiful and, to me, significant names lead as prosaic lives as we of New England. (p. 71)

The one aspect of French-Canadian experience for which Thoreau cannot find adequate compensation, however, is the French-Canadians' submission to British domination. "They are a nation of peasants" (p. 102), he remarks impatiently after describing the fortifications of Quebec and relating these symbols of the militaristic régime to the long tradition of feudal customs and institutions in New France. "How could a peaceable, freethinking man live neighbor to the Forty-ninth Regiment? A New Englander would naturally be a bad citizen, probably a rebel, there,—

certainly if he were already a rebel at home" (p. 102). In his walking tour to Ste. Anne and Montmorency, in farmhouses and villages remote from any signs of government and military power, Thoreau is able to forget about this aspect of Canada; but in Montreal and Quebec the ubiquitous scarlet coats, stone walls, cannons, and barracks continuously remind him of the ugly fact of foreign domination. To the author of "Civil Disobedience," that idealistic defense of individual integrity against arbitrary authority, these signs of imperial power reflect ignobly on both the weak-willed citizenry who tolerate them and the bureaucrats who sustain them. For the sake of lending rhetorical force to his point, Thoreau avoids any suggestion of similarity between the British presence in Canada and the recent American military adventures in Mexico, which had inspired his "Civil Disobedience." And in this context he finds himself granting almost completely unqualified praise for the political system of his own country:

> Give me a country where it is the most natural thing in the world for a government that does not understand you to let you alone.... What makes the United States government, on the whole, more tolerable,—I mean for us lucky white men,—is the fact that there is so much less of government with us.... In Canada you are reminded of the government every day. It parades itself before you. It is not content to be the servant, but will be the master; and every day it goes out to the Plains of Abraham or to the Champ de Mars and exhibits itself and toots. (pp. 101-02)

Elsewhere in "A Yankee in Canada" Thoreau concisely and effectively summarizes the differences between American and French-Canadian social traditions. In accordance with his perennial interest in the habitation as the epitome or symbol of a culture, he calls attention to the Canadians' circumscribed and introspective lives by describing their unusually constructed farmhouses, which he compares with the farmhouses of New England:

> ... these Canadian houses have no front door, properly speaking. Every part is for the use of the occupant exclusively, and no part has reference to the traveler or to travel. Every New England house, on the contrary, has a front and principal door opening to the great world, though it may be on the cold side, for it stands on the highway of nations, and the road which runs by it comes

from the Old World and goes to the far West; but the Canadian's door opens into his backyard and farm alone, and the road which runs behind his house leads only from the church of one saint to that of another. (p. 73)

Ironically, Thoreau's comparative meditation on America and Canada leads to a complex historical paradox. It would appear that the French came to North America as adventurers and traders and ended as unambitious farmers and townspeople, while the English came to establish farms and towns and emerged in the nineteenth century as adventurers and explorers. Thoreau offers some tentative suggestions towards solving this paradox, particularly by reference to a contrast between "Anglo-Saxon" libertarian traditions and continental European absolutism, a contrast that was to form part of the foundation of Francis Parkman's epic historical series on New France. But Thoreau was not interested in working out these ideas in the systematic way a historian might have done—at least not in "A Yankee in Canada," although he may have had some such plan in mind for the more elaborate work that remained unfinished. Ultimately, the most memorable impressions left by the narrative of his northern excursion are those involving suggestive, synthesizing images, such as his descriptions of the Montreal churches as caves inhabited by oxen, his comparison of a regiment of British soldiers to a colony of ants, his dreams of Provence and the troubadours inspired by Canadian place names, or his description of the typical Canadian house. In the concluding pages of the work he mentions how another tourist exclaimed, shortly after crossing the American border, "there's not so good a house as that in all Canada!" (p. 124). The American house, reflecting simplicity, directness, individualism—or at least the opportunity to cultivate these virtues—is preferable to the decadence and cultural stagnation suggested by its Canadian counterpart.

IV

THE CANADIAN PAST: THE IDYLL OF ACADIA

Thoreau's image of Canada is particularly distinguished by a detailed and informed interest in Canadian history. When he looked at the French Canada of 1850, Thoreau saw a priest- and soldier-ridden society that passively accepted foreign domination and seemed perversely indifferent to self-improvement and progress. When he contemplated the anterior chronicle of New France, however, he discovered a saga of exploration and adventure that, in spite of the totalitarian institutions that inspired it and ultimately brought it to a tragic conclusion, seemed to reflect a type of heroic individualism comparable to that associated with the westward movement of the nineteenth-century United States. In "A Yankee in Canada" Thoreau did not explore in detail the paradoxical similarities between the ages of adventure in totalitarian New France and republican America, but these similarities caught his attention, as they caught the attention of certain other American writers of his time.

As R. W. B. Lewis has observed, perhaps no nation has been so ambivalent in its attitude to history as the nineteenth-century United States: at the very moment influential figures like Ralph Waldo Emerson were proclaiming the emergence of a completely new and unprecedented era, writers like Hawthorne, Cooper, Longfellow, and even Emerson himself were more and more turning imaginatively to the past.[1] To compound the paradox, as Lewis further notes, the nineteenth century saw a prolific development in historiography in the United States, through the efforts of such scholars as George Bancroft, John Lothrop Motley, Richard Hildreth, William H. Prescott, and Francis Parkman. This paradox might be resolved by invoking the cliché that people study the past in order to understand the present and predict the future, but it would be more accurate to say that nineteenth-century Americans often scrutinized the past in order to confirm the rightness and inevitability of America's present and future. In fact, one can generalize further that the aim of nineteenth-century American historiography was the same as that of much of the poetry, fiction, and drama of the time: to create a national image or myth, or, more exactly, a world myth with the United States at the centre, since these historians, like many contemporary poets and novelists, did not confine their attention to the United States or even to the New World. The lines between history and imaginative fable were by no means clearly drawn in the nineteenth century, in spite of constantly increasing attention to scholarly methodology. With the concept of history as "social science" still to be developed in America, historians like Prescott and Parkman thought of themselves as having much more in common with Longfellow, Cooper, and Scott than with Agassiz, Cuvier, and Humboldt. Thoreau could think of moving naturally from his familiar essays, travelogues, and poems to a history of aboriginal America, while Bancroft, Parkman, and their colleagues dabbled in poetry and fiction, and wrote history with the narrative and dramatic energy of the best nineteenth-century imaginative literature.

The American version of Canadian history was episodic rather than comprehensive, and often the episodes chosen for emphasis were those that had particular relevance or parallels to the United States. One incident from Canadian history that nineteenth-century Americans found especially interesting was the story of the expulsion of the Acadians from Nova Scotia in 1755. Longfellow's tear-jerking poetic treatment of the topic in *Evangeline* (1847) is well known, but there are at least two other notable American versions dating from about the same time as Longfellow's poem, one a novelistic treatment, and the other a supposedly scholarly exposition by a historian. The novel, *The Neutral French: or The Exiles of Nova Scotia* (1841), was the work of a Rhode Island author, Catherine Williams (1787-1872). The earliest detailed historiographical treatment of the expulsion was that of George Bancroft (1800-91), in the fourth volume (first edition, 1852) of his *History of the United States* (1834-76, and many subsequent editions).

In a long introduction to *The Neutral French*, Catherine Williams represents the expulsion of the Acadians as a particularly heinous crime in a chronicle of British injustice against both the French and English settlers of North America. Then, in the early chapters of her narrative, she dramatizes the idyllic simplicity, happiness, and unsuspecting innocence of the Acadians, all of which are disrupted by the tyrannical British. But while she exploits a rather gruesome picture of suffering and endurance, she begins to develop an antiphonal theme involving the defiant self-possession of two young Acadian sisters. Separated from their family and transported to New England, the two sisters are transformed into Americans, a transformation that proceeds apace as their careers involve archetypal American patterns of revolutionary activity and economic and social success. The acceptance of American social ideals is followed by a rather incredible mass-religious conversion. The author obviously cannot bear to think of her Acadians as adherents of Roman Catholicism, so she represents them as continually expressing religious doubts; eventually all of the Acadian exiles in the novel—including even the parish priest—are converted to Protestantism.

As this summary suggests, *The Neutral French* is essentially a tract celebrating the rise of the American republic, with the Acadians serving first as innocent victims of British tyranny and subsequently as heroes of American independence. The movement from Acadia to America is obviously a fortunate fall in which native innocence is transformed into self-reliant moral strength. A similar development of the theme is evident in the work of George Bancroft.

As a historian, Bancroft made some effort to create the impression of scholarly comprehensiveness and objectivity, or at least to distinguish between his view of the past and that of the poet or romancer. In his version of the Acadian expulsion he makes no mention of Williams's novel (with which, indeed, he may not have been familiar) or even of Longfellow's famous poem, which had been published a few years before the completion of the fourth volume of Bancroft's history. A close consideration, however, of his version of the Acadian story indicates that he exploits the romantic and sentimental aspects of the story no less than the novelist and poet.

Bancroft's whole history is strongly anti-British, having as its theme the justification of American independence and the republican political system. Hence his brief survey of French North American history, interwoven in his third and fourth volumes with the stories of English and Dutch settlements in the American colonies, is treated as a prologue to the rise of individualism and libertarianism in New England. The Seven Years ("French and Indian") War prefigures the American Revolution, and great emphasis is placed on the cruel and arbitrary actions of the English government and army, not only towards the French, but towards the American colonial governments and militia forces. The Acadian episode is of particular value to Bancroft's thesis, and his indignant version of the story focuses on the tyranny of the British and the suffering of the exiles. Before the expulsion, says Bancroft, the Acadians lived in idyllic pastoral simplicity, in a kind of Golden Age of peace and contentment:

> No tax-gatherer counted their folds, no magistrate dwelt in their hamlets.... The pastures were covered with herds and flocks;... the meadows... were covered with grasses, or fields of wheat.... With the spinning wheel and the loom, their women made, of flax from their own fields, of fleeces from their own flocks, coarse but sufficient clothing.... Happy in their neutrality, the Acadians formed, as it were, one great family.[2]

Then suddenly and without reason—so Bancroft alleges—this idyllic existence was violently disrupted. Ignoring the possibility that the expulsion involved the connivance of New England administrators who had designs on the Nova Scotian farmland, and the fact that it was carried out by colonial militia, Bancroft excoriates the British "lords of trade, more merciless than the savages and the wilderness in winter," who "wished very much that every one of the Acadians should be driven out."[3] Most of his narrative involves similar extravagant rhetoric and categorical denunciations of the British motives and methods. Families were separated, says Bancroft, the refugees were subjected to indignities at the hands of the soldiers, and later, in the English colonies, the Acadian exiles "were cast ashore without resources."

> A beautiful and fertile tract of country was reduced to a solitude. There was none left round the ashes of the cottages of the Acadians but the faithful watchdog, vainly seeking the hands that fed him.[4]

Of particular significance in Bancroft's account of the Acadian expulsion are the intimations of lapsarian imagery that evoke a North American version of the Fall, with Acadia as Eden and the British as the intrusive agents of corruption. As numerous critics have pointed out, the lapsarian fable is a pervasive feature of the literature of the United States, and appears in both tragic and triumphant versions. In the tragic phase, an American Adam (or, frequently, an American Eve) is thwarted, deceived, or destroyed by sinister forces emanating from Europe—or from New England, if the protagonist is a westerner—or sometimes from inherent weaknesses of character and intellect. In the triumphant phase, the innocence of the American is an irresistible source of energy that eventually overwhelms opposing forces. Or, in a variation of the triumphant version based on the idea of the Fortunate Fall, the American loses his innocence but goes on to encounter and conquer adversity with a new intellectual and moral strength. Insofar as the Acadians fit into this American fabular structure, they obviously belong to the first version, as victims of European corruption and malevolence. But in the version developed by Bancroft—and later, at greater length, by Longfellow—the Acadians are unusually passive and pathetic victims, so lacking in such traditional American virtues as intuitive shrewdness and self-righteous moral energy that they are completely unable to defend themselves from the expulsion. The indigenous United States version of the tragic conflict between innocence and evil is seldom so uncompromising: even the naïve heroes and heroines of Henry James are not always passive, for their innocence is often related to a wilful refusal to adapt to foreign situations and ideas. The Acadians, however—at least as seen by nineteenth-century Americans—are given no opportunity for resistance. Even if they had the self-reliance and aggressiveness necessary to oppose the British, they would still be unable to resist the physical force arrayed against them. Ultimately, this extravagant image of the innocent Acadians recalls the condescending attitude of travellers such as Thoreau, Dana, John Cousens Ogden, and others, whose comparative tolerance towards the French-Canadians was related to an assumption that they would eventually be absorbed by the Anglo-North American population. The Acadians of nineteenth-century American memory, unlike the French-Canadians of nineteenth-century American observation, are much too good to exist in a fallen world, and their only alternative to complete extinction is assimilation into the irresistible historical evolution of the United States.

Longfellow's treatment of the Acadian theme, in contrast to Williams' and Bancroft's, does not at first glance appear to involve the idea of either the Fortunate Fall or of the triumphant historical development of the United States. His attention is absorbed by other aspects of the story, particularly the situation of the heroine. It was the sentimental and individual aspects of the story that first caught Longfellow's attention, not the anti-British implications or the suggestive movement of the refugees from Acadia to colonial America. When a friend related to him the allegedly true story of a young Acadian girl separated from her lover and spending most of her life searching for him, Longfellow is reported to have described it as "the best illustration of faithfulness and the constancy of woman that I have ever heard of or read."[5] In accordance with this first impression, Longfellow developed in the poem a close focus on the plight of the heroine, her pathetic weakness, and her dogged fidelity. Even in the expulsion episode the poet does not divert attention from his main character to give vent to anti-British sentiments: Evangeline and her people accept the cruel military edict with Christian patience. Indeed, the word "patience" is invoked repeatedly throughout the poem, emphasizing Evangeline's extremely passive attitude, which contrasts to the energetic actions of Catherine Williams's heroines.

But Longfellow devotes a substantial amount of attention to the community of Grand Pré as well as to his heroine, and his Acadia before the expulsion, like the images expounded by Bancroft and Williams, is a pre-lapsarian world of peace, contentment, and mutual benevolence:

> There in the tranquil evenings of summer when brightly the sunset
> Lighted the village street, and gilded the vanes on the chimneys,
> Matrons and maidens sat in snow-white caps and in kirtles
> Scarlet and blue and green, with distaffs spinning the golden
> Flax for the gossipping looms, whose noisy shuttles within doors
> Mingled their sound with the whir of the wheels and the songs of the maidens.
> Solemnly down the street came the parish priest, and the children
> Paused in their play to kiss the hand he extended to bless them.
> Reverend walked he among them; and up rose matrons and maidens,
> Hailing his slow approach with words of affectionate welcome.
> Then came the labourers home from the field, and serenely the sun sank
> Down to his rest, and twilight prevailed. Anon from the belfry
> Softly the Angelus sounded, and over the roofs of the village
> Columns of pale-blue smoke, like clouds of incense ascending,
> Rose from a hundred hearths, the homes of peace and contentment.
> Thus dwelt together in love these simple Acadian farmers—
> Dwelt in the love of God and of man. Alike were they free from
> Fear, that reigns with the tyrant, and envy, the vice of republics.[6]

Longfellow is said to have adapted this image of Acadia, like his rather somniferous metrical form, from Scandinavian sources—he never visited

Nova Scotia, presumably because he felt that the nineteenth-century British province would add nothing to his imaginative vision of the eighteenth-century French colony—but the ultimate origin of the poem's setting is pastoral and golden-age mythology. The benevolent figure of the parish priest and the reference to "smoke, like clouds of incense ascending" suggest a tolerance of Roman Catholicism unusual in nineteenth-century America—or rather, they suggest a design to absorb some of the features of Roman Catholicism into an atmosphere of languidly sensuous beauty.

This atmosphere predominates in the early, Acadian episodes of the poem, and a continuation or variation of it extends into later scenes where Evangeline carries her search into the hinterlands of the British American colonies and down through time into the post-revolutionary United States. The background to Evangeline's search is a panorama of American history from agrarian colony to urban republic, and a simultaneous panorama of geography encompassing the western and southern frontiers as well as the cities of the eastern seaboard. This movement from a static and idyllic Arcadia towards a constantly evolving, morally ambivalent, industrialized and urbanized society reflects the prevalent nineteenth-century American concept of progress, and the assumption that less dynamic cultures in this historical movement are doomed to extinction. But Longfellow's attitude to these ideas, unlike Catherine Williams' or Bancroft's, is elegaic. Acadia cannot exist in the modern world; Evangeline can be united with her Gabriel only in death; and in the disappearance of Acadia and of the innocence that informs the love of Gabriel and Evangeline, something has been lost for which such worldly gains as American political independence or modern social progress cannot entirely compensate.

V

THE CANADIAN PAST:
THE ROMANCE OF NEW FRANCE

Among early-nineteenth-century American literary conceptions of Canada, Longfellow's image of Acadia is perhaps exceptional for the intensity of its sentimentality, but the essential nature of the poet's attitude is typical of his time and place. In poems, travel narratives, histories, and historical romances, nineteenth-century Americans repeatedly express an ambivalence towards Canada, an ambivalence that is frequently resolved by their acceptance of what are believed to be the imperatives of New World history. On the one hand, Canada, in contrast to the United States, is sometimes seen as a more primitive and pure civilization, where man lives close to nature and the soil, where intimations of peace and innocence are still possible. On the other hand, the inexorable current of history seems to justify the disappearance of such primitivism and the evolution of the complex, progressive civilization of the United States. This historical development is often justified further by an appeal to the decadence of the French colonies, to their aristocratic social structure, and frequently to their Roman Catholicism.

The ambivalent attitude to the New World is evident in many of the historical romances written in the wake of the success of James Fenimore Cooper. Cooper himself never used specific Canadian settings, being committed imaginatively to his native region of upstate New York and a few other United States locales, but his evocation of the northern border wilderness during the eighteenth-century French and Indian wars is worth noting for its obvious analogies and occasional direct relevance to the nineteenth-century American image of Canada. Also important are his characterizations of Leatherstocking, his conception of the North American Indian, his exploration of the contrast between civilization and primitivism, and his consideration of the respective activities of the French and English in the New World.

The character of Leatherstocking is, in effect, the personification of Cooper's ambivalence towards the New World. Physically powerful, intrepid, intuitively virtuous, the epitome of American self-reliance and the westering impulse Cooper admired in his countrymen, Leatherstocking is at the same time the victim of historical inevitability, doomed to disappear as certainly as the forests and Indians with which he is constantly associated. In this respect he and his Indian companions are like Longfellow's Acadians, although the parallels do not go beyond their innate virtue, for unlike the Acadians, Cooper's characters are committed to action. The action to which they commit themselves, however, although admirable in terms of Cooper's favourable disposition to romantic heroism, is futile in its antagonism to the prevailing currents of history. As a moral force, this action is to be praised, especially for its opposition to the evil forces Cooper associates with the French and Indians of Canada, and to the irrational libertarianism of some elements among his countrymen. But in the long run, Cooper believes in progress, especially in the evolution of an American moral ideal, which he personifies in the "gentleman," a type of cultivated and conservative individual much like Cooper himself, who reflects the best features of Old and New World civilization. In Cooper's view, the facts of eighteenth- and early-nineteenth-century North American history—the defeat of New France, the gradual disappearance of the Indian, the westward withdrawal (and, in Cooper's own fiction, the eventual extinction) of the frontiersman—all bear out this conception of New World development.

In this imaginative scheme, Canada is associated not with primaeval innocence, as in Longfellow, but with the decadence of the doomed French colonial empire and the alleged barbarism of the northern Indian tribes who were allies of the French. Cooper evokes an indirect but ominous image of the northern country as the source and stronghold of a dark principle contrasting to the illuminating cultural forces arising in the colonies to the south. His Canadian Indians, such as the famous Magua of *The Last of the Mohicans* (1826), are incarnations of treachery; the French are represented as anonymous masses of white-clad troops, like the besiegers of Fort William Henry in the same novel, or as comic-opera stereotypes, like the wily and unctuous Captain Sanglier in *The Pathfinder* (1840). The only individual associated with Canada who is granted any substantial merit is the Marquis de Montcalm in *The Last of the Mohicans*:

> The Marquis of Montcalm was, at the period of which we write, in the flower of his age, and it may be added, in the zenith of his fortune. But, even in that enviable situation, he was affable, and distinguished as much for his attention to the forms of courtesy as for that chivalrous courage which, only two short years afterward, induced him to throw away his life on the plains of Abraham.[1]

The author subsequently condemns Montcalm for his failure to prevent the massacre at Fort William Henry, and describes him as "a man who was great in all the minor attributes of character, but who was found wanting when it became necessary to prove how much principle is superior to policy."[2] But in spite of this ultimately negative judgement, the brief scenes of the French general magnanimously conferring with his defeated enemies, and drifting incognito like Shakespeare's Henry v through his army encampment in the early morning, make him one of Cooper's more interesting minor characters, and reflect an admiration for the idea of gentility the class-conscious American author obviously felt, even as he claimed to reject it in its European forms.

In spite of its indirectness, its oversimplifications, biases, and errors of fact, Cooper's representation of Canada has greater cultural substance than the ostensibly more detailed and specific images of Canada created by several of his successors in the historical romance tradition. New France is the setting for about a dozen early-nineteenth-century American historical novels, but almost without exception these works rely on simplistic clichés of character and action, and do not pretend to much depth of cultural analysis. Nevertheless, these fictions provide both elaboration and contrast to Cooper's retrospective image of the New World. Also, like the anti-Catholic fictions discussed previously, they yield valuable intimations of American intellectual and emotional experience, particularly at the mass or popular level.

Politically, the Cooper imitators tended to be more committed to egalitarian democracy than Cooper was, although like him they were sometimes interested in the heroic possibilities of the French aristocrat. In a similar way, the northern forest wilderness elicited an ambivalent response: it was often simultaneously the retreat of primitive or retrogressive forces and the setting for the development of the American frontier hero. In addition, the northern setting might sometimes retain vestiges of the Edenic or pastoral imagery popularized by Longfellow. But unlike Longfellow and Cooper, many of these writers, like Catherine Williams of *The Neutral French,* were strenuously anti-Catholic, and they often attributed the prevalence of Anglo-American over French culture in the New World to the religious decadence of the French.

Many of these general features of the historical romance with a Canadian setting can be seen in *The Rivals of Acadia* (1827), written by a Bostonian named Harriet Vaughan Cheney. The "rivals" are the feudal proprietors Charles d'Aulnay and Charles de la Tour, whose squabble over seventeenth-century Acadia was of particular historical interest to Americans because it seemed to prefigure some aspects of the ideological and military conflict between democratic America and aristocratic Europe. La Tour was traditionally supposed to be a Protestant, which made him a sympathetic figure in American eyes, and the legends associated with him included an Amazonian wife who almost singlehandedly defended their stronghold during her husband's absence. All these elements and more, including frequent disguises, astounding revelations, and daring deeds modeled on the actions of Cooper and Scott characters, are featured in *The Rivals of Acadia.* As literature the work is without value, but it is interesting for its ambivalence towards the feudalistic society of New France. On the one hand, the main characters in the novel are obviously of genteel birth, and possess such traditional European signs of social superiority as good education, refined manners and authoritative demeanour. On the other hand, some of them incline towards a Protestant-inspired modern individualism and egalitarianism, and the novel ultimately resolves into a conflict between those characters who are prefigurations of Americans and those inflexible Europeans who are unable to attune themselves to the New World.

This theme is quite bluntly spelled out in a novella entitled "Castine," one of three *Tales of the Puritans* (1831) by Delia Salter Bacon (1811–59). Again, the French of Canada are mostly aristocrats: Baron Castine was an actual landowner and fur trader of the seventeenth century. But the hero, Castine's son, reveals that his English mother brought him up as a Protestant, and, in the end, he and a young female English captive escape to a new life in the British colonies.

Another occasionally popular subject for American historical romancers was the famous seventeenth-century governor of New France, Count Frontenac, who appears in four nineteenth-century American adventure narratives. He is the hero of a long, jingling narrative poem entitled *Frontenac* (1849) by the New York poetaster Alfred B. Street (1811–81). He figures also in a trilogy of dime novels by Ann Stephens (1813–86): *Ahmo's Plot; or The Governor's Indian Child* (1863), *Mahaska, The Indian Princess* (1863), and *The Indian Queen* (1864).

Both Street and Stephens deal with the same legend involving the French governor's affair with an Indian woman, and his subsequent tumultuous relationship with his half-breed daughter. The two authors also share a dominant interest in the Indians of Canada, who figure much more prominently than the French in their narratives. The Indians of Street and Stephens are conventional natural noblemen, marked by a taciturn and stoical hauteur and by an affinity with the wilderness. In the latter respect, particularly, they are the antithesis of the French-Canadian aristocrats like Frontenac, who are committed to their ceremonious and decadent civilization. While the Iroquois are depicted as the free and energetic children of the out-of-doors, the French are portrayed as the virtual prisoners of their social customs and institutions, confined to their walled cities and their châteaux. Throughout Street's poem, Frontenac is repeatedly depicted as sitting in his "usual room," glowering silently, as the poet rhymes it in his metronomic couplets, "with a brow of deepened gloom."[3] And in Stephens's novel *Ahmo's Plot*, Frontenac constantly broods over his exile from his native France in the wilds of Canada.

In the narratives of Street and Stephens, Frontenac is the epitome of the French failure to adapt to the New World. Not only do the French cling to the customs and institutions of Europe, they commit what in nineteenth-century American eyes appears to be the cardinal sin. Leslie Fiedler has pointed out in *Love and Death in the American Novel* how early American authors—most notably James Fenimore Cooper—seemed to be fascinated by the allegedly tragic consequences of miscegenation between white and Indian.[4] According to both Street and Stephens, Frontenac, in taking an Indian mistress, unleashes a chain of events involving disease, war, murder, and revenge. Thus the French of Canada (in contrast, so these authors imply, to the Anglo-Americans) not only establish an inappropriate social structure in the wilderness, they offend against nature in various ways—particularly the sexual—and bring themselves, their society, and the primitive inhabitants of the wilderness to destruction.

Yet just as Cooper saw Montcalm sympathetically, both Street and Stephens see Frontenac as a tragic hero. In spite of his apparent violation of some elemental principle in the relationship between man and nature, Frontenac is an admirable figure, for the values he imports from Europe are not entirely antagonistic to Americans. American civilization has supposedly triumphed where French-Canadian civilization failed because the Americans recognized and pursued the virtues called forth by the New World—virtues such as freedom, individualism, and, apparently, the preservation of racial purity. But the French devotion to authoritarianism, ceremony, and social complexity is to some extent an object of wistful envy for Americans, even as they assert the irrelevance of these entities to the New World experience. As Cooper observed of Montcalm, the French aristocrats can be admired for certain qualities of character even though they fail to recognize the exigencies of the North American situation.

The aristocratic hero was not always the central concern of the American forest romance set in New France, however. Some novelists preferred to use a more democratic type of protagonist, such as the Anglo-American woodsman modeled on Cooper's Leatherstocking, who becomes involved in the seventeenth- and eighteenth-century French and Indian wars and demonstrates prophetically the courage and ingenuity of the American frontiersman. *Haverhill; or, Memoirs of an Officer in the Army of Wolfe* (1831) by James A. Jones (1791–1854) is a breezy, picaresque story of the exploits of a young Cape Cod man who leaves home to seek his fortune and ends up in Wolfe's army at the siege of Quebec, in which, needless to say, he plays a vital rôle. *Ish-Noo-Ju-Lut-Sche; or The Eagle of the Mohawks* (1841), by J. L. E. W. Shecut (1770–1836), is an unabashed imitation of Cooper in which a Dutch settler in seventeenth-century New York joins a Dutch and Indian military campaign against the French and Indians of Canada. In a sequel, *The Scout; or The Fast of St. Nicholas* (1844), Shecut introduces a Leatherstocking imitation named Rawlee, who, in the course of a campaign against the French and Indians, holds forth like his prototype on a variety of political, religious, and ethnic topics.

Like Cooper, both Jones and Shecut are interested in comparing the American and Canadian historical experiences with respect to the conquest of the wilderness and the development of a distinctive New World type of individual. More specific than Cooper in their use of Canadian settings and French-Canadian characters, the two minor novelists demonstrate how Anglo-American and Dutch-American individualism and liberalism triumph over French autocratic and feudal traditions. Shecut, who uses his two novels to expound the benevolent doctrines of Universalist Christianity, is more tolerant towards the French-Canadians than Jones: in *Ish-Noo-Ju-Lut-Sche*, the inhabitants of the Canadian villages of La Chine and Montreal are represented as pious and simple peasants, whose Roman Catholicism, "bigotry and superstition apart... afforded as fair a field for the attainment of evangelical holiness as any other christian sect in the universe."[5] In Jones's *Haverhill*, however, the French are garrulous and silly, given to dancing jigs and chattering inanely.

Shecut, furthermore, is less tolerant when dealing with the administrative, military, and religious leaders of New France, whom he accuses of plotting to conquer the Five Nations Indian confederacy while pretending friendship and concern for their spiritual welfare.

In other American historical romances dealing with New France, the alleged religious and ethnic degeneracy of French-Canadians is quite crudely portrayed in narrative images comparable to those in *The Awful Disclosures of Maria Monk*. In a dime-novel trilogy by C. Dunning Clarke (also known as W.J. Hamilton)—*The Silent Slayer; or, The Maid of Montreal* (1869), *Despard, the Spy; or, The Fall of Montreal* (1869), and *Graybeard, the Sorcerer, or, The Recluse of Mount Royale* (1874)—the Canadian city with its Gothic churches, sinister ecclesiastics, and wily civilian and military populations is the setting for a tale of espionage and revenge during the eighteenth-century French and Indian wars. A somewhat more literate novel by Charles W. Hall, *Twice Taken: An Historical Romance of the Maritime British Provinces* (1867), deals with the political and military events associated with the Cape Breton fortress of Louisbourg, but much of the novel focuses on the grotesque fictional personage of Du Thet, a militant Jesuit priest who wields a ruthless sword, dabbles in mesmerism and prophecy, and even conjures up the spirits of the dead. *Lucelle: or The Young Iroquois!* (1845), by the prolific novelist Osgood Bradbury, is not explicitly anti-Catholic, but the inferiority of French-Canadians is emphasized (in a manner reminiscent of Washington Irving's treatment of the voyageurs in *Astoria*) in social and ethnic terms. Bradbury's French-Canadian heroine "sometimes dreamed of having a British officer of high rank and wealth for her husband, in case she could not obtain a French one."[6] In the end, however, she not only fails to attract a French or English husband, but she is united with an Iroquois brave, in a daring consummation of the miscegenation theme Cooper could resolve in *The Last of the Mohicans* only by giving his fated heroine a drop of Indian blood, then killing off both her and her Indian lover. But the marriage of Bradbury's Lucelle and the Indian is presumably acceptable, since, in the eyes of the author, a lower-class French-Canadian appears socially and ethnically equal to an Indian.

The ethnic, religious, and social calumnies against New France and the northern Indians in American historical romances prompted at least one novelist to attempt to redress the balance. James McSherry (1819–69), a Maryland Catholic author, produced *Père Jean; or, The Jesuit Missionary* (1847), based on the real-life exploits of Father Isaac Jogues. McSherry takes Cooper as his model, but reverses Cooper's ethnic and moral equations. The title character is accompanied on his mission by a French-Canadian version of Leatherstocking named Pierre, known as *l'Espion hardi,* who is, in turn, followed by a faithful Christian Huron, an exact opposite to the satanic Hurons Cooper depicted. *Père Jean* is a simplistic attempt to refute Cooper's statements about Canada and its inhabitants by adapting Cooper's own characters and situations to a series of contradictory propositions, and its relative success in this venture is perhaps reflected in the obscurity in which McSherry's hackneyed narrative rests.

As this brief survey suggests, the subject of New France did not inspire nineteenth-century American fiction writers to artistic and intellectual heights beyond the stereotypes of character and incident popularized by Cooper, or beyond the religious and ethnic prejudices widespread in their cultural environment. There was, however, at least one ambitious attempt to exploit the history of early Canada in fiction. Ohio-born Mary Hartwell Catherwood (1847–1902) was the author of a great many popular historical romances involving both North American and European settings, including four titles using characters and settings related to New France: *The Romance of Dollard* (1889), *The Story of Tonty* (1890), *The Lady of Fort St. John* (1891), and *The Chase of St.-Castin and Other Stories of the French in the New World* (1894). Catherwood was a talented and knowledgeable professional author who researched her historical backgrounds conscientiously and who attempted to endow her fictionalizations of historical episodes with some depth of characterization and idea. Her efforts appeared impressive enough in their time to win the approval of the historian Francis Parkman, who hailed Catherwood, in a preface to *The Romance of Dollard,* as "a pioneer in what may be called a new departure in American fiction":

> Fenimore Cooper, in his fresh and manly way, sometimes touches Canadian subjects and introduces us to French soldiers and bush-rangers; but he knew Canada only from the outside, having no means of making its acquaintance from within, and it is only from within that its quality as material for romance can be appreciated. The hard and practical features of English colonization seem to frown down every excursion of fancy as pitilessly as puritanism itself did in its day. A feudal society, on the other hand, with its contrasted lights and shadows, its rivalries and passions, is the natural theme of romance; and when to lord and vassal is joined a dominant hierarchy with its patient martyrs and its spiritual despots, side by side with savage chiefs

and warriors jostling the representatives of the most gorgeous civilization of modern times,—the whole strange scene set in an environment of primeval forests,—the spectacle is as striking as it is unique.[7]

Parkman's catalogue of the elements of early Canadian history—the contrasts of feudalism, the zealousness of Catholicism, the primitivism of the Indian and the forest—is a succinct indication of the narrative and dramatic possibilities of the subject. It is arguable, however, whether Catherwood succeeded as well as Parkman contends in her development of these possibilities. She does go beyond Cooper in her detailed representations of Canadian settings, characters, and events, and she refrains from indulging in the querulous religious and ethnic comparisons of other historical romancers. On the whole, however, her fictions are unsophisticated exploitations of the nineteenth-century sentimental and adventure-story traditions. Her heroes, like the legendary defender of Montreal in *The Romance of Dollard*, or the faithful follower of the explorer La Salle in *The Story of Tonty*, are anachronistic embodiments of the nineteenth-century American ideals of egalitarianism and individualism, and their unfailing courage and devotion leave virtually no room for complexities of characterization. Her favourite settings are not the Canadian forests, but various enclosed spaces: fortresses, cathedrals, chapels, châteaux, and, most frequently, the living quarters of her heroes and heroines, which create an impression not of the cultural panorama of which Parkman speaks, but of rather cramped domestic dramas. Her plots, furthermore, are often developed through bizarre Gothic elements, such as the dwarf who is believed to fly on a swan's back in *The Lady of Fort St. John*, the woman in the same novel who preserves the amputated hand of her husband, the transvestite religious hermit of *The Romance of Dollard*, and the werewolf apparition of the short story "The Beauport Loup-Garou." Some of these devices, it is true, are adapted from traditional French-Canadian superstition and folklore; but their use is so conventionalized that they bring the narratives in which they occur closer to the cruder elements of the Gothic novel than to the unique atmosphere of the historical setting from which they are supposedly derived.

Catherwood's interest in New France, furthermore, seems subordinated to her nineteenth-century political and social interests, particularly the cause of feminism, which she represents through a series of aggressive and independent heroines. In *The Romance of Dollard*, she provides the leader of the Long Sault expedition with an imaginary wife who zealously follows her husband to martyrdom; in *The Story of Tonty*, she provides La Salle's lieutenant with a resourceful young female companion; in *The Lady of Fort St. John*, she depicts the legendary Amazonian qualities of Madame de la Tour; and in her short stories she follows the careers of various historical and mythical heroines of New France. Of course, Catherwood has as much artistic licence to use the history and legend of New France for her feminist purposes as other romancers have to adapt this material to their various ethnic, religious, and nationalistic prejudices. Indeed, it is inevitable that her fictional image of New France should be a reflection of her individual background and interests, rather than an objective, impersonal representation of historical settings and events; but Parkman was clearly deceived about the nature and quality of her work when he credited her with a comprehensive artistic rendering of the exotic story of early Canada. Catherwood was perhaps the best of a rather undistinguished series of authors who approached this subject; but in treating the theme of New France, no nineteenth-century American fiction writer succeeded in rising very far above the level of stereotype, cliché, and social and religious prejudice. The most effective realization of this theme was achieved not in the medium of fiction, but in historiography, by Catherwood's mentor and advocate, Francis Parkman.

VI

FRANCE AND ENGLAND IN NORTH AMERICA

"The early history of Canada," wrote Francis Parkman to a Canadian historian in 1856, "is so full of dramatic incident and noble examples of devoted heroism, that it is a matter of wonder that American writers have, until lately, so little regarded it."[1] This history, as has been seen, was the object of the occasional and rather superficial notice of American romancers throughout the nineteenth century, but no serious American historian before Parkman gave it the rigorous scholarly and imaginative scrutiny that was accorded more nationalistic subjects. George Bancroft devoted some attention to New France in his *History of the United States*, but his brief and romanticized versions of the exploits of such heroes as Champlain, Frontenac, and LaSalle, and of such events as the seven-years war, the Acadian expulsion, and the fall of Quebec, were subordinated to the narrative of the emerging liberalism and independence of the American colonies. Henry Thoreau, after visiting Canada in 1850, began preliminary work towards a history of the North American Indian that was to make extensive use of his Canadian experiences and studies, but by the time of his death in 1862 this work had progressed no further than several notebooks of memoranda and extracts. French-Canadian scholars had devoted substantial attention to pre-Conquest history, but Parkman felt that their efforts were distorted by political and religious partisanship and limited by inadequate research. So when he turned his attention, in the 1850s, to the magnum opus that eventually appeared in seven parts between 1865 and 1892 under the series title *France and England in North America*, the Boston historian saw himself as the pioneer in an undeveloped subject.

As has been noted, during most of the nineteenth century, historiography was conceived primarily as a literary art, having affinities with fiction, poetry, and drama, rather than with scientific research. Parkman's own literary tastes inclined to the historical romance, particularly as practised by James Fenimore Cooper and Sir Walter Scott, both of whom he greatly admired. Cooper was a particular favourite, as Parkman indicated in his preface to Mary Catherwood's *The Romance of Dollard* as well as in a critical essay on the Leatherstocking tales, written in 1852. But Cooper, according to Parkman, had only an indirect and peripheral interest in Canada, and his primary achievement had been the realistic portrayal of the forest and a few American frontier character types.[2] Like Cooper, Parkman was fascinated by the North American wilderness; since his early youth when he developed his life-long enthusiasm for rambling in the woods, and especially since his years as a student at Harvard when he conceived the idea of writing the history of what was called "the Old French War," he was "haunted with wilderness images day and night."[3] Also like Cooper, Parkman was fascinated by the North American Indian, particularly as he existed in the early centuries of European exploration and settlement in the New World. But unlike Cooper, who created his Indians from conventional literary conceptions, Parkman was eager to recreate as accurately as possible the life and thought of the North American aborigine; so eager, in fact, that he endangered his health to pursue, on the Oregon Trail, the observation of tribes still living a nomadic life similar to that of the Indians of seventeenth- and eighteenth-century Canada. Most of all, however, Parkman was fascinated by the exotic and paradoxical panorama of New France. These three elements—the forest, the Indian, and the society of New France—form the main elements of *France and England in North America*.

Parkman's title implies an equal division of interest between the French and English colonies; but the overwhelming emphasis, as is suggested by the author's working title, "France in the New World" (given in his introduction to the first volume), is on New France. This disproportion recalls the attitude of Thoreau, who declared in "A Yankee in Canada" that "of all nations, the English undoubtedly have proved hitherto that they had the most business [in North America].... Yet I am not sure but I have most sympathy with that spirit of adventure which distinguished the French."[4] Throughout Parkman's history, the inevitability of English hegemony in the New World is stated in expository passages, while the dramatic focus is on the characters and exploits of the heroes of French-Canadian history.

Twentieth-century historians have complained that "Parkman was more concerned with telling a story than with understanding the underlying reasons [for the fall of New France],"[5] but this judgment is obviously made from the point of view of modern social-scientific historiography, with its emphasis on economic, geographical, and political factors. Parkman was perhaps not quite so indifferent to such factors as is sometimes claimed,[6] but it is true that his approach to the writing of history involved techniques and ideological assumptions that have become associated mainly with imaginative literature. This does not mean, of course, that Parkman relied exclusively, or even excessively, on invention, although he has been accused of distorting or suppressing evidence and of making grandiose leaps of inference.[7] Like a novelist, poet, or dramatist, Parkman used the generic conventions of literary art to reveal the essential and preconceived meaning of his subject. His story of New France and of the various leaders and adventurers associated with its rise and fall is particularly represented through formal and ideological concepts adapted from romance and tragedy.

One consequence of this approach to historiography is that the characters and events are presented in a deterministic light. When the concepts of tragedy are applied to the story of New France, the emphasis is placed on the inexorable movement towards catastrophe, a movement frequently prefigured by limited and localized disasters that also serve as dramatic points of departure or climaxes to the various episodes. "The story of New France opens with a tragedy," Parkman announces in a prefatory note to the first part of his series, *Pioneers of France in the New World* (1865) (p. 3).[8] The sixteenth-century Spanish massacre of Huguenot settlers is the first of several anecdotes from early French North American history that provide a dark counterpoint to the chronicle of exploration and settlement: Champlain's provocation of the Iroquois, who eventually brought Canada near to ruin; the wretched failure of the first Acadian colony; the French defeat in the first armed conflict with the English in the New World; and, as a climactic prefiguration of ultimate disaster, the temporary loss of Quebec to England in 1629. The second part of the series, *The Jesuits in North America in the Seventeenth Century* (1867), continues in the same vein, with the story of the tragically futile mission to the Hurons. In *The Discovery of the Great West* (1869; revised in 1878 as *La Salle and the Discovery of the Great West*), the emphasis is less on the ultimate significance of French westward exploration than on the frustration and disaster that marked the career of the ill-fated Robert Cavelier de la Salle. *The Old Regime in Canada* (1874) and *Count Frontenac and New France Under Louis XIV* (1877) describe the internal corruption and strife that contributed to the downfall of the French colonial empire. *Count Frontenac* also focuses on the rivalry with New England, which, by the late seventeenth century, was beginning to surpass New France in wealth and power. This rivalry, repeatedly flaring into open war, is followed to its catastrophe in one of the longest and most ambitious segments of the series, *Montcalm and Wolfe* (1884). Finally, in the only part written out of chronological order, Parkman goes back to consider crucial events of the rivalry during the early eighteenth century in *A Half-Century of Conflict* (1892).

Like the tragic heroes of Shakespeare, Parkman's French colonial leaders pursue inexorable careers through struggle, temporary and brilliant ascendancy, to swift decline and destruction. The source of this decline, Parkman argues, was the unique quality of French civilization in the New World, particularly as contrasted to its English or "Anglo-Saxon" counterpart. The basic formative principle of North American civilization, he declares, was the conflict between

> Liberty and Absolutism, New England and New France. The one was the offspring of a triumphant government; the other, of an oppressed and fugitive people: the one, an unflinching champion of the Roman Catholic reaction; the other, a vanguard of the Reform. Each followed its natural laws of growth, and each came to its natural result. *(Pioneers of France,* I, xcvi)

This explanation for the collapse of the French empire in North America remains the essential theme of the whole series, from *Pioneers of France in the New World* through *A Half-Century of Conflict*. This rather simplistic determinism, furthermore, reflects various nineteenth-century ideas about history, including the identification of Roman Catholicism with political reaction, the assumption that historical events follow "natural laws," and an organic metaphor that implies that societies follow a teleological development comparable to that commonly associated with plants.[9] In this deterministic conception of New World history, the emergence of the United States as an independent country becomes the ultimate "natural result" of the conflict between France and England in North America. Although his history ends with the fall of Canada in 1761, Parkman emphasizes in his concluding volumes the rise of a spirit of independence and a sense of national unity in the British American colonies, and suggests that the collapse of New France removed the main barrier to American independence. Freed from the menace of invasion from Canada, the colonies were able to concentrate on their own domestic interests, and these interests seemed to be increasingly incompatible with British imperialism.

But even though he saw the emergence of the United States as the inevitable climax to early North American history, Parkman was by no means an uncritical believer in the social and political structure of his native country. To his friend the Abbé Casgrain, professor of history at Laval University, he thus outlined his political beliefs:

> I have always declared openly my detestation of the unchecked rule of the masses, that is to say of universal suffrage, and the corruption which is sure to follow in every large and heterogeneous community. I have also always declared a very cordial dislike of Puritanism. I recognize some most respectable and valuable qualities in the settlers of New England, but do not think them or their system to be praised without great qualifications.... Nor am I at all an enthusiast for the nineteenth century, many of the tendencies of which I deplore, while admiring much that it has accomplished. It is too democratic and too much given to the pursuit of material interests at the expense of intellectual and moral greatness.[10]

And in the final paragraph of one of the last segments of his history, he declares:

> The string of discordant communities along the Atlantic coast has grown to a mighty people, joined in a union which the earthquake of civil war served only to compact and consolidate.... [The United States] has tamed the savage continent, peopled the solitude, gathered wealth untold, waxed potent, imposing, redoubtable; and now it remains for her to prove, if she can, that the rule of the masses is consistent with the highest growth of the individual; that democracy can give the world a civilization as mature and pregnant, ideas as energetic and vitalizing, and types of manhood as lofty and strong, as any of the systems which it boasts to supplant. (*Montcalm and Wolfe*, III, 260-61)

Thus the story of France and England in North America involves more than a bare conflict, with a foregone conclusion, between "liberty" and "absolutism." The rise of British America is a triumphant drama, qualified by grave character defects on the part of the protagonist. And conversely, the fall of New France is a tragedy, involving failure and defeat in spite of certain virtues.

The ambivalent qualities of New France and its heroes, which made them both magnificent and doomed, are conveyed particularly in one motif running through *France and England in North America*. Parkman, like Thoreau, was struck by the vestiges of mediaevalism in the society of French Canada. These vestiges Thoreau contrasted to the great age of French exploration and adventure, which seemed to him more modern than nineteenth-century Canada, in the sense that the explorers and *coureurs de bois* were comparable to the modern pioneers of the western United States. Parkman, who was more knowledgeable than Thoreau about the details of Canadian history, understood that mediaevalism had been pervasive in New France from the beginning. As a retrospective and regressive influence, it worked against the "natural" progress of the New World and contributed to the downfall of the French empire in North America. But at the same time, as Thoreau also recognized, it had an undeniable aesthetic appeal, by virtue of its relevance to the romance tradition. As Parkman suggests in his introduction to Mary Catherwood's *The Romance of Dollard*, and in various contexts throughout his own work, the history of New France seen from the perspective of the artist is a fascinating spectacle of pageantry, religious zeal, adventure, and heroism. From the cold and rationalistic eye of the chronicler of historical inevitability, however, it is a story of decadence, superstition, and defeat.

This dualistic attitude towards the mediaevalism of New France emerges early in the series. It is evident, for instance, in Parkman's presentation of the first prominent hero of New France, Samuel de Champlain:

> A true hero, after the chivalrous mediaeval type, his character was dashed largely with the spirit of romance. Though earnest, sagacious, and penetrating, he leaned to the marvellous; and the faith which was the life of his hard career was somewhat prone to overstep the bounds of reason and invade the domain of fancy. (*Pioneers*, II, 61)

Conversely, although the devotion to archaic ideals and beliefs led, in the long run, to social collapse, such devotion could contribute in a localized or temporary way to the cause of progress and civilization. This is the case with the Jesuit missionaries in Canada, who were "thoroughly and vehemently reactive" in their devotion to "the mediaeval type of Christianity, with all its attendant superstitions";

> Yet, on the whole, the labors of the missionaries tended greatly to the benefit of the Indians. Reclaimed... from their wandering life, settled in habits of peaceful industry, and reduced to a passive and childlike obedience, they would have gained more than enough to compensate them for the loss of their ferocious and miserable independence. (*Jesuits*, I, 257)

This mediaeval spirit of religious zeal and chivalric courage could also occasionally inspire enterprises of extraordinary boldness and resolution, which produced far-reaching and durable results, as Parkman demonstrates in his version of the legend of the "heroes of the Long Sault." In 1660, according to Parkman, a small band of adventurers led by a young nobleman named Adam Daulac (or Dollard) devoted themselves to a suicidal expedition against the Iroquois, an expedition that saved the little colony of New France from extinction. Daulac, says Parkman, "was a knight of the early crusades among the forests and savages of the New World" (*Old Regime*, I, 129). Equally remarkable were the religious zealots who defied the Iroquois to create in the wilderness a medical mission, which evolved into one of the most unusual cities in North America. "In many of its aspects," Parkman comments, "this enterprise of Montreal belonged to the time of the first crusades" (*Jesuits*, II, 23).

Ultimately, Parkman is unable to make any conclusive judgment on the mediaeval impulse that inspired the founders of Montreal, the Jesuit martyrs, and the heroes of the Long Sault. The New England historian's Unitarian upbringing and his personal agnosticism are unsympathetic to the mystical enthusiasm of the early Canadian Roman Catholic missions; yet some of the achievements of the church in New France make an irresistible appeal to his imagination. Parkman reveals his ambivalent feelings in his comment on the founding of Montreal:

> What shall we say of these adventurers of Montreal, of these who bestowed their wealth, and far more, of these who sacrificed their peace and risked their lives, on an enterprise at once so romantic and so devout? Surrounded as they were with illusions, false lights, and false shadows,—breathing an atmosphere of miracle, —compassed about with angels and devils,—urged with stimu-

lants most powerful, though unreal,—their minds drugged, as it were, to preternatural excitement,—it is very difficult to judge of them. High merit, without doubt, there was in some of their number; but one may beg to be spared the attempt to measure or define it. To estimate a virtue involved in conditions so anomalous demands, perhaps, a judgment more than human. (*Jesuits*, II, 22-23)

Parkman is equally inconclusive about the secular manifestations of mediaevalism in New France. The feudal system of society, established in Canada in the seventeenth century and consolidated under Louis XIV and his governor Frontenac, tended to promote the centralization of power at the expense of individualism and freedom. Yet, as Parkman demonstrates in *The Old Regime in Canada*, such a system was not inappropriate to a wilderness colony constantly threatened by Indians and by unfriendly settlements to the south. The ancient traditions that bound the settlers to *seigneur* and king were of inestimable value as a general source of social stability, and could be put to advantage during the frequent military crises that beset the colony, when an armed force could be quickly raised by arbitrary order from the government at Quebec. This situation, as Parkman points out in later volumes, differed strikingly from conditions in the more libertarian Anglo-American colonies, where attempts to raise troops were always accompanied by wrangling and dissension. In the long run, however, as Parkman acknowledges, Canadian feudalism failed to create a stable society. The aristocratic colonial administrators in New France were bent on establishing a miniature reflection of the mother country, but such a rigid and artificial social structure proved to be inappropriate to the New World. The Canadian settlers rejected the title of "peasant" and insisted on reserving to themselves the neutral appellation "*habitant*." They refused to take up the backwoods farms arranged in European fashion around the *manoir*, and defied the authorities and risked susceptibility to Indian attack to homestead on the more valuable land fronting the St. Lawrence River. In extreme instances—which became all too common as the population of the colony grew—they rejected the feudal society altogether and took to the woods, becoming *coureurs de bois* engaged in the outlawed independent fur trade.

With even more fatal consequences for the feudal society of Canada, many colonial aristocrats also responded to the appeal of the wilderness and preferred a life of bushranging, exploring, or guerilla warfare to the sedentary rôle of administrator or *seigneur*. The famous Baron Saint-

Castin, for instance, directed a huge illegal fur-trade operation from his stronghold in the woods of what eventually became the state of Maine. Even the governors themselves, notably the irrepressible Frontenac, were prone to neglect administrative duties in order to engage in clandestine fur-trade operations, or to lead hit-and-run raids against the Iroquois or the English, or to engage in exploration of the western frontier. The result, says Parkman, was that

> Canada was divided between two opposing influences. On the one side were the monarchy and the hierarchy, with their principles of order, subordination, and obedience.... On the other side was the spirit of liberty, or licence, which was in the very air of this wilderness continent, reinforced in the chiefs of the colony by a spirit of adventure inherited from the Middle Ages, and by a spirit of trade born of present opportunities; for every official in Canada hoped to make a profit, if not a fortune, out of beaver-skins. Kindred impulses, in ruder forms, possessed the humbler colonists, drove them into the forest, and made them hardy woodsmen and skilful bush-fighters, though turbulent and lawless members of civilized society. (*Half-Century of Conflict*, I, 347)

As in his portrayal of the mediaeval religious zeal that inspired the Huron missions and the founding of Montreal, Parkman does not offer a conclusive moral judgment on Canadian feudalism or its libertarian reaction. He disapproves of the lawlessness of the *coureurs de bois*, but his own fondness for the strenuous life in the wilderness inclines him to view their way of life sympathetically:

> Though not a very valuable member of society, and though a thorn in the side of princes and rulers, the *coureur de bois* had his uses, at least from an artistic point of view; and his strange figure, sometimes brutally savage, but oftener marked with the lines of a dare-devil courage, and a reckless thoughtless gayety, will always be joined to the memories of that grand world of woods which the nineteenth century is fast civilizing out of existence. (*Old Regime*, II, 113)

The wilderness itself is represented in ambivalent terms throughout *France and England in North America*. Parkman loved all his life to ramble through the New England and Canadian woods, and when he first conceived his epic work he thought of it not as the story of two warring civilizations, but as "the history of the American forest";[11] but his fascination with nature did not imply unqualified enthusiasm. Like Thoreau, he saw nature as an inspirational and restorative contrast to the worst developments of modern civilization; but, also like Thoreau, he recognized that the vast northern forests, with their implications of rampant primitivism, could be destructive of the higher moral and intellectual inclinations of humanity. Nature in *France and England* is associated with "dare-devil courage," "reckless thoughtless gayety," and with the liberal impulses that eventually lead to the triumph of New England over New France; but it is also associated with the extreme developments of such impulses, which, if left unchecked, move towards social and psychological chaos.[12]

Thus, on the one hand, the Canadian forest is frequently described in rather florid, idyllic terms, particularly when Parkman seeks to reinforce the more positive or creative aspects of French experience in the New World, and to suggest some measure of harmony between nature and human purposes. Jacques Cartier, approaching Quebec at the beginning of the great chronicle of exploration and conquest, comes to anchor "in a quiet channel between the northern shore and the margin of a richly wooded island, where the trees were so thickly hung with grapes that Cartier named it the Island of Bacchus" (*Pioneers*, II, 24). On the first arrival of the founders of Montreal to the site of the city that later was to so fascinate nineteenth-century American tourists, "spring flowers were blooming in the young grass, and birds of varied plumage flitted among the boughs" (*Jesuits*, II, 24). "The ribbon of rich meadow land" along the St. Lawrence near Quebec "... was yellow with wheat in harvest time" as the settlements began to flourish in the late seventeenth century (*Old Regime*, II, 35).

On the other hand, the Canadian wilderness is more frequently and more extensively characterized as an overgrown, dark, impenetrable place, standing ready to frustrate all petty human efforts at conquest. The remote retreats of the *coureur de bois* are described with a climactic accumulation of detail emphasizing mystery, violent conflict, monstrosity, and death:

> the stern depths of immemorial forests, dim and silent as a cavern, columned with innumerable trunks, each like an Atlas upholding its world of leaves, and sweating perpetual moisture down its dark and channelled rind,—some strong in youth,

some grisly with decrepit age, nightmares of strange distortion, gnarled and knotted with wens and goitres; roots intertwined beneath like serpents petrified in an agony of contorted strife; green and glistening mosses carpeting the rough ground, mantling the rocks, turning pulpy stumps to mounds of verdure, and swathing fallen trunks as, bent in the impotence of rottenness, they lie outstretched over knoll and hollow, like mouldering reptiles of the primeval world, while around, and on and through them, springs the young growth that battens on their decay,—the forest devouring its own dead.... (*Old Regime*, II, 114)

Similarly, the French-Canadian settler's first glimpses of his new country included the "vast piles of savage verdure" on the banks of the St. Lawrence, "till at length the mountain of Cape Tourmente upheaves its huge bulk from the bosom of the water, shadowed by lowering clouds, and dark with forests" (*Old Regime*, II, 34). And in his most substantial exposition of the formidable New World landscape, *La Salle and the Discovery of the Great West*, Parkman devotes most of an entire volume to the struggle between puny human beings and titanic nature, a struggle that ends in insanity and death.

All through *France and England in North America*, the North American wilderness is associated with what Parkman sees as the ambiguous elements in United States democracy. The wilderness suggests exhilarating freedom, individualism, and movement towards unknown frontiers; but it also suggests disorientation, confusion, anarchism, and chaos. But besides suggesting parallels between nature and human social structures, Parkman establishes contrasts. Like Thoreau, he points to a conflict between the village and the forest, or between modern social and technological developments and the world of primitive nature. This conflict, furthermore, involves a kind of reciprocal relationship, in which the better and worse features of each element are involved in a continual process of qualification. On the one hand, the imaginative or adventurous individual turns to the forest to escape the technological or bureaucratic tyrannies of society; on the other hand, he turns back to the ordered and humanistic structures of society to escape the primitivism of nature. In New France, according to Parkman, the tension between society and nature was particularly acute, and contributed to the downfall of the colony. The civilizing influences were constantly being carried to extremes of bureaucratic incompetence and tyranny, forcing the best individuals to seek refuge in nature; the attractions of nature, which carried explorers and traders to the far reaches of the western and northern frontiers, led ultimately to a brutalizing primitivism.

The primitivistic side of Parkman's image of Canada is represented particularly in his portrayal of the Indians. Unlike Cooper, who simplified the Indians by presenting them as either treacherous fiends or stoical heroes, Parkman struggled to present what he believed to be a comprehensive image of the aboriginal character. *The Jesuits in North America* begins with a long introductory essay on the native tribes of the continent, based on Parkman's wide reading and on his observations on the Oregon Trail. The result, however, is a categorization no less limited than Cooper's, for all its wealth of ethnological detail. In spite of his recognition of the many complexities involved in the historical analysis of people and events, Parkman ultimately accepted prevalent nineteenth-century notions about the inevitability of Europeanized technological and social progress. Thus his Indians are represented as occasionally admirable, frequently repulsive, and irrevocably doomed. Their closeness to nature, their jealous concern for personal freedom, their simple if ruthless ethics, their oratorical skills, elicit his admiration; but their undeveloped intellectual powers, their animalistic domestic habits, their indifference to higher forms of social organization, and their complete inability to adapt to change, are inimical to Parkman's nineteenth-century sensibilities. The history of the Indian in North America is only "a savage prologue" to the "American drama": a "glomy and meaningless" story of "extermination, absorption, or expatriation" (*Jesuits*, I, 8; II, 63).

Thus in Parkman's scholarly and imaginative study of early Canada, the Indians represent, in effect, a fatal extreme. Like the farthest reaches of the vast Canadian forest they inhabit, they stand for an antihumanistic primitivism, which, in spite of limited intrinsic virtues, must give way to the progressive forces of civilization. This surrender, furthermore, is to be complete and final: Parkman, like most nineteenth-century North Americans who turned their attention to the subject, was convinced that the Indian was destined to disappear utterly from the continent. In this respect Parkman distinguishes them from the French, whose destiny lies not in annihilation, but merely in defeat. The Indians are a doomed people whose overwhelming vices and feeble virtues prevent the modern observer from seeing them sympathetically; the French, on the other hand, are frequently presented as a dignified and idealistic—if sometimes foolish and decadent—people, whose defeat is worthy to be considered tragic.

The tragedy of New France, according to Parkman, is personified in various heroic individuals, such as Champlain, Frontenac, the Jesuits, and Montcalm. Parkman's choice of heroes generally conforms to popular tradition, but in a few cases his selections reflect his distinctive view of the subject. In dealing with the famous Acadian war between Charles d'Aunay (or d'Aulnay) and Charles de la Tour, for instance, American romancers Harriet Vaughn Cheney and Mary Catherwood preferred the bourgeois and alleged Protestant La Tour to the aristocratic d'Aunay. The Boston Brahmin Parkman, by contrast, comes down firmly in favour of d'Aunay. Although he admits candidly that "throughout this affair one is perplexed by the French official papers, whose entanglements and contradictions in regard to the Acadian rivals are past unravelling" (*Old Regime*, I, 28), Parkman proceeds to impugn La Tour as a dissembler and opportunist, and to praise his rival as a sincere and loyal devotee to the cause of French colonialism.

> He [d'Aunay] seems to have been a favorable example of his class; loyal to his faith and his King, tempering pride with courtesy, and generally true to his cherished ideal of the *gentilhomme Français*. In his qualities, as in his birth, he was far above his rival; and his death was the ruin of the only French colony in Acadia that deserved the name. (*Old Regime*, I, 49)

Just as he tends to prefer the stratified society of New France to the disorganized egalitarianism of New England, Parkman praises d'Aunay's gentility, loyalty, and devotion to duty over La Tour's supposedly democratic inclinations.

Another hero who is singled out for distinction is the title character of *La Salle and the Discovery of the Great West*. Like d'Aunay, La Salle was an aristocrat, and if not always devoted to the duty assigned to him by his official superiors, he was zealously committed to what he believed to be his mission in life. After describing in vivid detail the struggles, misfortunes, and tragic outcome of La Salle's career as explorer of the western frontier and discoverer of the mouth of the Mississippi, Parkman summarizes his hero's character by comparing him to other prominent figures in the history of New France:

> The enthusiasm of the disinterested and chivalrous Champlain was not the enthusiasm of La Salle; nor had he any part in the self-devoted zeal of the early Jesuit explorers. He belonged not

to the age of the knight-errant and the saint, but to the modern world of practical study and practical action. (*La Salle,* pp. 430-31)

As William R. Taylor has convincingly argued, Parkman personally identified with the explorer of the Mississippi. In general characteristics, La Salle appears to be a man very much like Parkman himself: aloof, scholarly, of distinguished family, fond of the wilderness and of adventure—and, perhaps most significant of all, prone to intermittent psychological problems. Furthermore, although Parkman was usually conscientious in his handling of primary source materials, he seems in his study of La Salle to have suppressed and distorted certain evidence to make his subject answer to a preconceived tragic image. Neglecting the accounts of La Salle written by the explorer's rivals and associates, Parkman takes La Salle's own account of himself at face value, and reports in a paraphrase of La Salle's own words that "this solitary being, hiding his shyness under a cold reserve, could rouse no enthusiasm in his followers.... His lonely and shadowed nature," he continues, "needed the mellowing sunshine of success, and his whole life was a fight with adversity" (*La Salle,* pp. 340-41). According to William R. Taylor, "Parkman... considerably improved the literary quality... of La Salle's letters in the translations he made of them from French documentary sources"[13] to prove that La Salle "was no rude son of toil, but a man of thought, trained amid arts and letters" (*La Salle,* p. 198).

But if Parkman became imaginatively involved with the character of La Salle to the point of distorting evidence, the instance is only an extreme example of the historian's attitude to his subject as a whole. The image of New France in *France and England in North America* is the unmistakably idiosyncratic product of the author's mind, with all its various social, ethnic, and political biases, as well as its unique creative energy. Because of these idiosyncrasies, as well as certain allegedly obsolete concepts of methodology, Parkman's history is no longer accepted as reliable by twentieth-century historians. But some of the very features that make his work unacceptable to modern social scientists make it valuable for students of imaginative literature. As a work of art, *France and England in North America* clearly belongs with the outstanding literary achievements of the nineteenth-century United States, such as the Leatherstocking tales, *Moby-Dick, The Scarlet Letter,* and the poetry of Whitman. With all its narrative vigour and descriptive vividness, Parkman's work is unquestionably the greatest American literary exposition of the French-Canadian past written in the nineteenth century, and might well be considered, without qualification, the foremost American literary exposition of the subject of Canada in general.

VII

ENGLISH CANADA: TRAVELLERS, PATRIOTS, AND FUGITIVES

The exotic elements of French-Canadian history and culture, as Parkman's work demonstrates, provided much greater stimulus to the nineteenth-century American imagination than the more prosaic chronicle of English Canada. But the predominantly Anglophone regions were not wholly neglected. The increasingly popular "northern tour," which featured the colourful landscape and society of Quebec, Montreal, and the Saguenay, frequently included excursions westward to Kingston, Toronto, and Niagara Falls. From the early post-revolutionary years, literary travellers like John Cousens Ogden and Joseph Sansom included brief reports on the settlements of Upper Canada, along with their more detailed accounts of the lower province, and they usually had some comments on the English-speaking populations of Montreal and Quebec. Occasional travellers, like the missionary Benjamin Mortimer, ventured into the more primitive regions west of Lower Canada. Before the United States Civil War, American literary interest in the province of Upper Canada—or, as it was known after 1841, the district of Canada West—can be traced to three main factors. First, and most obvious, was the continuing popularity of tourism, as population and rail and road communication continued to expand on both sides of the border. Second was the Upper Canada Rebellion of 1837-38, which briefly but dramatically riveted American attention on what momentarily appeared to be a new nation emerging through revolution to independence. Third, but by no means least in importance, was the influx into Canada of fugitive slaves.

The literary tourists who visited the upper province expressed much the same range of attitudes and ambivalence of tone as those who travelled to the French-speaking eastern regions. An 1844 guidebook, *The Picturesque Tourist; Being a Guide through the Northern and Eastern States and Canada,* warned its readers against the inhabitants of Toronto:

> The prejudice against the Americans, or *Yankees,* is easily perceived and easily accounted for, as most of the inhabitants are exceedingly loyal, have never visited "the States," and look upon their neighbours as a set of lawless republicans or disorganizers.[1]

In a similar vein, a novelist named Jesse Walker (1810-52) produced two travelogue novels, *Queenston* and *Fort Niagara* (both published in 1845, both subtitled "A Tale of the Niagara Frontier"), mainly devoted to demonstrating the inferiority of the Canadian land and people to their American counterparts. In both novels, an old sea captain and his twelve-year-old nephew ramble over the Niagara peninsula and discuss, in Socratic dialogue, the historical associations of the region. In *Queenston,* the two tourists climb to the top of Brock's monument to admire the view:

> On the east was to be seen the well cultivated fields of the western part of New York, and to the west the eye fell upon the domain of the British king. A striking difference was to be observed between these portions of the two countries. On the west there was less improvement than on the east, though the soil was equally fertile.
> "This difference may be owing," said the Captain, "to the different form of government and the different institutions existing in the two countries."
> "How," said Harry, "does the government have any effect on the cultivation of the fields?"
> "Because," said the captain, "men are not satisfied with the cultivation of the fields alone. They do that as a means of subsistence, but the most enterprising have some other purpose in view as the chief object to be accomplished. In the United States the highest offices are open to all, while in Canada their governors and many other officers are appointed by the government of a distant country, separated from them by thousands of miles of ocean. And though a man may never expect or hope to obtain any high station, yet he prefers to live in a country where

he is not excluded from it by custom, or by the organization of government."[2]

Other American visitors were less inclined to make invidious comparisons, but even the most amiable of visitors were sometimes disconcerted by the cultural incongruity of the province. Ralph Waldo Emerson, visiting the city of Hamilton on a lecture tour in 1855, noted briefly in his journal his surprise at "finding myself, in England, as it seemed, with English soft coal fire,... with English servant; & the hotel full of solid Englishmen talking London politics in the dear island tones."[3] The abolitionist and literary essayist Thomas Wentworth Higginson was in the same city, also on a lecture tour, in 1857, and recorded similar impressions:

> What's the use of going to England and using up excitement, all at once, when one can come to Canada and get enough here? I am as distinctly a foreigner here as in Sebastopol, and circumstances have enabled me to enjoy the experience more fully than I expected....
> Behold me, then domesticated at the City Hotel. Not a Yankee in it but myself—all straight, solid Englishmen, with deep, clear voices emerging from their fur-covered chests.[4]

But the number of occasional travellers and tourists who recorded their impressions of Upper Canada/Canada West were relatively few. Except for the spectacle of the Horseshoe Falls at Niagara, this part of the continent offered few striking attractions for Americans: the forest and the agrarian frontier were features common enough in their own country; the people spoke the same language as themselves, and differed only in their political orientation and in superficial social customs; and the settlements were economically backward compared to United States towns and cities. Unlike French Canada, there were no exotic elements to provoke the visitor's curiosity, nor any significant historical interest, except for fading memories of the War of 1812. This part of Canada, in brief, seemed to Americans slow and dull, lacking the exciting atmosphere or future possibilities of their own frontier. For a few brief months in 1837-1838, however, American interest in the northern province flourished remarkably.

Warfare seems to be a recurrent provocation for American interest in Canada: the pre-revolutionary French and Indian conflicts, the Revolution, and the War of 1812, all brought Canada to the forefront of American consciousness. The rebellions of 1837-38 provoked a surprisingly substantial American reaction—perhaps even more than any single preceding manifestation of warfare in the north. This is undoubtedly because, to many American observers in 1837, the time at last seemed ripe for Canada to throw off the yoke of imperialism and enjoy the advantages of United-States-style independence. The American interest was focused more on the upper province than on the lower, because French Canada still seemed to American observers to be isolated by language and religion from the mainstream of North American history. With United States attention thus aroused, in late 1837 and early 1838, by the rhetoric of William Lyon Mackenzie and other Canadian fugitives, Americans not only watched the rebellion, but in substantial numbers attempted to join it. Out of this martial enthusiasm a noteworthy series of American literary responses emerged.

Foremost among these responses are the autobiographical narratives of some of the would-be interventionists. At least nine such narratives were published in the decade following the rebellion: Thomas Jefferson Sutherland's *Loose Leaves from the Portfolio of a Late Patriot Prisoner in Canada* (1840), E. A. Theller's *Canada in 1837-38* (1841), Stephen S. Wright's *Narrative and Recollection of Van Dieman's Land* (1844), Linus W. Miller's *Notes of an Exile to Van Dieman's Land* (1846), Samuel Snow's *Exile's Return* (1846), Daniel D. Heustis's *Narratives of the Adventures and Sufferings... in Canada and Van Dieman's Land, during a Long Captivity* (1847), Robert Marsh's *Seven Years of My Life, or, Narrative of a Patriot Exile* (1848), William Gates's *Recollection of Life in Van Dieman's Land* (1850), and Jedediah Hunt's *An Adventure on a Frozen Lake* (1853).

As most of these titles suggest, the self-styled "patriots" who defied British and United States authorities to make armed incursions into Canada fared rather grimly, on the whole. Met by overwhelmingly superior forces of British troops and Canadian militia, and betrayed or harassed by unsympathetic Canadian settlers, the various groups of would-be liberators suffered swift military defeat with extensive casualties, and most of the survivors of the skirmishes were imprisoned. Several leaders of these expeditions were executed, and ninety-two volunteers were exiled for terms ranging from five to ten years in the British penal colonies of Van Diemen's Land.[5] The literary recollections of these interventionists tended to focus mainly on their experiences in captivity, although almost all included at least brief accounts of their battlefield experiences, and impressions of social and political conditions in Upper Canada. Few of these authors were skilled literary craftsmen, although most of them had literary pretensions, and in their attempts to explain and justify their experiences they had recourse to various forms of self-dramatization and rhetorical elaboration.

In attempting the literary rendering of their experiences, these authors were faced particularly with the problem of reconciling the disasters of the attempted intervention with the optimistic vision of New World history that prevailed in the post-revolutionary United States. Confident of the rightness and inevitability of United States republicanism in the New World, the American supporters of the rebellion were faced with the facts of the collapse of the Canadian revolutionary movement and the retrenchment of European colonial authority. In their literary records of events in Canada, most of the American interventionists simply assumed that the British victory was a temporary setback in the inevitable course of the Canadian movement towards liberty. In dealing with their own disastrous experiences, many of these writers used stylized rhetoric probably learned from such early-nineteenth-century authors as Byron and Shelley, involving the romantic rebel, bloody but unbowed, defiant in defeat and captivity, and confident of ultimate vindication.

Linus Miller's *Notes of an Exile to Van Dieman's Land* is typical of the interventionist narratives in these respects. A nineteen-year-old law student who entered Upper Canada early in 1838 as an emissary of the "Canadian Refugee Relief Association," Miller was arrested when he attempted to act under orders from one of the "Patriot" commanders and prevent a group of filibusters from making an unauthorized assault on Canada near Fort Erie. After narrowly escaping execution in Canada, he was transported to England for re-trial, and was sentenced to six years in a British penal colony. Throughout his narrative Miller admits to no regret about his experiences or doubts about the rightness of the Canadian cause, which he elevates rhetorically to the typical patriotic conception of the American Revolution. "The blight and mildew of misrule had repeatedly passed over [Canada].... In their distress [the Canadians] had turned their eyes to these United States; studied our glorious and peaceful institutions, until they imbibed the spirit of the heroes of the American Revolution, and felt the God-like divinity of liberty stirring within their souls and rousing their slumbering energies to action." The Canadian settlers, Miller insists, are decent and courageous people, deserving of American support. "It has been erroneously asserted that the Canadians are so unfeeling and selfish that sooner than do a noble deed, at the risk of property or life, they would cling to their hearthstones and see their nearest friends sacrificed. From close observation and experience, I know the reverse to be the case. A more generous, self-sacrificing people never lived."[6] The British garrisons that maintain imperial power in Canada are manned by pompous and blustering fools, as Miller illustrates when he describes his incognito movements in the town of Hamilton. Like the legendary heroes of the revolution, or like a character in James Fenimore Cooper's *The Spy*, Miller passes unrecognized among British officers, and even manages, by his personal magnetism and heroic demeanour, to elicit the sympathy of one officer who penetrates his disguise. In captivity, Miller becomes like Ethan Allan or Patrick Henry, titanic in his defiance of his captors and his unshakable commitment to liberty.

The same sorts of images of Canada, Canadians, and the heroic American "patriots" are evident in the narrative of E. A. Theller, whose *Canada in 1837-38* is a flamboyant account of the author's exploits as a "Brigadier General in the Canadian revolutionary service," including his escape from the Quebec Citadel.[7] Another "patriot" narrative, Robert Marsh's *Seven Years of My Life*, reflects in its concluding remarks the author's continued belief in the justice of the Canadian cause:

> Canada, wake up! Never submit or yield one inch to the tyrants who have been so long revelling and sporting on your inalienable rights. So long as you quietly submit, so long the abuses continue. I believe the rebellion of '37-38, though it did not succeed, yet had a tendency to open the eyes and ears of the tyrant clan, and to grant you some little indulgencies, but look out, be on your guard.[8]

William Gates's *Recollections of Life in Van Dieman's Land* is a more restrained but still militant account of the interventionist efforts, to which the author committed himself with idealistic zeal: "To the future I looked with imagination's eye, and fancied I might have the satisfaction of the future reflection, that I was one of those who aided in securing full liberty to Canada's sons and daughters."[9]

But Gates, like several of the "patriots" of 1838, also expresses reservations about the rebellion. His main complaint has to do with the failure of United States authorities to support the rebels and their American allies: "When Texas revolted from a sister republic, our men were permitted to organize companies and depart armed for the scene of the conflict.... The Canadian effort for liberty was quelled, not so much by her majesty's troops quartered in the provinces, as by that government which, above all others, boasts the truest freedom of any nation on the earth."[10] Robert Marsh similarly blames "tories" on both sides of the border for betraying the revolution, and attacks "corrupt aristocracy, which I fear is rapidly and to an alarming degree, extending its principles to this side of the Atlantic."[11] And Daniel D. Heustis, in one of the more balanced and detailed narratives of the 1838 events, also condemns American official interference with the cause, and provides revealing glimpses of internecine squabbling among the rebels:

> The man named T. J. Sutherland had been commissioned as a Brigadier-General by the provisional government.... General McLeod wished me to take a lieutenant-colonel's commission under Sutherland. Mackenzie advised me not to do so, as he had no confidence in the man. Subsequent events proved that Sutherland was totally unfit for the command to which he had been appointed.[12]

A recurrent suggestion in several of the narratives is that the rebellion failed because of qualities of inertia, unreliability, and submissiveness in the Canadian character, or because of vague, perhaps indefinable qualities that distinguish Canadians from Americans and render them unfit for freedom. The subject of Gates's suspicious comments, "Brigadier General" Thomas Jefferson Sutherland, thus describes his ultimate impressions of Canada and Canadians, in the earliest and one of the most self-consciously literary American responses to the rebellion, *Loose Leaves from the Portfolio of a Late Patriot Prisoner in Canada*. Most of this volume is taken up with miscellaneous fragments of poetry and fiction unrelated to the rebellion, composed while the author was held prisoner in the Quebec Citadel; but in two brief introductory essays, Sutherland reveals his disillusionment with the rebellion, and especially with the Canadian settlers, whom he recognizes as the "'blood and carnage' adherents of the British government.... About the first of February, I became satisfied there could be no chance of success for any of the proposed movements of the revolutionists in Upper Canada, and relinquished my connection with the Patriots...."[13]

Similarly, Samuel Snow, in his *Exile's Return*, complains of the indifference and deceit encountered by the American volunteers who attempted to attack the garrison at Windsor, in December of 1838. "Not a Canadian met us on our arrival save a few who joined us in Michigan, and some of these turned traitors soon after."[14] And Daniel Heustis, while persisting in his belief in the ideals of revolution, came to the conclusion that "the Canadian people, in whose behalf we fought, were less true and faithful to the cause of liberty than our revolutionary sires...."[15]

The futility of the rebellion is forcibly expounded in *An Adventure on a Frozen Lake*, by another American participant in the "battle of Windsor," Jedediah Hunt, Jr. The last and one of the most disastrous border skirmishes of the rebellion, the Windsor affair is seen by Hunt in terms of battlefield violence and desperate struggles for survival that crudely prefigure the anti-war naturalism of *A Red Badge of Courage*. After the raiders in Hunt's narrative are defeated by overwhelming forces of British regulars and Canadian militia, the survivors flee towards Lake St. Clair through a cold and hostile wilderness peopled by equally hostile and treacherous settlers and Indians. Although professing his continued opposition to "the potent power of unholy usurpation and despotic tyranny,"[16] Hunt observes that on the wintry Canadian frontier, humanity and nature seem to join in opposition to the revolutionary impulses that might liberate the northern colonies.

Although Hunt insists on the literal truth of his story, *An Adventure on a Frozen Lake* was printed in a format resembling the dime and nickel novels of later decades. By the 1850s the possible appeal of stories about the Canadian rebellion for the readers of cheap fiction was evident to at least a few American writers and publishers; in the same year as Hunt's narrative, a novel appeared entitled *The Empress of the Isles; or, The Lake Bravo. A Romance of the Canadian Struggle in 1837*. The author, signing himself "Charley Clewline" (identified as George S. Raymond, author of other novels, about Great Lakes and ocean sailors),[17] claims in the narrative to have participated in the Battle of Pelee Island in March of 1838. But the work does not convey an impression of first-hand experience, for it is a compilation of such popular fiction clichés as a hero of mysterious birth, lecherous villains who seek to seduce virtuous young heroines, false marriages, forged documents, and elaborate schemes of revenge. Like some of the authors of autobiographical narratives, Hunt is ambivalent about the rebellion, seeing the northern colonists as perhaps justified in their resistance to oppression, but sceptical about the motives of the interventionists:

> On the American side, the sympathy for the Canadians was unbounded, and fifty thousand daring, reckless men (twenty true patriots perhaps out of the whole number) were ready to shoulder their rifles and march into Canada.... They had little else to occupy their leisure hours during the winter, and so they

were anxious to become brigands and invade Canada—never once reflecting, perhaps, that what was perfectly justifiable on the part of the Canadians themselves, would be an act of downright piracy on their part.[18]

A more skilful work of fiction dealing with the rebellion is Peter Hamilton Myers's *The Prisoner of the Border* (1857). Myers (1812–78), a New York lawyer, was interested, like James Fenimore Cooper, in the pre-revolutionary and early-nineteenth-century history of his native state, and particularly in the Dutch settlers and the Indian wars on the northern frontier. His heavy debt to Cooper, plus his devotion in later years to grinding out dime novels, have contributed to his obscurity in literary history; but *The Prisoner of the Border*, which was his eighth novel, has a vigorous narrative and a cultural sophistication comparable to the best of Cooper's work.[19]

Myers' novel deals with the best-known—and probably the bloodiest—skirmish between American interventionists and British troops, the Battle of the Windmill, near the village of Prescott, across the St. Lawrence River from Ogdensburg, New York. In this battle, approximately two hundred would-be invaders were defeated by twice that number of British regulars and Canadian militia. The British authorities dealt severely with the prisoners: eleven were hanged, including their dashing leader, a European soldier of fortune named Nils Von Schoultz; all the prisoners languished for various lengths of time in jail at Kingston; and sixty were sent to Van Diemen's Land.[20] In *The Prisoner of the Border*, Myers focuses on a fictional American named Harry Vrail, who is among those sentenced to death, but who is spirited out of jail and across the border at the eleventh hour by a bold group of sympathizers.

Myers is interested in extolling individual courage and in exploiting love interest and courtroom drama, but he also offers some trenchant reflections on the moral and political significance of the rebellion. The disasters that befall the interventionists are blamed partly on their careless enthusiasm, as when Harry Vrail joins his foolhardy brother in the Canadian struggle for little reason other than fraternal loyalty and boredom with life at home. More emphatically condemned, however, are the American rabble-rousers who recruit volunteers in the cause of Canadian independence, while they cautiously avoid the fighting themselves. Myers' clownish villain, Barak Jones, is, furthermore, like similarly cowardly characters in James Fenimore Cooper's novels, a New Englander of uncertain family background and barbarous dialect. But the Canadian people are also condemned: the settlers of the Kingston-

Prescott region who assist the militia in pursuing American fugitives are exposed as ignorant boors, unfit for the advantages of American liberty. Like Cooper, Myers takes a patrician view of society: only cultured aristocrats, such as his Dutch Patroon-class central characters, or occasionally natural noblemen, such as the real-life Canadian river pirate William Johnson, whom Myers transforms into a Leatherstocking-type adventurer, are capable of appreciating true freedom.

Thus the American narratives, both fictional and non-fictional, of the Upper Canada rebellion, provide further examples of the ambivalence of United States attitudes towards Canada. If in 1838 most Americans were still committed to the abstract ideal of revolution and to the inevitability of republicanism in North America, many of those who observed or reflected on the rebellion had doubts about the inclinations or abilities of Canadians to fulfil their rôle in New World destiny. The continuing subservience to British power was seen as evidence of the degrading force of imperialism, which seemed to drain people of the energy and the will to independence. By no means all early-nineteenth-century American responses to English Canada were anti-imperialistic and anti-British, however. Writers of conservative or aristocratic sympathies, such as the 1799 traveller John Cousens Ogden, or like Richard Henry Dana, expressed occasional admiration for the order, benevolence, and even the greater liberalism of the British colony as compared to the American republic. And in the 1850s a small group of writers appeared who were particularly committed to the belief in the greater freedom of the colonies. These were the literary chroniclers—novelists, biographers, and autobiographers—of the fugitive slave experience.

The most famous of these writers is, of course, Harriet Beecher Stowe. *Uncle Tom's Cabin* (1853) deals directly with Canada only very briefly, but throughout the novel the country is a distant ideal of freedom. George and Eliza, after all their tribulations with overseers, slave catchers, and partly frozen rivers, finally land on "the blessed English shores" at "the small town of Amherstburg, in Canada."[21] Later, they are briefly shown living a life of domestic bliss in Montreal. Canada as a place of refuge and an ideal of freedom is particularly set in antithesis to the northern United States, where Simon Legree originates, and where public indifference, avarice, and cruelty help perpetuate the evils of slavery. Some white southerners, on the other hand, are seen as the mildly benevolent but ineffectual victims of an inherited social system and a languid climate, which have sapped their will to benevolent action. The aristocratic plantation owner St. Clare is associated with Canada in a way that suggests a direct link between the South and the visions and possibilities of freedom associated with the northern provinces. "Augustine St. Clare," says the author, "was the son of a wealthy planter of Louisiana. The family had its origin in Canada."[22] Little Eva's full name is Evangeline, a suggestive but cryptic allusion, creating a further association with Canada, but invoking Longfellow's myth of passive endurance, suffering, and pathetic death, and the Arcadian dream of a prelapsarian world in the north that can never be recaptured.

Stowe's rather vague thoughts about Canada are clarified in her other anti-slavery novel, *Dred: A Tale of the Great Dismal Swamp* (1856). More concerned with the effect of slavery on whites than with the tragic circumstances of the slaves, this novel shows how the enlightened white southerner might take the initiative by freeing his slaves and by helping them to rise above the degradation of their former condition. In *Dred*, the repentant plantation owner, Clayton, liberates his slaves and leads them to Canada, where he establishes an agricultural colony in the southwestern part of Upper Canada. At the end of the novel, Stowe gives a brief account of this benevolently feudal settlement:

> It is a striking comment on the success of Clayton's enterprise, that the neighboring white settlers, who at first looked coldly upon him, fearing he would be the means of introducing a thriftless population among them, have been entirely won over, and that the value of the improvements which Clayton and his tenants have made has nearly doubled the price of real estate in the vicinity.
>
> So high a character have his schools borne, that the white settlers in the vicinity have discontinued their own, preferring to have their children enjoy the advantages of those under his and his sister's patronage and care.[23]

Canada as an undeveloped region where Americans might make a new beginning free from the evils of their own society is a recurrent imaginative ideal in United States writing, and appears sporadically from the time of the United Empire Loyalists, through the nineteenth century and on into the twentieth. In Stowe's fiction, this ideal is brief and tentative, but it becomes more detailed in other works, particularly those based on the actual experiences of fugitives. With their educational disadvantages, not many of the former slaves could write about their experiences, but some of them were able to do so, and there were a few white people ready to write biographies, "as-told-to" autobiographies, and histories.[24]

The Life of Josiah Henson, Formerly a Slave, Now an Inhabitant of

Canada, as Narrated by Himself (1849), a purported source for Mrs. Stowe's "Uncle Tom," was dictated to a Boston abolitionist named Samuel A. Eliot. Henson's autobiography, like most such works, is mainly concerned with depicting the horrors of slavery in the United States; but the image of Canada serves, as in Stowe's novels, as a climactic vision of freedom and future possibilities. "When I got on the Canada side, on the morning of the 28th of October, 1830, my first impulse was to throw myself on the ground, and giving way to the riotous exultation of my feelings, to execute sundry antics which excited the astonishment of those who were looking on."[25] But Canada is only momentarily the land of jubilee; calming down, Henson sets out to make his way in this country of supposedly equal opportunity. This is mainly what Canada represents to Henson: a place where the American ideal of striving and succeeding can be pursued without the impediments of racial prejudice. Unlike Mrs. Stowe, with her suspicion of New England avarice and selfishness, Henson is whole-heartedly committed to American materialism and the myth of success. "It was precisely the Yankee spirit which I wished to instil into my fellow slaves, if possible,"[26] says Henson, as he describes his efforts to encourage cooperative agricultural development schemes among the blacks of Canada.

But if Henson sees Canada as merely a modified Yankee-land, other black fugitives see the northern provinces in different terms. For Samuel Ward, the educated author of *Autobiography of a Fugitive Negro* (1855), Canada is valued for its affinities with England, and particularly for the social stability and personal refinement, which contrast to the raw and racially discriminatory frontier egalitarianism of the United States. True distinction between persons, suggests Ward, should be based on social accomplishment: "I never saw the slightest appearance of [racial prejudice] in any person in Canada recognized there, or who would be recognized [in England], as a gentleman." Ward does acknowledge, however, that there is some anti-Negro feeling in Canada, as a result of the proximity to the States and the presence of large numbers of "Yankee" immigrants. "Canadian Negro-haters," he admits, "are the very worst of their class." But he suggests that the cosmopolitan make-up of the Canadian population may eventually relieve the racial problem: "In Canada, whose population must of necessity become more or less mixed, the maintenance of distinct nationalities is certainly exceptionable."[27]

Most fugitive autobiographers saw Canada in terms of three basic images, which were all emphasized, to varying degrees, in their testimonies. On the ideal level, and, to some extent, on the experiential level, it was the land of opportunity for American-style self-reliance and self-fulfillment. More fundamentally, it was the land of freedom, a refuge from slavery; then, more realistically, it was a place of occasional encounters with racial discrimination, deception, and oppression. These are the main impressions conveyed by the series of oral testimonies collected by the Boston abolitionist, Benjamin Drew, in *A North-Side View of Slavery. The Refugee: or, the Narratives of Fugitive Slaves in Canada, Related by Themselves...* (1856). Almost all of the refugees interviewed by Drew report experiences of racial prejudice in Canada, particularly in the larger settlements such as London, Hamilton, and Toronto. Many of them also reported experiences of isolation, struggle, disappointment, and poverty. Their over-riding conviction, however, is conveyed in the comment of one refugee: "I then made up my mind that salt and potatoes in Canada, were better than pound-cake and chickens in a state of suspense and anxiety in the United States. Now I am a regular Britisher. My American blood has been scourged out of me...."[28]

The fugitive slaves, like the partisans of 1838 and the casual tourists of the pre-Civil-War period, thus expressed a significant range of response to the landscape and people of Anglophone Canada. The country north of Lake Ontario was variously an interesting tourist resort, a hostile and economically backward society, a potential but unreliable part of independent America, a refuge for victims of United States social evils, and a newer New England offering freedom and economic opportunity. By the 1840s and 1850s, this variety of response, which stemmed from the diversity of social and cultural background among the observers, was being complicated by the steadily expanding social and geographical scope of British North America. Upper Canada/Canada West was second to French Canada of the Montreal-Quebec region as a focus of American interest; but travellers and other observers were also discovering the maritime provinces. Nova Scotia and New Brunswick received a certain degree of attention; so did Prince Edward Island, Newfoundland, and even Labrador. Indeed, an important part of the American discovery of "English Canada" in this period was the discovery of the region that stretched vaguely and mysteriously along the eastern coast and inland towards Hudson Bay and beyond, a formidable yet alluring frontier.

VIII

THE NORTHEASTERN FRONTIER

The idea of Canada as a geographically vague frontier of forest and frozen wastes, stretching northward towards the top of the world, might seem as if it should be quite prominent in the American imaginative conception of the country. As many early-nineteenth-century autobiographical and fictional accounts demonstrate, however, the main impressions were social and political, rather than geographical: Canada was a decadent vestige of Europe, a bastion of British imperialism, a refuge for fugitive slaves, and so forth. But almost all writers acknowledged, however briefly, the sense of remoteness and northern wildness evident even in travelling through the settled regions. Longfellow set *Evangeline* against the background of "the forest primeval"; and Thoreau remarked, in describing his walking tour, that "We had only to go a quarter of a mile from the road, to the top of the bank, to find ourselves on the verge of the uninhabited, and for the most part, unexplored wilderness stretching toward Hudson's Bay."[1] In Parkman's work, the northern forest is a constantly emphasized backdrop for the violence, savagery, and decadence of early Canadian history. Some travellers and novelists who turned to Upper Canada/Canada West and the maritime provinces were similarly aware, at least tentatively, of the vast, primitive frontier; and a few placed the images of vastness and primitivism at the centre of their writings.

The image of the northern wilderness and of the English-Canadian as a frontiersman appears in suggestive combination in a novel by Owen Duffy entitled *Walter Warren; or The Adventurer of the Northern Wilds* (1854). Ironically, most of this novel is set in and around the town of Hamilton, the urban centre that Ralph Waldo Emerson and Thomas

Wentworth Higginson found so Anglophone in atmosphere. In *Walter Warren*, however, Hamilton is a frontier village, to which the young hero's father has immigrated, like a latter-day Leatherstocking or Daniel Boone, "in his desire to get as far as possible from the prying curiosity of his neighbours."[2] The basic conflict in the novel derives from the familiar Cooper-inspired contrast between forest and settlements. The Canadians who befriend Walter after his father is murdered by Indians are musket-toting, Indian-hating backwoodsmen, indistinguishable from their American counterparts of literary and folk traditions. The town of Hamilton, on the other hand, where the orphaned Walter is taken by an evangelical preacher, is an enclave of iniquity and hypocrisy. After suffering the preacher's abuse, and subsequently falling prey to sensual temptations in the Irish slum of Corktown, Walter follows the example of his father (and of Boone and Leatherstocking), and escapes to a more remote frontier, the region northwest of Lake Superior. But the author of *Walter Warren* does not ultimately uphold the exaltation of the wilderness against the creeping decadence that is overtaking the cities and towns of Canada. At the end of the story, the hero is reunited with his long-lost wealthy uncle, thereby gaining the means to return to civilization and enter a social stratum where he will presumably be able to avoid the problems that drove him into the wilderness.

Thus in *Walter Warren*, Canada is a new frontier offering the same opportunities for escape and invigoration that Americans associated with their own western frontier; but like many popular romancers of the nineteenth century, the author resolves his plot through success-story clichés, which do not follow logically upon the theme of the exaltation of nature and individualism. A slightly more consistent development of the pattern is evident in another novel of mid-century, *The Renegade: A Tale of Real Life* (1855), by John B. Coppinger. Set mostly in the forest wilderness north of Lake Ontario, the novel concerns two young Americans who have come to Canada to test certain ideals associated with nature and the primitive life. Frank Bramley believes that the retreat to nature is valuable only insofar as it affords the opportunity for contemplation in solitude and tranquillity, so that one can return to civilization with increased self-understanding and renewed religious sensibilities. His friend Dick Wood, on the other hand, has come to Canada to get away from the "selfishness and ingratitude of man" and to study the Indians, whom he takes to represent human beings "as they were created... in their primitive simplicity."[3] To settle their disagreement about the respective value of primitive and civilized societies, the two Americans join a nomadic tribe of Indians who are just about to set off into the wilderness. The rest of the novel is a compound of didactic colloquy, crude allegory, and fantasy, wherein the wanderers meet a band of Indians on a "prairie" near Lake Muskoka, and eventually pursue their researches to the remote retreat of an articulate Indian prophetess north of Lake Superior. The prophetess expounds the moral illustrated by the career of the title character, an Indian who is the personification of Dick Wood's misogyny carried to its logical conclusion. No individual or race is innately good or evil, but protracted solitude and resentment against mankind will eventually pervert the moral nature. With the sermon of the prophetess and the object-lesson of the renegade fresh in his memory, Dick Wood returns to the United States, determined to follow the more optimistic philosophy of his friend.

Literary tourists who ventured into the wilderness north of the Great Lakes were more restrained in their written impressions than the novelists, but their impressions nonetheless reflect familiar American preoccupations. The eminent poet William Cullen Bryant took a steamer voyage in 1846 from Buffalo across Lake Erie, through Lake St. Clair and the St. Clair River into Lake Huron and up to Sault Ste. Marie, a journey he describes in *Letters of a Traveller; or, Notes on Things Seen in Europe and America* (1850). Stopping from time to time on the "British" side, Bryant notes the sparse signs of social and economic progress, as compared to life in the American ports. At a fuel depot near the mouth of the St. Clair River, he sees a row of unprepossessing cottages, beyond which stands "the original forest...like a long, lofty wall."[4] Having a special interest in native Indian life, he notes—with what seems to be nationalistic satisfaction—that British efforts to turn a local remnant of the Chippewa tribe towards a domesticated agrarian life have been unsuccessful. At Sault Ste. Marie, however, his admiration for bureaucratic efficiency and economic progress, regardless of political affiliation, is expressed in his description of the Hudson's Bay Company outposts: "The walks are graveled and well-kept, and the whole bears the marks of British solidity and precision."[5]

A similar respect for economic achievement, combined with a devotion to an ideal of the primitive life in the wilderness, is featured in another travel book, *Adventures in the Wilds of the United States and British American Provinces* (1856), written by a journalist friend of Bryant named Charles Lanman. "I hate cities," Lanman announces. "I have not visited Canada for the purpose of examining its cities, but solely with a view of hunting up some new scenery and having a little sport in the way of salmon fishing."[6] In his two-volume compendium of travel and sporting sketches, Lanman includes accounts of his expeditions to

Sault Ste. Marie and along the shore of Lake Superior, into the Saguenay region northeast of Quebec, and to the Restigouche region of New Brunswick. In all of these outposts of British North America, he admires the purity and titanic strength of the wilderness, while deploring the exploitive human activity such as the speculative copper mining around Lake Superior. With uncertain consistency, however, he reveals his admiration for other business enterprise that is destructive of nature: William Price, the Saguenay "lumber king," is heartily praised for his "Yankee" commercial spirit and energy.[7]

Lanman was one of several American travellers and novelists who turned their attention to the Atlantic provinces of British North America in the 1850s and early 1860s. Some were attracted, like Lanman, by the remoteness and wildness of this region, but others came in search of the "forest primeval" and the peaceful Acadian villages of *Evangeline*. Throughout the late nineteenth century American tourists inspired by Longfellow's poem came to Nova Scotia in search of the countryside that had become a fragment of the American mythology of pastoral innocence and peace associated with rural life; and some of these tourists wrote sentimental magazine articles and little books on the subject. One of the earliest and more intellectually substantial of these books was a work entitled *Acadia; or, A Month with the Bluenoses* (1859) by Frederick S. Cozzens.

Cozzens (1818-69), a New York merchant, publisher, and author of humorous magazine sketches, came to Nova Scotia partly to look for Longfellow's Acadia, partly to explore an unfamiliar back-country frontier, and partly to gather material for more of the comic articles on which his modest literary reputation was based. The multiplicity of his purpose and the discrepancy between his expectations and his experience are reflected in the erratic tone of his book, which wanders from chuckling condescension to bemusement, indignation, and stern moral superiority. But for all its eclectic tone, Cozzens's *Acadia* is a noteworthy effort, with perceptive comments not only on the Atlantic region, but on British North America as a whole.

Cozzens discovered that Longfellow's Acadia still existed, at least vestigially; but it was only one small element in a confusing social and geographical mosaic. Within an easy ride of the sleepy town of Halifax he could encounter a small settlement of French-speaking peasants clad in much the same costumes, and living much the same kind of life, as Longfellow described. But only a few miles farther on, this pastoral image was shattered by the spectacle of a settlement of escaped slaves, living in extreme poverty and apathetic drudgery:

> In a few minutes we saw a log house perched on a bare bone of granite that stood out on a ragged hill-side, and presently another cabin of the same kind came in view. Then other scare-crow edifices wheeled in sight as we drove along; all forlorn, all patched with mud, all perched on barren knolls, or gigantic bars of granite, high up, like ragged redoubts of poverty, armed at every window with a formidable artillery of old hats, rolls of rags, quilts, carpets and indescribable bundles, or barricaded with boards to keep out the air and sun-shine.
>
> "You do not mean to say those wretched hovels are occupied by living beings?" said I to my companion.
>
> "Oh yes," he replied, with a quiet smile, "these are your people, your *fugitives.*"
>
> "Are all the negro settlements in Nova Scotia as miserable as this?" [Cozzens asks his companion, after they have talked to one of the inhabitants, and looked around at the dilapidated log huts.]
>
> "Yes," he answered; "you can tell a negro settlement at once by its appearance."
>
> "Then," I thought to myself, "I would, for poor Cuffee's sake, that much-vaunted British sympathy and British philanthropy had something better to show to an admiring world than the prospect around Deer's Castle."[8]

Cozzens' disdain is provoked not only by the black settlements, but also by the economically backward, unprogressive communities of Acadians, Micmac Indians, and Scots Highlanders scattered throughout the province, all of which suggest to him the inferiority of the British colony to his own country. But his comparison between Nova Scotia and the United States is based more on social than on economic factors. What particularly strikes him as offensive about the province is its fragmented social structure: the French, blacks, Scots, and others live in their own isolated, homogeneous communities, within easy access of each other, yet avoiding interaction. This fragmentation of society is antagonistic to Cozzens' American ideals of national unity:

> I must confess to no small amount of surprise at the complete isolation of the people of these colonies; the divisions among them; the separate pursuits, prejudices, languages; they seem to have nothing in common; no aggregation of interests; it is existence without nationality; sectionalism without emulation;

a mere exotic life with not a fibre rooted firmly in the soil. The colonists are English, Irish, Scotch, French, for generation after generation....

A mere aggregation of tribes is not a great people. Take the human species in a state of sectionalism, and it does not make much difference whether it is in the shape of the Indian, proud of the blue and red stripes on his face, or the Scotchman, proud of the blue and red stripes on his plaid, the inferiority of the human animal, with his tribal sheep-mark on him, is evident enough to any person of enlarged understanding.[9]

Cozzens' interest in Nova Scotia was focused almost entirely on the social situation of the settlements. Other travellers to the maritimes, particularly those not affected by *Evangeline*, were more aware of the remoteness, wildness, and frontier-like atmosphere, although most authors tended to think in terms of the familiar assumptions about the inevitability of industrial and social progress, and to compare the British provinces adversely with their own country. Nova Scotia and Prince Edward Island seemed quite settled, and, in some ways, even appealing in their rural and village societies; but just a few hours' voyage eastward from Halifax was the barren, rocky island of Newfoundland; and to the north was Labrador.

Newfoundland came briefly to American attention in 1855, when its ports became important to the laying of the trans-Atlantic cable. One of the members of the engineering party working on the Cape-Breton-Newfoundland portion of the cable was an Irish-American named John Mullaly, who recorded his impressions of the region in *A Trip to Newfoundland* (1855). A thoroughly committed disciple of technological progress, Mullaly is uninterested in the harsh spectacle of nature presented by the region and contemptuous of the inhabitants' indifference to modern technology and subservience to British political authority. "The day that sees the bond of Union between Newfoundland and the Mother Country severed," says Mullaly, "will be one of the brightest in the history of that island."[10]

A clergyman named Louis L. Noble (1813–82) ranged even further afield, incorporating his experiences in *After Icebergs with a Painter: A Summer Voyage to Labrador and around Newfoundland* (1861). More sympathetic than Mullaly towards the inhabitants, he speculates benevolently on their spiritual welfare; but as the title of his book suggests, his main interest is in the pictorial qualities of the natural setting. The icebergs and the rugged Labrador coast are described in florid terms derived from the English romantic poets he obviously admires; and his commitment to a genteel, literary civilization is indicated when he describes an evening spent with the Anglican bishop of Newfoundland, "where the conversation was about Oxford, and Keble, English parsonages, and Christian art."[11]

A more complex and more literarily skilful response to the North Atlantic regions of Canada is reflected in a five-part account of a trip to Labrador by David A. Wasson (1823-87) entitled "Ice and Esquimaux," published serially in the *Atlantic Monthly* in late 1864 and early 1865. Wasson has been described as a neglected genius of the Transcendentalist movement, "a corrective to Emerson and Thoreau,"[12] and if his writings do not entirely justify this praise, his contacts with Emerson, Thoreau, and other notable New England authors are certainly of historical interest. Particularly significant is his ideological debate with Thoreau, which was stimulated by personal acquaintance between the two authors while Wasson lived in Concord in the 1850s.

The basic terms of this debate are outlined in the first chapter of "Ice and Esquimaux," where Wasson describes the appeal Labrador holds for him:

> The mystic North reached forth the wand by which it had fascinated me so often, and renewed its spell. Who has not felt it? Thoreau wrote of "The Wild" as he alone could write; but only in the North do you find it,—unless you make it, as he did, by your imagination. And even he could in this but partially succeed. Talk of finding it in a ten-acre swamp! Why, man, you are just from a cornfield, the echoes of your sister's piano are still in your ears, and you called for a letter as you came! Verdure and a mild heaven are above; *clunking* frogs and plants that keep company with man are beneath. But in the North Nature herself is wild. Of man she has never so much as heard. She has seen, perchance, a biped atomy creeping through her snows; but he is not Man, lording it in power of thought and performance; he is a muffled imbecility, that can do nothing but hug and hide its existence, lest some careless breath of hers should blow it out; his pin-head taper must be kept under a bushel, or cease to be even the covert pettiness it is. The wildness of the North is not scenic and pictorial merely, but goes to the very heart of things, immeasurable, immitigable, infinite; deaf and blind to all but itself and its own, it prevails, it is, and it is all.[13]

Wasson is presumably thinking of *Walden* in his allusion to the "ten-acre swamp." Perhaps he had not read Thoreau's *The Maine Woods*, which was published in 1864 (although parts of it had appeared earlier in periodicals), and which might have more adequately satisfied his criteria for the retreat to the wild. In any case, he is hardly being fair to Thoreau, who deliberately chose Walden Pond, rather than some more remote retreat, because an important part of his purpose was to juxtapose and compare civilization and the wild. To explore this comparison, he would inevitably have to rely on his imagination, and most readers of *Walden* would argue that he more than "partially" succeeded. Indeed, it might be argued that Thoreau's imaginative wild is more clearly realized than Wasson's supposedly literal one. Wasson retreats to one of the most isolated and primitive regions on the continent, but he is unable to project himself imaginatively into this environment. There is a suggestion of irony in the fact that he was accompanied on his expedition not only by a painter, as Louis L. Noble was, but by a photographer as well. His view of Labrador, in spite of the implied promise of metaphysical explorations in the reference to the "immeasurable... infinite," is largely "scenic and pictorial."

Wasson's inability to probe beyond a superficial pictorial level is evident in his contemplations of the inhabitants of Labrador. He devotes part of a chapter to the Innuit, "an original and pre-Adamite man," who is depicted as an enigmatic and rather inhuman figure, completely unself-conscious, and almost indistinguishable from the landscape and the animals of the region.

> Not only is he original, but one of the most special of men, related more strictly than almost any other to a particular aspect of nature. Inseparable from the extreme North, the sea-shore, and the seal, he is himself, as it were, a seal come to feet and hands, and preying upon his more primitive kindred.[14]

In his contemplation of the Inuit, Wasson reveals his preference for civilization and progress over the "pre-Adamite" world. Similarly, in another chapter of the narrative, entitled "Birds and Boys' Play," the author suggests that the experience of hunting belongs, in effect, to the childhood of the human race, and although it may afford temporary amusement, the cultural and intellectual values of civilization are the proper pursuits of modern man.

Thus Wasson, like Louis L. Noble and other American travellers in the maritime north, relies largely on the clichés of romantic poetry to embellish his superficial impressions, and ultimately uses his literary exposition of his experience to defend the values of modern American civilization. The same tendency is reflected in what is evidently the only significant pre-Civil-War American attempt to adapt the north Atlantic region to fiction, a novel entitled *The New Priest in Conception Bay* (1858) by Robert Traill Spence Lowell (1816–91).

The brother of James Russell Lowell and grandfather of the twentieth-century poet, Lowell served as an Episcopal missionary from 1843 to 1847 in the fishing village of Bay Roberts, Newfoundland. Besides writing the novel, Lowell used his Newfoundland experience in a short story and several brief lyric poems. Although his poetry is undistinguished, it is perhaps remarkable for its prefiguration of some of the less attractive affectations of Walt Whitman. Lowell attempts to imitate, by means of apostrophes and unusual verse forms, the rough and violent features of the Atlantic landscape. The opening stanza of "Newfoundland" (written in 1847) exclaims:

> O rugged land!
> Land of the rock moss!
> Land whose drear barrens it is woe to cross!
> Thou rough thing from God's hand!
> O Stormy land!
> Land where the tempests roar!
> Land where the unbroken waves rave mad upon the shore:
> Thine outwalls scarce withstand![15]

But *The New Priest in Conception Bay* is a more subtle and detailed attempt to present both the landscape and the society of Newfoundland. The novel begins with a prefatory chapter that unites terrain and inhabitants in a comprehensive picture of primeval starkness and elemental struggle:

> Up go the surges on the coast of Newfoundland, and down again, into the sea. The huge island, in which the scene of our story lies, stands, with its sheer, beetling cliffs, out of the ocean, a monstrous mass of rock and gravel, almost without soul, like a strange thing from the bottom of the great deep, lifted up, suddenly, into sunshine and storm, but belonging to the watery darkness out of which it has been reared. The eye, accustomed to richer and softer scenes, finds something of a strange and almost

startling beauty in its bold, hard outlines, cut out on every side, against the sky....

In March or April almost all the men go out in fleets to meet the ice that floats down from the northern regions, and to kill the seals that come down on it. In early summer a third part or a half of all the people go, by families, in their schooners, to the coast of Labrador, and spend the summer, fishing there; and in the winter, half of them are living in the woods, ... to have their fuel near them. At home or abroad, during the season, the men are on the water for seals or cod. The women sow, and plant, and tend the little garden, and dry the fish: in short, they do the land-work; and are the better for it.[16]

Lowell particularly succeeds in presenting a sympathetic and convincing picture of the Newfoundland fishermen and villagers with their naïve piety and their uncritical acceptance of the stern natural conditions of their lives. Some of the characters—particularly the garrulous Skipper George, with his intuitive moralizing and dogged acceptance of Christian principles—are perhaps too heavily idealized. But Lowell qualifies some of their virtues by pointing out that their simplicity of character can occasionally be united with abysmal ignorance, and by introducing a comic "Yankee" named Elnathan Bangs (an avatar of James Russell Lowell's Hosea Bigelow) who calls attention to the Newfoundlanders' alleged lack of initiative and energy.

The Newfoundland fishermen and their struggle with nature are not, however, the central focus of *The New Priest*. The plot involves the violent quarrels between the Anglo-Newfoundland Protestants and the Catholics of Irish descent, which periodically shook the island in the nineteenth century. This theme was perhaps not an unwise choice for Lowell, who as a missionary would have detailed, first-hand knowledge of the island's religious controversies, while his experience of the fishermen's professional lives would be limited. Certainly the detachable episode, "Skipper George's Story," which concerns a tragedy in the fishing fleet, suggests that an extended sea narrative in Lowell's hands might have been intolerably sentimental and didactic. Lowell also wrote a very compelling short story about the Newfoundland seamen, a story that suggests he might have been capable of something far more impressive than the doctrinal controversies of *The New Priest*. "A Raft That No Man Made" (published in the *Atlantic Monthly*, March, 1862) tells the story of a Newfoundland seal hunter cast away on an ice floe, whose harrowing experience leads to a resolution to forsake his cruel and violent occupation. The hunter's discovery, in a barren world of ice and sea, that the moral principle of the universe is love rather than the survival of the fittest reflects the author's debt to "The Ancient Mariner" and indicates that Lowell was capable of amalgamating his literary background, his observations of the Newfoundland inhabitants, and his experience of their environment. In *The New Priest*, however, he chose to focus more exclusively on matters related to his clerical pursuits, and the results are far from satisfying. Incapable of religious objectivity, he depicts his Catholics as devils, weaklings, or fools, while his Protestants are paragons of virtue and patience. An even more serious flaw in the novel is the love story involving two "genteel" characters obviously derived from the tradition of domestic sentimental fiction. In addition, the plot of the novel is carried along almost entirely by melodramatic contrivances such as kidnapping, mysterious apparitions, and midnight rendezvous. Nevertheless, in spite of the conventional characters and events that dominate the foreground, *The New Priest* (as one of Lowell's few modern commentators has declared) "should have honorable mention ... as a distinguished study of character and environment in a time when one could count the first-rate productions of American fiction on his two hands."[17]

Lowell's image of the northeastern frontier, whatever its artistic merits, deserves careful comparison with other American literary responses to Canada. The stark and rugged landscape of Lowell's Newfoundland, like the barren vistas of Wasson's Labrador, suggests the continuing awe and revulsion with which Americans face the far north. Even in the hearty melodrama of popular fiction, as in Duffy's *Walter Warren* and Coppinger's *The Renegade*, the North is a place to compare adversely with the southern regions of the continent, or one to reject altogether. Even the more settled outposts, like Cozzens' Acadia, suggest remoteness and barrenness—or at least a lack of the qualities Americans associate with the higher forms of political and social existence. Although curious or adventurous Americans are drawn to these outposts, their ultimate commitment is to urban culture. In the pre-Civil-War period, especially, this apprehensive attitude towards the North is evident. Not until after the war, with the "opening" of the American West, did this attitude to remote frontiers change markedly. And even then, the change was qualified by counteracting tendencies. In the American literary exploitation of Canada, the counter-acting tendencies derived particularly from the continuing interest in the cultural and political comparison of the two societies.

IX

POST-CIVIL-WAR LITERARY TRAVELLERS

In the years between the outbreak of the American Civil War and the end of the nineteenth century, a great many political, social, and literary developments affected the American image of Canada. Both countries were rapidly changing and expanding. Both, almost simultaneously, achieved a new sense of the importance of national unity: the United States through the ordeal of civil war; Canada through the less drastic, but precarious, process of confederation of the British North American provinces. Both countries were looking with new eagerness towards the vast frontiers of unsettled land to the west and north. As political and geographical demarcations opened outward, cultural activity in the two countries was energetic and innovative. In the United States, while literary conventions of the New England genteel tradition continued to dominate certain segments of the creative and reading population to ensure the persistence of such genres as the historical romance, new forms and themes were emerging. Chief among innovative trends was the complex series of developments that came to be encompassed by the label "realism." The American realist movement was associated particularly with the novel, although its ramifications were evident in other genres, including travel writing. Emphasizing a supposedly democratic exposition of common-place modern experience, realism also developed in conjunction with a flourishing interest in regional or "local-colour" elements. Inevitably, most American realist writers tended to relate this democratic mythology and localism to the United States, but they did not neglect foreign settings, particularly when the foreign settings offered opportunities for comparisons with their own country.

In the exultant and prosperous post-war atmosphere, pleasure travelling and travel writing received new impetus. In *The Innocents Abroad* (1869), Mark Twain concluded from the hordes of Americans rushing to get passage on the trans-Atlantic steamers that "everybody was going to Europe";[1] but, as always throughout the nineteenth century, a significant segment of the travelling population—including, eventually, Mark Twain himself—was making more economical tours of the northern provinces. In the closing months of the war, one of Mark Twain's literary predecessors, "Artemus Ward" (Charles F. Browne), reported that he was "travelin' among the crowned heds of Canady," and went on, in *Artemus Ward: His Travels* (1865), to poke fun at the usual objects of American curiosity. "Altho' this is a monikal form of Gov'ment," says Artemus, "I am onable to perceive much moniky. I tried to git a piece in Toronto, but failed to succeed." "Quebeck is full of stone walls, and arches, and citadels and things. It is said no foe could ever git into Quebeck, and I guess they couldn't. And I don't see what they'd *want* to get in there for." Artemus views with satirical contempt the British loyalism as well as the ceremonial militarism of Canada, but in view of his own country's internal strife, he cannot help admiring the relatively tranquil atmosphere of Quebec. The Canadians, he says, "don't enjoy the priceless boon of a war"; and he concludes, half-seriously, that he "wouldn't mind comin' over here to live in the capacity of a Duke, provided a vacancy occurs...."[2]

The Innocents Abroad is the best known of the breezy type of comic travel narrative in which a folksy American tourist comments irreverently on foreign customs and locales, and satirizes both the subject of such observations and the stilted conventions of traditional travel writing. Among the few other writers of such works who dealt with Canada was Mark Twain's friend and one-time collaborator Charles Dudley Warner. Warner's *Baddeck, and That Sort of Thing* (1874) described a journey by boat, train, and stagecoach from Boston to the village of Baddeck, on Cape Breton Island. In spite of Warner's repeated attempts at jocosity, however, the main tone conveyed by his little book is rather like that of Frederick Cozzens' *Acadia; or, A Month with the Bluenoses*. To Warner, as to Cozzens, this part of the country seemed a fragmented outpost, having no cultural or political relevance to the rest of North America or to any larger community. If this region is typical of the new Dominion of Canada, Warner suggests, its circumstances do not bode well for the country's future:

> I could not resist a worrying anxiety about the future of the British Provinces, which not even the remembrance of their

hostility to us during our mortal strife with the Rebellion could render agreeable. For I could not but feel that the ostentatious and unconcealable prosperity of the "States" overshadows this part of the continent. And it was for once in vain that I said, "have we not a common language and a common literature, and no copyright, and a common pride in Shakespeare and Hannah More and Colonel Newcome and Pepys' Diary?" I never knew this sort of consolation to fail before; it does not seem to answer in the Provinces as well as it does in England.[3]

Mark Twain visited Canada in 1881; he spent two weeks in Montreal and made a brief trip to Quebec, mainly for the purpose of fulfilling legal requirements to secure Canadian copyright for his new novel, *The Prince and the Pauper*. His notebook entries of the trip are sparse and often trivial, although the occasional thoughtful or tentatively humorous comment suggests that he may have considered working them into a travel sketch for publication.[4] His reactions to Montreal and Quebec City, like his comments on Europe in *The Innocents Abroad*, include objections to the sub-standard hotel accommodation, burlesques of the French language and of his own attempts to speak it, and brief descriptions of the tedious procession of churches, cathedrals, and other attractions considered compulsory viewing for tourists. Notre Dame Cathedral in Montreal is "huge and gaudy with gilding & vivid & variegated color." Other religious aspects of the city are equally unimpressive: "There is an average of one clergymen [sic] per sinner here, I judge." The much-touted natural spectacles are not worth inconveniencing oneself for: "Drove half way to Falls of Montmorency, then came back & bought a photograph. The wind down on the low ground was mighty cold. The photograph is very satisfactory."[5]

Canada was an object of American humour throughout the nineteenth century in pre-Civil-War works like *Major Jones's Sketches of Travel*, Cozzens' *Acadia*, and more incidentally, in Thoreau's "A Yankee in Canada," as well as in the post-war works of Browne, Warner, and Twain. The more pervasive tendency, however, among travel writers and novelists, was to take the country seriously. The most perceptive and detailed post-war commentaries were by authors skilled in the close analytical methods of "feature" writing for the burgeoning magazine industry, or by adherents to the realist theories of writing. Most travel writers working in this changing literary atmosphere aimed at the judicious selection of detail, including the supposedly common-place and familiar, which might serve even better than the ostensibly striking or dramatic element to convey the significance of the subject.

This approach to Canada can be seen in four noteworthy works: an essay on French Canada by E. L. Godkin, an essay on Quebec City by Henry James, and two travelogue novels by William Dean Howells. All three of these authors wrote about the familiar routes and attractions that had appealed to American curiosity for almost a century; yet in their respective writings can be discerned a vitalization of the American image of Canada. At the same time, there is a continuation between many of the responses of these writers and the responses of their pre-war predecessors. This is particularly true in the case of Godkin, who shares many of the rather condescending attitudes of earlier travellers.

E. L. Godkin (1831-1902), owner and editor of the New York magazine *The Nation*, visited Quebec City and environs in the summer of 1868 and wrote his impressions in a two-part article entitled "French Canada," published in the magazine in August of that year. An erudite social critic and historian, Godkin was a friend and intellectual associate of Howells, James, and Parkman, and had probably read the two volumes of *France and England in North America* that had appeared by 1868. Godkin mentions Thoreau in his essay, and had evidently read "A Yankee in Canada," which was published for the first time in its entirety in 1866. Like Thoreau, Godkin is interested in the religious and secular vestiges of the past in French Canada, although his reflections on them are quite different from those of the author of "A Yankee in Canada."

In spite of the implication of the title of his article, Godkin divides his attention between the two linguistic communities of Quebec province. He begins, in fact, with a speculative commentary on the English-Canadians of Quebec City, a commentary that suggests his affinity with the new realist attitudes and modes of expression. Reporting on his scrutiny of the faces of people in the streets of the northern city, he notes rather facetiously, "The first question which presents itself to an observer on entering Canada is, why do the Canadians look so fat and chubby compared to Americans?" (p. 128).[6] Continuing to focus on physical appearance and social custom, Godkin emphasizes the Anglophilia of the English-Canadians, who, by virtue of "the well-known colonial tendency to out-Herod Herod," are "considerably more English... than the English themselves" (p. 128). This observation of Canadian imitativeness leads to the first expression of his rather pessimistic outlook for Canada as a whole. The imitation of foreign customs, Godkin insists, will inevitably impede the development of any nation:

> One cannot remain very long in Canada without having the idea very strongly presented to one that even a slight political connection between a colony and "the mother country" is a curse to the colony. As long as they are bound together, even by the light silken tie of allegiance, really healthy political and social life seems to be impossible for the latter. A people whose manners are not the natural result of its own character and culture, but a laborious copy of those of another people, differently situated and in a different stage of development, of course suffers much both morally and mentally, no matter what amount of political freedom it may enjoy. (p. 128)

Godkin is slightly more sympathetic to the French-Canadians than to the English-Canadians, although both linguistic communities seem to him to lack any sense of national pride or identity. Cut off from the past, uncommitted to the present and future, a large percentage of the Canadian population has rejected the possibilities of the new Dominion to seek economic and social advancement in the United States. The southward exodus "has even reached the French, to whom the United States has been hitherto a land as far off as when the Indians came down from the St. Lawrence to harry the New England heretics" (p. 129). Canadian indifference to national traditions and ideals is epitomized for Godkin by the monument to Wolfe and Montcalm in Quebec City, a symbol potentially expressive of the tragic conflict and triumphant resolution of Canadian history, but which has been left to crumble into ruins, its tribute to the heroes of the Plains of Abraham overshadowed by an irrelevant inscription commemorating the governor-general under whose patronage it was built. "The impression left on the mind of the spectator by the monument is, in fact, that it was a far finer thing to build it than to die sword in hand on the Plains of Abraham..." (p. 128).

Like Thoreau and many other American travellers, Godkin is able to praise the relative simplicity of the way of life of the French-Canadians, who are "as little troubled about stocks, bonds, railroads, mines, and the other 'big things' of American progress as if [they] lived in Paraguay, instead of within a few hours of Maine and Vermont" (p. 129). But on the other hand, Godkin relates this unworldliness to the same social and religious decadence that Parkman identified as among the main causes of the collapse of New France: "society in French Canada even now rests largely on feudal ideas, and is held together by medieval laws" (p. 129). Godkin is not anti-Catholic to the same extent as many earlier travellers, but he does see the church as a retrogressive social force, binding the *habitant* to the past, and excluding him from the currents of progress that shape modern life. The French-Canadian, according to Godkin, is perhaps more self-reliant than his European counterpart: "Priest-ridden and seigneur-ridden though he has been, the free air of the wilderness has given the Canadian a dignity and self-respect in which the French peasant, in spite of the Revolution, is still wanting" (p. 147). But in the long run, French-Canadian social and religious traditionalism, along with English-Canadian adherence to British customs and institutions, will probably lead to the extinction of Canada as a separate nation. The French-Canadians, Godkin concludes, "will probably preserve their language and manners intact till the whole country is annexed to the United States. Both will probably then disappear rapidly before the terrible solvent of American ideas and institutions" (p. 148).

But as these remarks indicate, Godkin views the prospective fate of Canada—or, at least, of French Canada—with an ambivalence comparable to Parkman's dualistic view of New France. "The terrible solvent" of American democracy will eventually engulf the whole continent, in that irresistible historical process that decrees a constant development of technology and social institutions. But in this process, something of value will be lost.

A slightly more congenial, but also ultimately pessimistic, evaluation of Canada is evident in a brief essay on Quebec City written in 1871 by the young novelist Henry James. Originally published in *The Nation*, and revised for inclusion in his book of travel articles, *Portraits of Places* (1884), "Quebec" constitutes James's only literary use of Canada, but its suggestive insights and images make it well worth detailed consideration. Like Godkin, James had read Parkman, whose *The Jesuits in North America* he had reviewed in *The Nation* a few years before visiting Quebec, and with whose ambivalent evaluation of the history of New France he generally agreed. The French, James observed in the review, wasted their time ranging the wilderness and trying to convert morally unregenerate savages, while in the British American colonies "prolific Dutch farmers and Puritan divines were building up the state of New York and the commonwealth of Massachusetts." Nevertheless, the "faith, patience, and courage" of such zealots as the Jesuit missionaries "form a very interesting chapter in the history of the human mind."[7]

James agrees with Godkin that modern French Canada is probably destined to go the same way as New France; but just as he shares Parkman's fascination with the "interesting chapters" of early Canadian history, so does he find nineteenth-century Quebec to have many appealing features. The modern society does not reflect the epic qualities of its predecessor, which so fascinated the historian; but it does have qualities that engage the interest of the artist attuned to the illusions of fiction, painting, and stagecraft. "The old world rises in the midst of the new in the manner of a change of scene on the stage," James reports of his first glimpse of Quebec City (p. 350).[8] He emphasizes the city's pictorial and dramatic "effects" (as James himself emphasizes the word, p. 350), and various features, which he repeatedly describes as "picturesque." The most striking impression James has of Quebec is that of fictive illusion: in "the little residential streets... some of the houses have the staleness of complexion which Balzac loved to describe" (p. 357); strolling through these streets, he encounters "little old Frenchmen who look as if they had stepped out of Balzac" (p. 358). This referral of the setting and characters of Quebec to one of his beloved French realist authors suggests that James finds Quebec fairly convincing in its "effect" of reality; but on at least one occasion he is reminded of a literary polarity to realism, suggesting that the illusion is not always successful. Of the *habitant*'s docile submission to the church, he remarks: "It is, perhaps, not Longfellow's *Evangeline* for chapter and verse, but it is a tolerable prose transcript" (p. 359). And in the village of Château-Richer, where he looks in vain for the "elderly manor which might have baptised" the town (p. 361), he discovers that much of French Canada, as convincing as it may be, conveys merely the illusion of antiquity after all: "in such pictorial efforts as this Quebec breaks down; one must not ask too much of it" (pp. 361-62).

The most successful "effect" is produced not by the quaint populace or by artificial antiquities, but by the natural setting of Quebec, "perched on its mountain of rock, washed by a river as free and ample as an ocean-gulf, sweeping from its embattled crest, the villages, the forests, the blue undulations of the imperial province of which it is warden..." (p. 355). But the contrast between the picturesque artifice of the pseudo-European city and the primitive reality of the vast northern wilderness forcibly evokes the idea of the tenuousness of the city's existence. If the deliberate quaintness of Quebec makes it appear more like a novel or a painting than a reality, its geographical position raises the questions of how and why the city exists at all. Yet for all his ironic comments on the "effects" of Quebec, James is grateful that it does exist, and hopeful that it will continue to do so. "As it has managed from our scanty annals to squeeze out a past," he remarks, "you pray in the name of all that's majestic that it may have a future" (p. 355). But James is not optimistic about this future; like most nineteenth-century Americans, he sees his country's ultimate political domination of the continent as inevitable. Even more forcibly than Godkin, however, he expresses his regret at this prospect:

> I suppose no patriotic American can look at all these things, however idly, without reflecting on the ultimate possibility of their becoming absorbed into his own huge state. Whenever, sooner or later, the change is wrought, the sentimental tourist will keenly feel that a long stride has been taken, roughshod, from the past to the present. The largest appetite in modern civilization will have swallowed the largest morsel. What the change may bring of comfort or of grief to the Canadians themselves, will be for them to say; but, in the breast of this sentimental tourist of ours, it will produce little but regret. The foreign elements of eastern Canada, at least, are extremely interesting; and it is of good profit to us Americans to have near us, and of easy access, an ample something which is not our expansive selves. Here we find a hundred mementoes of an older civilization than our own, of different manners, of social forces once mighty, and still glowing with a sort of autumnal warmth. (pp. 362-63)

Thus in Quebec City and the surrounding countryside James discovers what appears to be a possible alternative to the raw and often ruthlessly self-centred society of the United States; but the peculiar historical situation of Canada, and the apparent commitment of much of its populace to a quaint, fictive existence, make the continued existence of the country a matter of extreme doubt. Although his attitude, like Parkman's attitude to New France, is regretful rather than complacent, James is in effect saying what American observers had been saying throughout the nineteenth century: that Canada had failed to attune itself to the inevitable direction of life in the New World.

A somewhat more hopeful, and more substantial, literary response to Canada can be found in the work of James's friend and fellow realist, William Dean Howells. In contrast to James's limited experience of Canada, Howells' personal and literary involvement with the country was quite extensive. He made his first visit to the northern provinces in July 1860, as a side-trip to the famous first visit to New England described in *Literary Friends and Acquaintance* (1900). His impressions of Niagara Falls, Toronto, Montreal, and Quebec were included in two series of travel letters, "Glimpses of Summer Travel" and "En Passant," published in 1860 in the *Cincinnati Gazette* and the *Ohio State Journal* respectively. Much of the material gathered for these articles, supplemented by notes from another trip made in 1870, was incorporated into his first two novels, *Their Wedding Journey* (1872), and *A Chance Acquaintance* (1873).

In presenting the chronicle of common-place events in the wedding journey of Basil and Isabel March, Howells attempted what was perhaps the purest and most thorough application of his theories of literary realism.

> As in literature the true artist will shun the use even of real events if they are of an improbable character, so the sincere observer of man will not desire to look upon his heroic or occasional phases, but will seek him in his habitual moods of vacancy and tiresomeness. To me, at any rate, he is at such times very precious; and I never perceive him to be so much a man and a brother as when I feel the pressure of his vast, natural unaffected dulness. (p. 55)[9]

This "dulness," which was by no means a pejorative term for Howells, was in his view the most characteristic feature of life in nineteenth-century United States. Stories of war, heroism, and mass suffering were outside the ordinary course of modern life. Or, as he suggested later in *Criticism and Fiction* (1891), such stories belonged to the decadent, undemocratic Old World. Even after the Chicago Haymarket affair of 1886, which opened his eyes to the fact that severe injustice could exist in his own country, Howells could still say that

> in a land where journeymen carpenters and plumbers strike for four dollars a day the sum of hunger and cold is comparatively small, and the wrong from class to class has been almost inappreciable.

"Though all this," he added in a terse reflection on recent events, "is changing for the worse."[10]

Thus the early chapters of *Their Wedding Journey* are devoted to a discursive and leisurely account of travel in the modern United States, with all its minor inconveniences and occasional delights: the Marches resignedly accept the rudeness of railway and hotel employees, suffer the terrible heat wave of 1870 in New York City, indulge themselves with the splendour of a stateroom on a Hudson River steamboat. Occasionally, the author calls attention to what might be considered a more serious aspect of life. As the Marches proceed on their journey, they catch glimpses of urban slums, with 'rows of ashbarrels, in which the decrepit children and mothers of the streets were clawing for bits of coal" (p. 17); they witness the misery of a victim of heat prostration on a New York street; and they discuss with momentary solemnity the enigmatic cataclysm of a small boat rammed and sunk in the night on the Hudson River. But this background of extraordinary or exceptional circumstances does not seriously disturb the orderly and leisured progression of Howells' two characters along the course of their unremarkable journey, which, in its placid routine of domestic detail, interrupted by only brief inconvenience or by the impersonal spectacle of misfortune, might be considered Howells' metaphor for the course of middle-class life in late-nineteenth-century United States.

At Niagara Falls, a new thematic element is introduced. Here, at what is perhaps the most famous geographical phenomenon in North America, and is certainly the most famous border point between the United States and Canada, Basil March reflects on the historical associations evoked by the setting:

> [Niagara's] beauty is relieved against an historical background as gloomy as the lightest-hearted tourist could desire. The abominable savages, revering the cataract as a kind of august devil, and leading a life of demoniacal misery and wickedness, whom the first Jesuits found here two hundred years ago; the ferocious Iroquois bloodily driving out these squalid devil-worshippers; the French planting the fort that yet guards the mouth of the river, and therewith the seeds of war that fruited afterwards in murderous strifes throughout the whole Niagara country; the struggle for the military posts on the river, during the wars of France and England; the awful scene in the conspiracy of Pontiac, where a detachment of English troops was driven by the Indians over the precipice near the great whirlpool; the sorrow and havoc visited upon the American settlements in the Revolution by the savages who prepared their attacks in the shadow of Fort Niagara; the battles of Chippewa and of Lundy's Lane that mixed the roar of their cannon with that of the fall; the savage forays with tomahawk and scalping-knife, and the blazing villages on either shore in the War of 1812; these are the memories of

the place, the links in a chain of tragical interest scarcely broken before our time since the white man first beheld the mist-veiled face of Niagara. (pp. 88-89)

As Howells goes on to state, this meditation has been partly inspired by his reading of Parkman. "Those precious books," he says of the four volumes of history Parkman published by 1870, "... make our meagre past wear something of the rich romance of old European days, and illumine its savage solitude with the splendor of medieval chivalry, and the glory of medieval martyrdom" (p. 89). Howells' basic literary ideal was the celebration of the common man in modern America, but he did not reject the epic and romance traditions with their European-derived conventions, and their emphasis on the pre-eminent hero and on extraordinary incident. Indeed, he indicates in *Their Wedding Journey* his gratitude to Parkman for having shown that North America has a historical tradition comparable to the epic and romance mythology of Europe. The important point about this tradition as it concerns North America, however, is that it belongs to the past. The Indians have vanished, or appear to be on the point of extinction; French military power has disappeared from the continent; and in place of the savage war parties along the border in 1812, peaceable American tourists come to view the natural and artificial vestiges of an earlier era.

Thus Canada represents in the first instance for Howells a kind of fossil of the heroic North American past. Unlike James, Godkin, or Parkman, however, Howells does not contend that the significance of Canada relates entirely to the past, or that the northern country has no future as a nation. More than most American travellers to Canada, Howells is eager to scrutinize the country closely, to see how it differs from his own, and to see what it offers in the way of alternatives to life in the United States.

In line with the realist inclination to define experience in terms of the common-place and routine elements of every-day life, Howells forms his conception of modern Canada not from a detailed study of its political and social structures, but from encounters with ordinary Canadians who come within his observation. In general, he claims to find a more amiable and leisurely manner in the Canadian people as compared to Americans. The porter on the St. Lawrence boat

> was so civil that he did not snub the meekest and most vexatious of the passengers, and Basil mutely blessed his servile soul. Few white Americans, he said to himself, would behave so decently

in his place; and he could not conceive of the American steamboat clerk who would use the politeness towards a waiting crowd that the Canadian purser showed when they all wedged themselves in about his window to receive their stateroom keys. (p. 107)

Like James and Godkin, Howells is particularly struck by the bicultural qualities of Montreal and Quebec, and notes the observable distinctions between the Anglophone and Francophone populations:

> Our friends... knew [the other American tourists] at a glance from the native populations, who are also easily distinguishable from each other. The French Canadians are nearly always of a peasant-like commonness, or where they rise above this, have a bourgeois commonness of face and manner; and the English Canadians are to be known from the many English sojourners by the effort to look much more English than the latter. (p. 124)

In spite of the large French-speaking population, the most prominent feature of Montreal, from the American tourist's point of view, is the political and cultural attachment to England. "At dinner [the Marches] spent the intervals of the courses... in wondering if the Canadians did not make it a matter of conscientious loyalty to out-English the English even in the matter of pale-ale and sherry, and in rotundity of person and freshness of face, just as they emulated them in the cut of their clothes and whiskers" (p. 134).

On the basis of these random observations of the populace of Montreal, Howells offers a general summary of the political and social status of Canada, a summary that reveals his ultimate devotion to the ideal of North American independence from Europe. Basil and Isabel March gradually come to the opinion that

> its overweening loyalty placed a great country like Canada in a very silly attitude, the attitude of an overgrown, unmanly boy, clinging to the maternal skirts, and though spoilt and wilful, without any character of his own. The constant reference of local hopes to that remote centre beyond seas, the test of success by the criterions of a necessarily different civilization, the social and intellectual dependence implied by traits that meet the most hurried glance in the Dominion, give an effect of meanness to the whole fabric. Doubtless it is a life of comfort, of peace, of

irresponsibility they live there, but it lacks the grandeur which no sum of material prosperity can give; it is ignoble, like all voluntarily subordinate things. Somehow, one feels that it has no basis in the New World, and that till it is shaken loose from England it cannot have. (p. 135)

Unlike Henry James, however, Howells does not assume that American annexation of Canada is inevitable. There is still a possibility that Canada will find a distinctive national identity independent of both England and the United States:

> It would be a pity... if [Canada] should be parted from the parent country merely to be joined to an unsympathetic half-brother like ourselves; and nothing, fortunately, seems to be further from the Canadian mind. There are some experiments no longer possible to us which could still be tried there to the advantage of civilization, and we were better two great nations side by side then a union of discordant traditions and ideas. (p. 135)

Political independence, Howells recalls, is by no means a magical guarantee of social perfectibility. The United States continues to be plagued by a profusion of difficulties derived from its status as a republic.

> But none the less does the American traveller, swelling with forgetfulness of the shabby despots who govern New York, and the swindling railroad kings whose word is law to the whole land, feel like saying to the hulking giant beyond St. Lawrence and the Lakes, "Sever the apron strings of allegiance, and try to be yourself, whatever you are." (pp. 135-36)

But as the uncertain wording of this excerpt suggests, Howells finds it difficult to come to any conclusions about Canada. In spite of the careful and leisurely scrutiny his realist perspective brings to bear on the subject, he can only repeatedly express his bewilderment at the paradoxes and enigmas of Canada. The sense of inconclusiveness is aggravated by his experience of Quebec, which, as Godkin and James discovered, presents to the American eye a particularly striking series of contradictions. The fortifications, monuments, and antique buildings evoke the splendid chronicle of discovery and adventure associated with Cartier, Champlain, the Jesuits, and Wolfe and Montcalm; but the modern city with its tranquil Francophone population seems out of place in its northern wilderness setting:

> Quebec, in fact, is but a pantomimic reproduction of France; it is as if two centuries in a new land, amidst the primeval silences of nature and the long hush of the Northern winters, had stilled the tongues of the lively folk and made them taciturn as we of a graver race. They have kept the ancestral vivacity of manner; the elegance of the shrug is intact; the talking hands take part in dialogue; the agitated person will have its share of expression. But the loud and eager tone is wanting, and their dumb show mystifies the beholder almost as much as the Southern architecture under the slanting Northern sun. It is not America; if it is not France, what is it? (pp. 158)

Thus the methods of realist fiction, focusing on the observable details of the setting and the supposedly representative populace, rather than on abstract political and social facts or concepts, are unable to come to any conclusion about Canada. Repeatedly throughout *Their Wedding Journey* Howells' meditations move towards statements of uncertainty ("try to be yourself, whatever you are"), or questions ("if it is not France, what is it?").

Howells made further use of Canada in *A Chance Acquaintance*, his second work of fiction and the beginning of a series of novels involving emotional conflict and domestic crisis, a series climaxed by his first important achievement, the "divorce novel," *A Modern Instance* (1882). *A Chance Acquaintance* is set entirely in the Quebec City and Saguenay regions; but instead of getting involved in the subtle and elusive question of Canada's national identity, Howells uses the northern scene as a backdrop for a slight but subtle tale of American tourists in a fleeting situation of infatuation and disillusionment. In depicting the brief romantic interlude involving young Kitty Ellison of Eriecreek, New York, and the world-weary Miles Arbuton of Boston, Howells deals with a theme that is prominent throughout his work, the cultural conflict between New England and the western American frontier. Indeed, the two lovers are almost allegorical representatives of their respective regions: Kitty, the daughter of a militant abolitionist, has been brought up in an atmosphere of "fierce democracy"; Arbuton, educated in New England and Europe, is unreflectively aristocratic, "an exclusive by training and by instinct" (pp. 39-40).[11]

The contrast between these two Americans and the regional viewpoints they represent is mainly developed in terms of their respective responses to Canada. To Kitty, who has seen very little of the world beyond Eriecreek, the province of Quebec appears simultaneously a foreign country and an epitome of what she has read and thought about the North American wilderness and the heroic past associated with it. On the boat trip up the Saguenay, she is impressed by "the sad great river of the awful north," the ominous grandeur of which evokes visions of the continent as it must have been before the coming of Europeans. The first feeble attempts of the white man to gain a foothold on the continent are evoked by the towns and villages, like Tadoussac, "where early in the sixteenth century the French traders fixed their first post, and where still the oldest church north of Florida is standing" (p. 16). These geographical and historical associations appear to Kitty, fresh from her reading of Parkman and the guidebooks, part of a common heritage of both Canada and the United States, a heritage worthy of comparison to the more venerable traditions and the more famous scenery of the Old World.

The Bostonian Miles Arbuton, by contrast, is disdainful of the scenery. "I should like to see an American landscape that put one in mind of anything," he tells Kitty when she praises Quebec City and the surrounding countryside (p. 21). "The great drawback to this sort of thing in America," he complains as their boat moves down the Saguenay, "is that there is no human interest about the scenery, fine as it is" (p. 43). Even when Kitty repeats to him the legend she has learned from Parkman of the party of French explorers who "left their comrades at Tadoussac, and came up the Saguenay three hundred years ago, and never were seen or heard of again," Arbuton persists in his preference for "famous rivers abroad" (p. 43). He acknowledges the magnificence of Cape Eternity with only grudging admiration; "Mr. Arbuton," Howells confides in a sly authorial intrusion, had "an objection to the exaggerations of nature on this continent, and secretly thought them in bad taste" (p. 44). As for the "local colour" of the settlements and the inhabitants, Arbuton is bored and embarrassed by the interest his companions show in them. The more he sees of Canada, the more his hostility increases; and although he extends his stay at Quebec to pursue his infatuation with the charming girl from Eriecreek, there is little doubt about the outcome of the flirtation. Kitty's enthusiastic response to Canada reveals her to be more cosmopolitan than the closed-minded Bostonian whose travels have only served to confirm a narrow set of prejudices.

Howells made brief literary use of Canada on two further occasions, in the novel *The Quality of Mercy* (1892), and in an article on Ottawa published in *Harper's* in 1907. The novel, which involves an aging American businessman who flees to Canada after embezzling company funds, includes only a brief episode in the northern country. But the Canadian episode is quite striking in its dramatic detail, and interesting in terms of both Howells's earlier attempts to explore Canada in fiction, and the attempts of other American authors to deal with the subject. As Howells' embezzler proceeds on his journey into the sparsely populated, snow-covered wilderness of the Saguenay region, he begins to feel as if his sense of purpose and his identity, which have been defined mainly in terms of his personal and business relationships back in New England, were slipping away:

> At first his mind worked clearly but disobediently; then he began to be aware of a dimness in its record of purposes and motives. At times he could not tell where he was going, or why....
>
> As his carriole slipped lightly over [the snow], Northwick had a fantastic sense of his own minuteness and remoteness. He thought of the photograph of a lunar landscape that he had once seen greatly magnified, and of a fly that happened to traverse the expanse of plaster-like white between the ranges of extinct volcanoes.[12]

Like David A. Wasson's "Ice and Esquimaux" (1864-65), or John B. Coppinger's *The Renegade* (1855), *The Quality of Mercy* uses the northern wilderness of Canada as an antithesis to the civilized society that constitutes the modern American's familiar element. As Thoreau and numerous other American visitors to Canada concluded, prolonged experience with wildness has a detrimental effect on the civilized sensibility.

In 1907, Howells returned briefly to the possibilities of Canada as a social and political alternative to the United States in an "Editor's Easy Chair" article for *Harper's*, written after a visit to Ottawa to see his sister, who was married to a Canadian civil servant. Certain passages in the article suggest that the visit may have prompted Howells to reread *Their Wedding Journey*, and to reconsider aspects of Canadian politics and society he had addressed in that novel. In *Their Wedding Journey*, for instance, he apostrophized Canada: "sever the apron strings of allegiance, and try to be yourself, whatever you are." In the *Harper's* article, he wrote that Canada had successfully managed "to throw off the guidance of the Mother Country, without severing the political ties which one need not be so offensive as to call apron strings." Although no more able to make a succinct characterization of Canadians in 1907 than he had been in 1872, Howells at least accepted the Canadians' evident satisfaction with their situation: "They are so rather bouncingly pleased, those Dominion folk, to be just what they are in their own way...." Using the city of Ottawa, with its northern locale and its bicultural atmosphere, as an epitome of the country as a whole, the American novelist suggests that Canada is perhaps not so distinctive as Canadians think it is, for much of its political and social life was only made possible (according to Howells) by the example of United States experiences. Nevertheless, he finds in Canada "an effervescence which has more or less subsided with us," and concludes with the suggestion that the "forced torpor" of its winter weather "may be all that prevents the neighboring power annexing the States to the south of her."[13]

Howells, like James and Godkin, responded to Canada and Canadians with many of the familiar ideas and images that pervade nineteenth-century American writing about Canada. The northern country is an intimidating wilderness, an exotic and inexplicable society, and a minor variation on United States experience, useful in the evaluation of American achievements. But the post-Civil-War writers bring to the comparison between the two countries a range of implication that reflects the concerns of a new cultural era. For these writers of the late 1860s and the 1870s, America represented the grim realities of Civil War, post-war industrial expansion and political corruption, and the general decline of early American idealism, sometimes to the point of complete disillusionment. In this cultural atmosphere, the exotic elements of Canada suggest an unreality, a romantic or idealistic quality that provides welcome relief from the realities of the United States. Thus, in Artemus Ward's brief monologue, the comic-opera militarism of Quebec is set against the grim facts of the Civil War; in Godkin's and James's essays, the picturesque elements of Quebec City are wistful reminders of the appeal of fantasy and romance in an oppressively materialistic world. Even Howells's more comprehensive scrutiny of Canada usually resolves towards a similar tendency to associate Canada with fantasy and the United States with reality. Canada is an enigma, a remote spectacle, an element in an ironic reversal of the perennial American obsession with continental domination. To suggest facetiously that Canada might annex the United States, or to use Canadian tourist attractions as a means of evaluating the tension between the American East and West, is to provide imaginative relief from the immediacies of American experience. For these writers, Canada is, in effect, a means of escape, albeit a temporary escape, which ultimately compels a return to the obsessive contemplation of the meaning of America.

X

SPORTSMEN AND TOURISTS

For certain other post-Civil-War American writers, Canada was obviously and simply a means of escape. Of all the various types of nineteenth-century American literary reactions to Canada—historical romance, narrative history, sentimental poetry, realistic novel—by far the most popular was the tourist narrative. Most of the post-Civil-War American tourists in Canada were interested, like Howells and James, in the foreign and picturesque elements of the society; but in the last three decades of the nineteenth century, American travellers of a slightly different sort became increasingly evident in the northern provinces. These were the sportsmen or outdoorsmen: the hunters, fishermen, canoeists, campers, and general wilderness seekers, whose growing numbers contributed to the emergence, in the twentieth century, of the prevalent American conception of Canada as (in Edmund Wilson's words) "a kind of vast hunting preserve convenient to the United States."[1] The distinction between the "tourist" and the "outdoorsmen" is, in some cases, misleading, since many of these visitors experienced and wrote about both sight-seeing in the settled regions and nature-seeking in the wilderness. But it is possible to point out degrees of emphasis, at least, and to make certain consequent generalizations. As a rule, the "tourist narrative" tended to emphasize sight-seeing as a family or communal activity, and to be concerned with cultural, social, and political topics. The "outdoors" narrative was usually more concerned with solitary and supposedly "masculine" pursuits, and less obviously interested in communal issues.

The emergence in the American imagination of the idea of the northern wilderness as a pleasure ground, as opposed to a formidable frontier, can be fairly precisely dated. Of course, such an idea was sporadically evident in earlier years, as can be seen from Charles Lanman's *Adventures in the Wilds of the United States and the British American Provinces* (1856), for instance, or even in David Wasson's "Ice and Esquimaux," which includes a boisterous account of bird hunting along with its meditations on the intimidating vastness of the North and the superiority of urban civilization. But the idea of the North as a playground for sportsmen became more common after the Civil War, and received particular impetus in 1869, with the publication of a book entitled *Adventures in the Wilderness*. In this book, a minor novelist and travel writer named William Henry Harrison Murray revealed to thousands of Americans the apparently unsuspected news that there existed, within relatively easy access, a vast and undeveloped region of forest, lakes, and rivers, with unlimited possibilities for hunting, fishing, and camping. Murray's book—much to the author's surprise—provoked a rush of northward travellers, and announced a new era of outdoor recreation in the "North Woods."[2] *Adventures in the Wilderness* was concerned not with Canada, but with the Adirondacks of northern New York State; but it took very little time for the devotees of this new cult of the outdoors to discover that the "North Woods" extended into New Brunswick, Quebec, Ontario, and the more remote reaches of the North.

This fascination with the forest wilderness in the closing decades of the nineteenth century can be related also to the emerging conservationist movement, and to the naturalists and sportsmen of whom Theodore Roosevelt eventually became the public representative. This conception of conservation was related not to the ideal of pristine preservation, but to recreational use: the woods and waters of the North were to be preserved because men needed a place to withdraw temporarily from the bustle and anxiety of urban civilization and to live (in Roosevelt's famous phrase) "the strenuous life."

The search, if not exactly for "the strenuous life," at least for a temporary closeness to nature, brought one noteworthy literary visitor to Canada in 1877. John Burroughs (1837-1921), ornithologist and prolific essayist, the friend and first biographer of Walt Whitman and eventually a close associate of Roosevelt, visited Quebec City, then set out on an excursion into the wilderness stretching northward towards Lake St. John. His descriptive and meditative essay on the trip, "The Halcyon in Canada," was published first in *Scribner's Monthly*, and was included in his collection of essays *Locusts and Wild Honey* (1879). "Halcyon" is an alternate name for "king-fisher," so Burroughs's title suggests, by a slight play on words, that he was attracted to Canada mainly by the prospects for bird-watching and fishing.

In the "bush" north of Quebec City, the veteran woodsman Burroughs discovers a face of nature that is both familiar and strange: the birds and trees are mostly recognizable, yet everything seems on an extravagant, awe-inspiring scale. The distance between settlements is vast, and for hours on end the road is empty of life. The sense of desolation is increased by the stretches of stunted spruce interspersed with the boulders of the Laurentian shield, and by the stretches of fire-blasted wasteland.

> Early in the afternoon we entered upon what is called *La Grand Brûlure*, or Great Burning, and to the desolation of living woods succeeded the greater desolation of a blighted forest. All the mountains and valleys, as far as the eye could see, had been swept by the fire, and the bleached and ghostly skeletons of the trees alone met the gaze.... For three hours we rode through this valley and shadow of death.

Even the cheerful experience of trout-fishing adds to the sense of strangeness, for the fish conform to the enlarged design of the surroundings: the first trout taken "would have swallowed any three we had ever before caught." But unlike David Wasson in Labrador, and other earlier travellers in the northern wilderness, Burroughs ultimately finds that the recreational value of the experience compensates for the sense of desolation. "Seated upon my raft and slowly carried by the current or drifted by the breeze, I had many a long, silent look into the face of the wilderness, and found the communion good. I was alone with the spirit of the forest-bound lakes, and felt its presence and magnetism."[3]

Burroughs's combination of trout-fishing and transcendentalism is one of the more suggestive literary exploitations of sporting experiences in Canada. By the 1870s, articles on fishing and hunting, often dealing with Canada, were regular features of prominent American magazines such as *Scribner's*, *Harper's*, and *The Atlantic Monthly*; but most such articles usually revealed the authors' insensitivity to nature and indifference to Canada. George W. Pierce's "Two Weeks' Sport on the Coulonge River," in the September 1873 *Atlantic Monthly*, is a jovial account of the author's rather inept and sadistic attempts at such activity as shooting beaver from a boat; A. G. Wilkinson's "Notes on Salmon Fishing," in the October 1876 *Scribner's*, complains of the Canadian bureaucracy that imposes catch-quotas and travel restrictions on American fishermen. A feminine perspective, in Janet Chase Hoyt's "Babes in the Wood: Through Maine to Canada in a Birch-Bark Canoe" (*Scribner's*, August 1877), is refreshingly concerned with non-destructive recreation. And Charles C. Ward's "Moose Hunting," in the February 1878 *Scribner's*, is a knowledgeable, if drily factual account of the ways of moose and of general woods lore, based on the author's experiences in New Brunswick.

These representative articles by literary amateurs suggest the general tenor of much of the "outdoor sports" writing about Canada. Such prosaic, or artificially rhapsodic, or awkwardly facetious efforts did little to enhance the American conception of Canada as aesthetically significant, but they contributed to the growing idea of the "northern playground" in the popular imagination. Even writers of more literary reputation or pretensions — with a few exceptions, such as John Burroughs — seldom rose above the popular clichés associated with the subject. John Habberton (1842–1921), a New York journalist and bestselling novelist, was co-author of *Canoeing in Kanuckia, or, Haps and Mishaps Afloat and Ashore of the Statesman, the Editor, the Artist, and the Scribbler* (1878), whose title suggests the strained comic tone and tedious structure of the book. Describing a canoe trip in New Brunswick, Habberton and his collaborator, C. L. Norton, report a series of misadventures as a result of their ineptness as canoeists and campers, and try to force comedy from their encounters with French-speaking inhabitants and with the signs of British loyalism.

Canoeing in Kanuckia provides an example of the blending of the "outdoor sports" essay with the familiar tourist narrative: setting out in search of the wilderness, American travellers pause along the way to observe the quaint elements of Canadian society. Several late-nineteenth-century American authors thus combined Canadian local colour with outdoor-recreation experiences in informal essays and fiction. The New York clergyman Henry Van Dyke, author of many volumes of stories and essays on village and backwoods life, spent several fishing vacations in Quebec and northwestern New Brunswick in the 1880s and 1890s. His rather sentimental literary adaptations of these experiences were published over several years in *Scribner's Magazine*, and collected in *Little Rivers: A Book of Essays in Profitable Idleness* (1895), *The Ruling Passion: Tales of Nature and Human Nature* (1901), and *The Unknown Quantity: A Book of Romance and Some Half-Told Tales* (1912). Like other American travellers, Van Dyke is impressed by the titanic proportions of the Canadian forest: the Lake St. John country of northern Quebec "is not a little pocket wilderness like the Adirondacks, but something vast and primitive." The sparse settlements in the region invoke a sense of antiquity unfamiliar to American experience: his French-Canadian guides are "descendants of the men who came to New France with Samuel de Champlain,"[4] and the curé of a village reminds him of an earlier age of spiritual history. In the short stories, emphasis is placed on the picturesque qualities of the French-Canadian villages and their inhabitants, who are repeatedly presented in episodes of romantic love, social rivalry, and domestic conflict, usually seen from the detached and slightly ironic perspective of a visiting American tourist, who serves as narrator. Van Dyke claims to avoid the over-simplification of characterization, which "happens only in books,"[5] but in fact his essays and tales are heavily dependent on sentimental and melodramatic elements.

The Illinois regional realist "Octave Thanet" (Alice French) attempted at least one "tourist" story of French Canada, similar to the stories of Van Dyke. Thanet's "The Ogre of Ha Ha Bay," included in her *Knitters in the Sun* (1877), uses the detached perspective of a vacationing American, but attempts to reveal the fallacies of American sentimentality towards the inhabitants of the backwoods. "How peaceful it is," says the young American bride in the story when she first sees the Saguenay village where she is to spend part of her wedding journey; ". . . they seem so pastoral and childlike, like people in poems. One can hardly imagine any one's being very unhappy here."[6] But this naïve impression is soon obliterated by the spectacle of a domestic conflict among the villagers, whose lives are revealed as no less petty and sordid than those of people in the more populous regions to the south.

Two other noteworthy examples of tourist and recreation fiction in the last decades of the century are the novels *Jack in the Bush: or A Summer on a Salmon River* (1888) by Robert Grant, and *When All the Woods are Green* (1894), by S. Weir Mitchell. Grant (1852–1940), a distinguished New York lawyer, friend of Edith Wharton and author of several realistic novels of social criticism, began his writing career with a series of light juvenile books about "Jack Hall," an all-American boy who loves the outdoors and various related kinds of recreational activities. Set in the Restigouche salmon-fishing region of New Brunswick, *Jack in the Bush* tells how a group of American boys learn various skills related to fishing, hunting, camping, and wilderness survival, as well as the moral qualities supposedly related to these skills. Included among the virtues illustrated by the novel is American patriotism, which the author extols at appropriate opportunities to his young readers. Jack Hall and his friends, while eagerly pursuing the strenuous life in the woods, are surprised and sometimes disgusted by the Canadians they encounter. The villain of the story, Pete Labouisse, is a silent, half-French, half-Indian squatter, who ignores the rules of sportsmanship and shoots sitting ducks and spears salmon at night. By implication, his villainous conduct is related to his racial inferiority; at least, the American boys are not surprised by his behaviour. They are surprised, however, by the English-Canadians they encounter. They are interested to learn that the Restigouche region is populated by the descendants of United Empire Loyalists, and that many of the inhabitants carry such respectable old New England names as Patterson and Coffin. One of their guides, George Coffin, has "much of the Yankee in his build and manner."[7] To the boys' surprise, however, George and his helpers have never even heard of the Fourth of July. As woodsmen they are equal to the best of Americans; but politically they are benighted Canadians who have not had the advantages of American democracy.

The Restigouche region and its inhabitants are given more serious consideration in a novel by the eminent Philadelphia physician and author S. Weir Mitchell (1829-1914). *When All The Woods Are Green* is one of a series of "conversation" novels by Mitchell in which various characters discuss moral and metaphysical topics, and occasionally become involved in slight situations that serve to illustrate or complement their discussions. Like Henry Van Dyke, who included an essay on *The Compleat Angler* in *The Ruling Passion,* Mitchell had perhaps been reading Isaac Walton, for the imaginary conversations of *When All The Woods Are Green* often take place in the languid atmosphere of fishing excursions, and the subject discussed is often the spiritual values of fishing. More generally, the novel is about life in the wilderness and the influence of nature on the human personality. Mitchell accepts the common assumptions about the restorative value of a temporary withdrawal to the wilderness: like Thoreau, he has discovered that going to the woods is a valuable ritual of purification, whereby the individual divests himself of all the trivia and impediments of civilization. As one of Mitchell's characters says:

> "In the woods, away from men and their struggles and ambitions, with the absence of need to be this or that, as duty, work, or social claims demand, we lose the resultant state of tension, of being on guard. It is readily possible to notice this effect in the rapid erasure from the faces of the constantly strained, intellectual workmen of the lines of care which mark the features of those on whom, in one or another position, the world relies to carry its burdens."[8]

But in spite of this tribute to the salutary effects of life in the woods, Mitchell comes to the conclusion that civilization and progress provide a more appropriate situation for humanity than primitivism and wildness. The native Canadian, Mitchell's tourists agree, presents certain admirable qualities in which the urbanized American is possibly deficient; but there is some ambiguity about the value of these qualities:

> "Yes," said Lyndsay, "these Gaspe men are most interesting. They are clever, competent, and inherently kindly, really good fellows; but their trouble is, and it does not trouble them, that they have no persistent energy. I confess that, being myself, at least while here, without energy, I like its absence."
>
> "Isn't it a vast relief, after all the endless restlessness of our people," said Anne, "to fall among folks who are contented, and home-loving, and so uncomplicated?" "I certainly think so," said Carington. "And what a surprise it is to meet the stray descendants of loyalists hereabouts.... Some of the best of the Canadians are descendants of those people; but for the most part, those who settled in certain quarters of Lower Canada are down again to the level of mere laborers and fishermen."[9]

Mitchell illustrates the disadvantages of a life of unrelieved primitivism with the story of a shiftless middle-aged couple who have never lived anywhere but in the Canadian backwoods. Brutish in their manners and speech, they are dishonest, suspicious, and selfish, completely lacking in self-reliance and "persistent energy" which, according to Mitchell, characterize the American backwoodsman. The latter contention is illustrated in the person of a Quaker woman who has emigrated from Pennsylvania to the backwoods settlement on the Restigouche. Although uneducated and rustic in habits, she is, in most respects, a complete antithesis to the Canadian couple. Her self-reliance is illustrated in the fact that her small backwoods farm prospers, while the Canadian couple, with a similar portion of land and virtually identical opportunities, are unable to sustain themselves. Furthermore, the Quaker woman is almost instinctively charitable, and persists in offering to help the indigent Canadians, even when they display their ungratefulness. And finally, unlike the Canadians, she is intellectually curious: hearing about Shakespeare from the American tourists, she eagerly reads the play about "Mrs. Macbeth."

Another "tourist novel" that attempts a more ambivalent exploration of the comparison between the United States concept of civilization and the Canadian experience of wildness is *The Lady of the Flag-Flowers* (1899) by the minor poet Florence Wilkinson Evans. In this novel, a young man joins the northward procession of American tourists with the vague idea of finding a rural retreat "where, like Tolstoi, he could live simply, and labor alike with his hands and his head,"[10] while preparing himself for a life dedicated to social reform. In Quebec, he falls in love with a half-breed girl, and the plot develops into a Madame-Butterfly-like situation when the American returns to his own country. "And in his young, confident way, Pierce imagined himself returning a year, two years later, still with the same ideals in his head—as he never was to return—and finding Yvonne, with the black hair and earnest gaze, basket-weaving—as he never was to find her again."[11] In Canada the young American finds opportunities for recreation and contemplation that help him in his subsequent career as a reformer, but he also brings a form of corruption to the idyllic northern setting. The corruption spreads and is followed to a tragic conclusion when the half-breed girl goes to the United States, where she achieves superficial success, but is eventually murdered by an unrequited lover. In a historical prologue, the author suggests that the corruption that leads to tragedy was inherent in the earliest encounters between Europeans and the North American aborigine. The United States becomes the centre of this corruption; and although American moral and social progress can lead to the improvement of modern urbanized life, this progress is achieved in part through the continuing destruction of primitive innocence and wildness.

XI

CHARLES HAIGHT FARNHAM AND WALT WHITMAN

A noteworthy literary tourist of the closing decades of the century was Charles Haight Farnham (1841-1929), who wrote a series of magazine articles on Canada based on his experiences "canoe-cruising" in Quebec and the maritime provinces. Rather unjustly neglected by literary history, Farnham was a witty and literate writer, the son of two professional authors, a frequent contributor to major American magazines and newspapers, and the authorized biographer of his friend and camping companion, Francis Parkman.[1] Like Parkman, Farnham was fascinated by the primitive northern wilderness and its reciprocal influence on the character and society of the white man in the New World; but he was especially interested in one aspect of the subject Parkman had rather neglected, the modern remnant of the French empire in North America. All of his "canoe-cruising" articles, with the exception of one dealing with the Scots Highlanders of Cape Breton, focus on French-Canadian life and character. Unlike most American travellers who turned their attention to this rather overworked subject, Farnham was both comprehensive in his observations and scrupulously balanced in his judgements. Speaking French fluently, and willing to cultivate the acquaintance of representatives of all levels of the rural and urban Quebec population, Farnham was able to get closer to the subject than most of his predecessors. He not only made the standard excursion to the two major cities of the province ("The Gibraltar of America," *The Century*, October 1882; "Quebec," *Harper's*, February 1888; "Montreal," *Harper's*, June 1889), he went beyond the usual tourist routine to spend "A Winter in Canada" (*Harper's*, February 1884). He made canoe trips along the north shore of the St. Lawrence ("Labrador," *Harper's*, September-October 1885), and the south shore ("The Lower St. Lawrence," *Harper's*, November 1888). His studies of the inhabitants of Canada included sympathetic portraits of the French-Canadian villagers and farmers ("The Canadian Habitant," *Harper's*, August 1883), backwoodsmen ("Canadian Voyageurs on the Saguenay," *Harper's*, March 1888), and the remnants of Indian tribes in the wilderness once dominated by the Huron and Iroquois ("The Montagnais," *Harper's*, August 1888).

"Canada," says Farnham, "with an arctic winter and the greater part of its soil almost sterile, seems designed by nature to be the Norway of America, a land of forests."[2] Throughout his narratives of travel in the North, he emphasizes the cold, barren hostility of the Canadian landscape: the Saguenay region in winter is an "expanse of cold white death," and the vast wilderness lying just beyond the ramparts of Quebec City is "a penetration of desolation into the very heart of man."[3] Like other sensitive observers of nature, such as Parkman and Thoreau, Farnham is capable of a positive response to the spectacle of wildness: "The surroundings of Quebec have become familiar to me by years of observation, and still I always look abroad with pleasure from the Citadel or the Terrace, at the great St. Lawrence Valley, walled in with mountains, cloven by a vast arm of the sea, and still watched over by primeval forests."[4] And, like Thoreau, he is inclined to use ecclesiastical or religious imagery in his descriptions of the wilderness, which suggests a sort of romantic pantheism: "Nowhere has nature spoken to me more directly, both in the majestic storm service and in the unutterable peace of this vast and rugged temple."[5] But ultimately, he echoes Thoreau and other Americans in his belief in the importance of civilization as a counteraction to the oppressive and destructive force of wildness. "In looking across this immense flood [the Gulf of St. Lawrence]... I am glad to be ashore among a people living close together for shelter and warmth under an arctic winter."[6]

In Farnham's essays, as in Thoreau's "A Yankee in Canada," the inhabitants and habitations of the North constitute, with nature, equally important subjects of study. In the remote outposts of "Labrador" (Farnham applies the name loosely to the north shore of the St. Lawrence, including that part of the region belonging to Quebec province), he finds an exotically varied population of outcasts and devotees of the wilderness, including an Irishman who has lived in New York, a French-Canadian monarchist priest, a European French emigré, and an Italian jeweller. In the less distant region of the Saguenay, he observes the modern descendants of the *coureurs de bois,* who are mostly tame and conventional loggers and boatmen. But to get a close view of the French-Canadian people, Farnham visits (as Thoreau did) the farmers of the St. Lawrence Valley.

Farnham is especially interested in the Canadian attitude to the United States, and he reports the suspicion and hostility with which the *habitants* regard the country to the south. In one household where he has found lodging,

> One of the sons had passed two years working in a brick-yard at Haverstraw, and like many of his countrymen, he had returned with some heretical admiration of our more progressive civilization. Emigration to the United States is energetically opposed by church and state, so in praising the wonders of New York I became an emissary of the devil, which increased the interest of my position.

He describes the *habitants*' devotion to religious charms and rituals, their subservience to the parish priests, and their tendency to subordinate individual personality to the customs of the community: "The whole parish dresses as one man and one woman; you feel the extraordinary unity of Canadian life in this external monotony of the people." In this atmosphere of conformity, superstition, and cruel physical labour, "there is not even the beginning of intellectual life."

> Canada is our twin brother in chronology and geography; and yet no other contiguous lands differ more widely. You can scarcely believe yourself in this age when you pass from our luxurious, elaborate, and practical existence to the poor, primitive, and poetic life of Canada.

"And yet," Farnham admits elsewhere, "this civilization has many attractive features."

> [It] rests on the labor of the hand alone, unaided by mechanical powers; and its narrow, slow, economical, but self-supporting life thus acquires something of the dignity of manhood. It is a very human civilization, as distinguished from a mechanical and commercial one. Here you come in direct contact with human needs and human efforts. This phase of life, when man

stands out as in the old hand-to-hand encounter, is a strange contrast to our existence, where man seems to retire behind his engines and improvements.[7]

Finally, however, Farnham is unable to grant that the dignity of the primitive life is preferable to the cultural advantages of a civilization based on belief in material progress:

> The Canadian is an excellent pioneer up to a certain point: no one surpasses him in enduring hardships, labor, want; he lives and increases where others will not remain. But when he has cleared a few acres and won half of a living he feels satisfied, and generally fails to carry his civilization to the higher plane of comfort, cleanliness, and taste.[8]

Thus Farnham arrives at the familiar conflict between primitivism and progress that repeatedly characterizes the nineteenth-century American attitude towards Canada. Like many of his countrymen, he is caught between the polar attractions of his own technically advanced culture and a life of ostensible simplicity close to nature, and his mind can only range back and forth between them. Like his mentor Parkman, he is both attracted and repelled by the northern wilderness and the paradoxical civilization that has arisen within it. Both the wilderness and Canadian society seem to appeal to some vital aspiration in the human spirit, while at the same time threatening to stultify or destroy that spirit.

Farnham's ambivalence towards Canada was shared in one form or another by most nineteenth-century American literary artists who took up the subject. The northern provinces and their inhabitants were seen as unregenerately primitive in contrast to their progressive, modernistic counterparts to the south; or alternatively, they were seen in terms of a remote, aboriginal innocence that was corrupted by European and modern American civilization. At least one American literary tourist, however, visiting Canada about the same time as Farnham, saw Canada in terms that departed significantly from familiar American images of the northern country, and pointed towards possibilities for a new and original conception.

As might be expected of the most innovative and energetic poetic imagination to emerge in the nineteenth-century United States, Walt Whitman saw Canada not as an entity to be observed and analyzed, but as an image to be expressed in the language of poetry. Whitman was only a casual tourist in Canada, like many of his countrymen; his experience of the country, furthermore, led only to some rough notes and fragments, which he never got around to developing into a polished work of art. Yet these obscure notes and fragments constitute an important indication of the literary possibilities inherent in Canada when the country was conceived as a unified imaginative concept, as opposed to a mere conglomeration of empirically observed details.

In June of 1880, Whitman travelled by train from his home in Camden, New Jersey, to London, Ontario, in response to an invitation from Dr. Richard Maurice Bucke, a Canadian physician of wide scientific, philosophical, and literary interests, who was eventually to become one of Whitman's literary executors. The poet spent most of June and July in and around London; then he accompanied Dr. Bucke on a three-week expedition to the familiar tourist attractions of Niagara, Kingston, Montreal, Quebec, and the Saguenay. Unlike most American tourists, Whitman was able to give the northern country a leisurely scrutiny, with particular attention to the less frequently noticed regions of western Ontario, as well as the more popular tourist resorts to the east.

"Calm and glorious roll the hours here," Whitman writes in the opening pages of the diary as he observes his surroundings from Dr. Bucke's suburban home. "... A perfect day, (the third in succession) cloudless, the sun clear, a faint, fresh, just palpable air setting in from the Southwest, temperature pretty warm at midday, but moderate enough mornings and evenings" (pp. 611-12).[9] Throughout the diary there is an emphasis on the exquisite qualities of the light and air in rural Canada. "Such a procession of long-drawn-out, delicious half-lights, nearly every evening," the poet remarks of his stay in London; and in the nearby village of Sarnia he finds "A lovely, soft, soothing, voluptuous scene,—a wondrous half-hour for sunset and then the long rose-tinged half-light with a touch of gray..." (pp. 612-14). In conjunction with these invocations of the delicate atmosphere is an emphasis on the neatly cultivated rural landscape with human figures going about their field work, the whole scene observed as from a distance:

> Any hour I hear the sound of scythe sharpening, or the distant rattle of horse-mowers, or see the loaded wagons, high-piled, slowly wending toward the barns, or toward sun-down groups of tan-faced men, going from work. (p. 620)

The detached, objective point of view is reminiscent of the mystical poetic persona of "Song of Myself," who observes and describes the landscape in minute detail before moving outward towards an attempt to merge verbally and emotionally with the whole of creation. Except for the emphasis on sound, the impression conveyed is also reminiscent of nineteenth-century landscape painting, with the subdued light and colour and the remote but high-lighted human figures. As F. O. Matthiessen has observed, Whitman was familiar with the work of contemporary landscape painters such as W. S. Mount and Thomas Eakins, and he strove to invest his poems with painterly qualities.[10] The Canadian diary is, in effect, a preliminary sketch in which the artist establishes his perspective and lighting, and sets down the main outlines of his scene, including some of the human figures in the foreground.

Other eminent literary travellers showed some interest in exploiting Canada artistically, but their writings seldom conveyed the unity of impression and empathy with the subject implied in the type of landscape painting admired by Whitman. Thoreau's narrative, for instance, with its satirical allusions and idiosyncratic selection of detail, is reminiscent of caricature; and James's essay, in spite of the author's repeated invocation of the word "picturesque," tends to invoke not pictorial models, but literary ones, such as the fiction of Balzac and Longfellow's "Evangeline." Both Thoreau and James, furthermore, like most nineteenth-century American observers of Canada, are mainly interested in noting and evaluating the good and bad features of Canada, and in comparing Canada with the United States. Whitman does neither: his response to the country is entirely benign, and his interest is wholly absorbed in incorporating Canada into his poetic image of the continent as a whole.

Whitman does, however, in spite of his interest in the Canadian landscape, ultimately share his countrymen's emphasis on the human aspects of his subject. Even the great river of the Saguenay is glossed over rather perfunctorily as "dashes of the grimmest, wildest, savagest scenery on the planet, I guess" (p. 636), while the poet's attention lingers on the colourful costumes of the *habitants,* the black soutanes of the priests, and the neat rows of whitewashed farmhouses along the banks of the St. Lawrence. The houses of Canada were a frequent object of interest to Americans, who saw the supposedly more primitive habitations of the northern country as a reflection of its economic and cultural inferiority to the United States. Thoreau, it will be recalled, particularly noted the position of the farmhouses along the St. Lawrence, with their backs to the highway, as if rejecting the links with the outside world that homes in the United States had so energetically forged. Whitman, however, saw these farmhouses not from the road, but from one of his favourite perspectives, the deck of a boat, as he made his way on his tourist excursion down the river. And as he gazes at the Quebec villages from the water he comes to a conclusion virtually opposite to Thoreau's with regard to the historical experiences and prospects of Canada:

> I see, or imagine I see in the fu[ture] A race of 2,000,000 farm-families, 10,000,000 people,—every farm running down to the water, or at least in sight of it—the best air and drink and sky & scenery of the globe the sure foundation-nutriment of heroic men & women (p. 646)

Thus the seemingly endless rows of whitewashed farmhouses become in Whitman's imagination a vision of social progress and human perfectibility comparable to similar visions the poet derives from observations of his own country. The "heroic men and women" of Canada are the same optimistic and strenuous Americans who march towards the future and the western frontier in *Leaves of Grass*. In the Quebec portion of the diary, Whitman takes note of the foreign language, colourful costumes, distinctive habitations, and exotic religion of the *habitants*, but unlike most other American travellers, he does not see these details as antagonistic to American ideals of racial and cultural homogeneity. The Canadians, both French and English, are part of the unity-plurality paradox of America, part of the endlessly diverse panorama of "Yankee... Kentuckian... Hoosier, Badger, Buckeye... Kanadian" (as section sixteen of "Song of Myself" enumerates representative elements in the North American population), which yet make up a single, unified American identity.

On one level, this casual absorption of Canada into the rhetoric of American unity can be seen as the crude language of "Manifest Destiny," which assumes that the whole of North America—indeed, the whole of the western hemisphere—must eventually submit to the political and cultural hegemony of the United States. Whitman, as Thomas L. Brasher has demonstrated, was not above this kind of political simplification, especially in his early journalism days, when he was writing for the chauvinistic Brooklyn and New York tabloids.[11] Even in his later years, as for instance at the time of his visit to Canada, he tended to hold a rather naïve faith in American continental unity, as he revealed with questionable judgement in an article published in the London (Ontario) *Advertiser*, to the undoubted annoyance of many of its local readers:

> (It seems to me a certainty of time, sooner or later, that Canada shall form two or three grand States, equal and independent,

with the rest of the American Union. The St. Lawrence and lakes are not for a frontier line, but a grand interior or mid-channel.)[12]

Such statements, seen in the context of political and social history, appear naïve and trite; but seen in terms of Whitman's poetic vision, this faith in North American continental unity becomes one further image of the transcendental, cosmic unity that encompasses all elements of creation, all fragments, variations, alternatives, opposites, and antagonisms in one grand, mystic, ideal whole.

Whitman's Canadian writings, even in their rough and superficial form, thus reflect the theme of unity in diversity that pervades all his work. Unlike most travellers, Whitman was much less interested in describing the specific details of landscape and society than in evoking a sense of the atmosphere of Canada as an intrinsic part of the America of his imagination. Hence the detached point of view that dreamily contemplates the pastoral scenes of Ontario and Quebec is much the same as the poetic mind that broods over the American scene throughout *Leaves of Grass*. Similarly, there is throughout the diary, as throughout the poetry, an emphasis on nature, usually in its most tranquil and most aesthetically pleasing facets. The "delicate, almost *flavored* air" (p. 612), the fruitful hayfields, the exquisite sunlight, the flowers and birds of Canada, are part of Whitman's vision of an organic natural world. In the diary, as throughout his poetry, Whitman focuses on the microcosm of nature—the sprig of lilac, the "leaf" of grass, the circle of sunlight reflected in the water—to represent the purity and unity of creation.

A superficial response to Whitman's Canadian writings might object to his totally uncritical attitude to the country, which, like his belief in continental unity, is indisputably naïve. Whitman, to be sure, praises everything in Canada—the rural fields; the streets of Toronto, "a lively, dashing place" (p. 625); the Thousand Islands; Montreal and Quebec; the school system of Ontario, "one of the best and most comprehensive in the world" (p. 649); the various benevolent institutions for the mentally and physically disabled. Even the spectacle of poverty and disease on a native Indian reservation provides him with an opportunity to expatiate on the benevolent policies of the Canadian government (p. 617). But this unity of moral judgment is like the unity of his aesthetic response: Canada is a moral and social whole, just as it is a natural whole.

Whitman's image of Canada, with its emphasis on the benevolence of nature and the spiritual unity and perfectibility of mankind, is thus an important innovation in the nineteenth-century American literary image of the northern country. The poet never found time to write a more polished essay or poem on the subject, probably because in 1880 his imagination was committed to numerous other poetic experiments and continuing projects, which he feared he might not live to complete. But his diary offers valuable indications of what a strenuous poetic imagination might do with the idea of Canada. The travellers and novelists who continually complained about the Canadian failure to adapt to American ideals, or who sentimentalized Canadian primitivism, could not get beyond the surface observations of social criticism and local colour. Whitman went to the heart of his subject, and produced a sensuous and lyrical image that reveals the unique possibilities for the interaction of the artistic imagination with the empirical world.

XII

THE NORTHWESTERN FRONTIER

Whitman's image of Canada, with its emphasis on unspoiled nature, infinite vistas of human achievement, and the ideals of continental unity and the unity of humankind as a whole, suggests associations with the nineteenth-century American conception of the West. Such an association seems at first paradoxical, in view of the eastward direction of most of Whitman's Canadian travels, but the image of the West and its various implications pervades Whitman's writings. As poems such as "Passage to India" demonstrate, all movement, both spatial and temporal, becomes subsumed in the westward vision: even a journey eastward and northward merges imaginatively with the infinite vistas associated with the American frontier. Whitman's fascination with the image of the West is an epitome of the great obsession of his countrymen, who, throughout the nineteenth century, were eagerly turning, both imaginatively and literally, towards the great plains, the Rocky Mountains, and beyond.

The westward movement in the United States was essentially a nationalistic experience, a part of the ongoing search for and expression of the American identity. For the most part, the imaginative and literal involvement with the West tended to be focused on regions within United States borders, or to which the republic laid claim. But the Canadian west—or the "British Northwest," as it was called throughout much of the nineteenth century—was by no means entirely ignored. Even at the height of the immense migration beyond the Mississippi towards California and Oregon in the closing decades of the nineteenth century, travellers and imaginative authors cast occasional glances northward. This peripheral interest in the Canadian west is to be found in a numerically small but sometimes insightful and evocative series of fictional and non-fictional works.

Because of the noticeable differences in purposes and emphasis among these Americans who wrote about the Canadian west, it is useful to divide their works into the three generic categories of adventure fiction (usually in the dime- and nickel-novel formats), travel narratives, and promotional magazine articles. This generic division suggests also certain basic distinctions of conception as well as of purpose: to the novelists, the Canadian west is merely a northward extension of the American "Wild West" with slight modifications; to most travellers, the region is another tourist attraction to be compared with their own country; to the promotional writers (and to some authors of travel books), many of whom were hired to sell Canadian land to would-be settlers or speculators, the country is an abundant frontier that can supplement the gradually disappearing region of free land in the United States.

The American fictional use of western Canada appears as early as 1859 in a novel entitled *Pathaway; or, The Mountain Outlaws*, by John Hovey Robinson. In *Pathaway*, as in the handful of similar productions, the setting is only vaguely characterized as "the Northwest" in the region of "the southern branch of the Saskatchewan."[1] In two other dime novels, Joseph E. Badger's *The Lone Chief; or, The Trappers of the Saskatchewan* (1873), and its sequel, *Death Trailer, The Scourge of the Plains Crees* (1873), the setting is more specifically identified as "many miles north of the line that divides the United States from the British possessions,"[2] again in the region of the Saskatchewan River. The Saskatchewan seems to have been a favoured choice among settings for northwest adventure stories; it figures also in W. J. Hamilton's *Mountain Gid, The Free Ranger* (1878), which is set in "the foothills of the Saskatchewan."[3] It was, however, the exotic sound of the name rather than any considerations of geographic authenticity that led to its repeated use, for the mythic region of the Saskatchewan created by these novelists lacks both consistent local features and a clear relationship to the larger context of North American geography, except as such elements might be useful to the plot. In fact, plot creates landscape in this kind of fiction, for the authors conjure up a variety of environments, including thick forests for tracking and Indian fighting, rivers or lakes for canoe chases, foothills and mountains to inspire sentimental expressions of romantic sublimity, and open prairie for peaceful travel. The dominant landscape, however, seems to be a kind of badlands, as in *Pathaway*, where "the ground which the parties were now traversing was cut up and rendered dangerous by yawning chasms, jagged rocks, rifts, and gulches. There were marks everywhere around... of volcanic convulsions, that had at some period of the world's history, upheaved the foundations of the mountains."[4]

The vague unrealism of the northwestern frontier is reflected also in its political and social structures, or rather the lack of them, for only occasionally is the setting identified in terms of national demarcations. *Pathaway* seems to be set in the Alberta-Montana frontier, but few place-names are mentioned, and all the characters, except one French-Canadian trapper, are evidently American. Badger's *The Lone Chief* and *Death Trailer* are explicitly set north of the border, but except for a brigade of French-Canadian voyageurs in *Death Trailer*, all the characters are American; and only in *The Lone Chief* is there any specific use of a northern setting, as the action takes place in a snow-bound winter landscape. Edward L. Wheeler, the author of *Canada Chet*, seems to have had some interest in the idea of Canada as a separate country, but this interest was developed in a comic direction. *Canada Chet* seems almost to be a clumsy fable of the vicissitudes of Canadian-American relations, for the title character is a fiery, American-hating British loyalist who lies in wait in his secret stronghold on the Manitoba prairies, ready to seize unwary American travellers and put them to work as slave labourers in his counterfeiting shop. One of Wheeler's later novels, *Deadwood Dick Jr.'s Desperate Strait; or, The Demon Doctor of Dixon's Deposit* (1892), is set in a prairie town that "enjoyed one distinction: namely it did not know positively whether it belonged to the States or to the Dominion."[5] But the town's location on the international boundary is the occasion only for some incidental humour, while the main plot has to do with a mad doctor's plan to infect various people with hydrophobia.

The northwest of these adventure novels is thus little more than a minor variation on the stylized fictional American west. The landscape is that of the remote and limitless frontier; the heroes are rugged individuals, usually Americans, often modeled on Cooper's Leatherstocking, who impose rough frontier justice on evil-doers. Canadian or British institutions are seldom in evidence. Even the Northwest Mounted Police are generally excluded from these novels, for the American fictional romanticization of the scarlet force belongs to a later period, particularly to the early-twentieth-century efforts of the popular Michigan novelist James Oliver Curwood. Wheeler, in *Canada Chet*, makes brief use of the Mounties, bringing them in towards the end of his story like the United States Cavalry to effect a last-minute rescue; but his ambiguous references to them as "the Mounted Police" and "mounted Manitoba volunteers" suggest that his knowledge of the force was uncertain.⁶

Yet perhaps it is an oversimplification to say that these writers "Americanized" the Canadian west. Certainly they used stereotyped characters and social traditions with which they and their readers were comfortably familiar. But it seems that their purpose was not to suggest that the Canadian prairies were or should have been part of the United States; they implied, rather, that on the northwest frontier, far from eastern customs and institutions, such labels as "American" and "Canadian" lost much of their significance. On the free and open frontier, where a man's worth was related primarily to the art of survival, national pride—like that of Wheeler's militant Canada Chet—was sometimes even a character defect.

Some of the various Leatherstocking avatars in the fictional northwest are identified in terms that suggest their liberation from narrow political and social structures. The reputation of Nick Whiffles, the old frontier scout in Robinson's *Pathaway*, extends "up the Big Red," "down the Columby," "on the southern slopes of the Rocky Mountains," and "'cross the lakes to Montreal."⁷ Similarly, W. J. Hamilton's Mountain Gid, the "free ranger," "had wandered from the shores of the Golden Horn off San Francisco, to Halifax on the east, and from the uttermost regions penetrated by the trappers to the north-west of Hudson's Bay to the mouth of the Rio Grande."⁸

The dime novelists' emphasis on the vastness and openness of the western landscape can also, of course, be seen simply as a commitment to the idea of a continental unity dominated by the United States. The heroes of these novels are all American, and their adventures reflect such values as rugged individualism and intuitive virtue that are associated in popular culture with the frontier United States. Most American authors of narratives of travel in the Canadian west were obliged by the accepted conventions of the genre to be more explicit about geography and political and social structures, although in detailing their observations and impressions they often revealed their commitment to some form of American domination of the continent. Some travellers, on the other hand, were quite receptive to the idea of an independent Canada and were prepared to contemplate the possible alternatives to American society that Canadians might achieve in the west.

Early American travellers into the Canadian plains included government and military officials, explorers, and surveyors, all of whom seem to have assumed that the region would eventually become a part of the

United States. Governor Alexander Ramsey of Minnesota visited the Red River of the North in 1851; in 1855 an Indian-affairs agent ventured into what later became Alberta; and a group of explorers looking for a route through the Rockies included British territory in their 1859 expedition.[9] In 1860, an editor of the *New York World* named Manton Marble contributed to *Harper's New Monthly Magazine* a three-part narrative entitled "To Red River and Beyond," describing his overland trek from St. Paul to Fort Garry. Unlike the dime novelists, Marble is more interested in the processes of cultural and economic development than in the opportunities for anarchistic individualism and adventure on the prairies. Like a tourist in Montreal or some other eastern settlement, he inspects the Roman Catholic cathedral in St. Boniface and the English church in Fort Garry. Also unlike most of the novelists, he is interested in comparing the relative achievements of Americans and Canadians on the frontier, noting with satisfaction signs of inefficiency and slow development north of the border. At Fort Garry, he observes two workmen labouriously using a heavy rip-saw while a steam-powered circular saw stands idle nearby, and comments that such a thing would not be allowed to happen "in an American settlement."[10]

Ten years later, another contributor to *Harper's*, Brigadier-General Randolph B. Marcy of the United States Army, visited and wrote of the same region, in more disparaging terms. Vehemently anti-British, Marcy argues that the slow and inefficient development in the Canadian northwest is the fault of the short-sightedness of "English capitalists," who, "... when called upon to loose their purse strings for any purpose involving the slightest hazard, are as alien in their instincts to their descendants in the United States as if their lineage had no approximation since the flood."[11] In a similar vein, Marcy condemns the English policies towards the plains Indians, and accuses the British of opposing immigration into the northwest in order to perpetuate the fur trade and the Hudson's Bay Company monopoly. Another American visitor to Manitoba, in the years before the opening of the Canadian Pacific Railway, was the clergyman author Henry Van Dyke, who, like Marble and Marcy, noted the primitive stages of settlement and development on the Canadian prairies, and reported the disillusionment of many British and English-Canadian immigrants. "Large numbers, being dissatisfied, have recrossed the line, and settled in Dakota and Minnesota. In Pembina County alone the number of Canadians is reckoned at one-half the population."[12]

In contrast to these travellers, the Boston novelist and historian Charles Carleton Coffin found south central Manitoba and the burgeoning settlement of Fort Garry as worthy of praise as the farming regions of Illinois and Minnesota, which he had come west to publicize. In his travel book *The Seat of Empire* (1871), which described his 1869 expedition from Chicago to Duluth, Coffin's only complaint is directed against "the pusillanimity of President Polk" for the resignation of American claims to the Saskatchewan Valley.[13] Even without republican political and economic advantages, the northern Red River Country, according to Coffin, was fostering the same prosperous and self-reliant agrarian society as was developing in the northern American middle west.

The Riel rebellions of 1870 and 1885 provoked some American interest in the Canadian prairies, particularly among journalists and expansionist politicians, who saw the possibility of repeating the experience of Oregon in mid-continent. But except for a few vociferous demagogues and sensationalist reporters, Americans were cautious in their attitudes to Canadian political events, and suspicious of the French-speaking Métis rebels. After only a few heated speeches and articles, American attention wandered from the subject, particularly after the apparently successful resolution of northwestern problems effected by the Canadian government.[14]

Even the completion of the Canadian Pacific Railway did not at first cause a great increase in American interest in the region. As the historian James B. Hedges has pointed out, Americans who immigrated westward until about 1892 were almost exclusively interested in the land still available in the United States;[15] and most American tourists likewise were more interested in their own national experience than in the Canadian scene. There were, however, a few exceptions, including the authors of three noteworthy book-length travel narratives on western Canada.

William Henry Harrison Murray (1840–1904) travelled the Canadian Pacific Railway from Montreal to Vancouver, and described his experiences in an episodic, idiosyncratic, alternatively facetious and bombastic volume entitled *Daylight Land* (1888). Murray was a prolific but imitative author, who, after his early literary success with his Adirondacks book, *Adventures in the Wilderness* (1869), wrote several novels and short stories, some of them with Canadian settings, exploiting the rather antiquated model of James Fenimore Cooper's Leatherstocking tales.[16] A militant advocate of continental unity, Murray undertook a leisurely excursion, with many stop-overs, on the newly opened Canadian Pacific Railway line from Montreal to Vancouver, for the purpose of publicizing in the eastern United States the Canadian west and the advantages of annexation. In a speech delivered in Boston in December

1888, after his return from western Canada, he expounded his vision of an American empire stretching "from Northern to Southern gulf" and "from Prince Edward's Island to Vancouver."

> Never did man see a lovelier evidence of God's design and Nature's unity, than stretches, green as a sleeping sea, from Southern gulf to the white lines of Northern snow, making in itself a prairie empire that would feed half a world.[17]

Unfortunately, Murray's zeal for his subject was not matched by his literary abilities. *Daylight Land,* which describes his excursion to Vancouver, seems to be modelled on Mark Twain's *The Innocents Abroad,* complete with semi-picaresque structure, outrageous jokes, barely relevant digressions, Gothic tales-within-the-tale, and far more emphasis on the attitudes and comments of the narrator and his travelling companions than on the landscape and society they are passing through. The book often reads, furthermore, like an unconscious satire on the behaviour of insensitive American tourists. The travellers seem to encounter no one in Canada but Americans; they refer to the country carelessly as if it were merely a regional adjunct of their own; and they are particularly inclined to speculate on the advantages American investment, enterprise, and immigration would ultimately bring to the Canadian west. The latter subject is, indeed, the main concern of the book. Like Murray's Boston speech, *Daylight Land* is essentially an exposition of the doctrines of Manifest Destiny, prophesying the inevitable Americanization of the prairie provinces and British Columbia. "The productive area of this western Canada," declares one of Murray's travellers, "is ten times larger than the State of Illinois. Two hundred millions of people can be supported, richly supported, north of the forty-ninth parallel" (p. 99).[18] "I wish our countrymen would learn the facts about this huge empire of opportunity to the north of them," says another, "or that the Canadians had knowledge of it themselves, faith in, and the right connections with us. Then you would see this western land jump to the front of continental observation" (p. 145).

The same character injects a possibly ominous or pessimistic qualification to these expressions of American expansionism and boosterism when he suggests that one function of the Canadian west must be to compensate for the inevitable depletion of American agricultural lands. "As the soil to the south under our silly system of agriculture becomes exhausted, as it soon will be, and the average yield per acre shrinks more and more, the wheat growers must and will move northward" (pp. 146-47). By implication, similar processes of exhaustion must overtake the open lands to the north as they are filled up with American settlers and brought under cultivation. There is another qualification to the American observers' approval of progress in the northwest: in the midst of an exclamation over the rapid development of the city of Vancouver, the narrator briefly laments the destruction of the great trees of the British Columbia rain forests. "Alas that life must forever feed its growth on death, and human progress advance only over the ruins of the perfect" (p. 314). On the whole, however, Murray does not pursue in *Daylight Land* the dialectic of the conflict between human progress and unspoiled nature, nor does he give more than implicit consideration to the ultimate consequences of unlimited immigration and exploitation in the Canadian west. Essentially, his vision of Canada, like his vision of the continent as a whole, implies an infinitude of space and time, a blurred and indefinable vista extending outward beyond any imaginable limitations.

Murray's vision of the Canadian frontier, as has been indicated, is related to his belief in Manifest Destiny, the conviction that the Canadian lands, population, and potential for the future would eventually be absorbed into the United States. This conviction was shared by many of his countrymen in the closing years of the nineteenth century, especially by journalists and political orators; but as A. K. Weinberg has shown, there was a considerable discrepancy between this kind of rhetoric and the realities of American domestic and foreign politics. If they had been presented with the opportunity of annexing Canada, post-Civil-War American politicians would probably have decided that internal problems took precedence over the assumption of the additional administrative responsibilities of a new and vast expanse of territory.[19] Conversely, as at least some Americans realized at the time, the majority of Canadians were opposed or at least indifferent to the idea of annexation. Thus, seen in the perspective of the improbability of an early political union between the two countries, the Canadian west appeared not as a spatial and temporal continuation of American progress, but, like the eastern regions, as a rather curious alternative to American experience. This is the conception of the country conveyed by Charles Dudley Warner in his *Studies in the South and West, with Comments on Canada* (1890).

Warner made the same railway excursion as Murray, from Montreal to Vancouver, in September 1888. The resulting three-part travel essay of about eighty pages was serialized in *Harper's Magazine* in 1889 and published in book form the following year, with fourteen other articles, previously published in *Harper's*, on the American south and west. Although "Comments on Canada" includes statistical and descriptive summaries of the political, social, and geographical features of the country as a whole, the main emphasis in the essays is on the regions that most obviously stimulated Warner's imagination, the prairie provinces and British Columbia. Accordingly, Warner collected his Canadian travel observations in a volume dealing with two other frontier regions, and although the "Studies" and the "Comments" are separated in the volume by sub-title pages, the author obviously conceived some degree of unity between the two works. "Comments on Canada" does not include explicit comparative reference to the earlier American travel pieces, but the reader is implicitly invited to note certain parallels and contrasts.

The most obvious points of comparison involve the development of the three regions. In one sense, as Warner suggests, all three can be considered frontiers, since although the South includes some of the oldest settlements on the American continent, its vast stretches of sparsely settled land and its basically agrarian orientation bring it much closer economically and socially to the west than to the urbanized, industrialized centres of New England and other northeastern states. In another sense, too, the South and West are closely linked: the processes of urbanization and industrialization have recently been accelerated by the Civil War and its aftermath, in the one case as a result of the determination of a defeated population to put past troubles behind them and commit themselves to the future, and in the other case because of a post-war economic boom and the sudden availability of a large, mobile force of workers and would-be settlers. In western Canada, however, the building of cities and the development of manufacturing and service extensions to the agrarian economy can, in 1888, hardly be said to have begun. Warner notes the recent rapid growth of Winnipeg and Vancouver, but he observes also that the builders of the Manitoba capital have perhaps been overly ambitious, since the city's facilities seem too elaborate for the sparsely inhabited area. "At present it is in a condition of subsided 'boom'; the whole province has not more than 120,000 people, and the city for that number is out of proportion. Winnipeg must wait a little for the development of the country" (p. 434).[20] In a similar way, Vancouver is establishing itself as a northwest-coast trade and shipping centre, with a degree of enthusiasm that perhaps overlooks the actualities of population growth, especially since, as Warner reports, "there is a constant 'leakage' of emigrants, who had apparently promised to tarry in Canada, into United States territories" (p. 450).

Like most post-eighteenth-century thinkers, Warner associates the idea of progress mainly with population growth, the rise of cities, the diversification of regional economies, and the various cultural and material advantages this rise and diversification bring. All his essays on the South and West celebrate the rapid growth of American cities; his admiration for rural or backwoods landscapes, like those of Louisiana and Kentucky, for instance, is frequently qualified by adverse remarks on the retarded economic and social development of the regions. As might be expected of the co-author of *The Gilded Age,* he makes occasional objections to rapacious investors and corrupt politicians in the West; but nowhere in the "Studies in the South and West" or in the "Comments on Canada" does the author suggest that non-urban life involves any kind of Arcadian simplicity or natural virtue contrasting with the decadence of life in the cities. Warner associates progress, furthermore, with a process of national uniformity, whereby the disjunctions caused by traditional southern isolationism and more immediately by the Civil War will gradually be transcended as the various regions come closer together in purpose, economic achievement, and general quality of life. "When," says Warner, "we have made all allowance for difference in climate, difference in the way of looking at life for a century, it is plain to be seen that a great transformation is taking place in the South, and that Southern society and Northern society are becoming every day more and more alike" (p. 34). The same is true of the western territories, which are coming more and more to be typified not by the cattle ranges and farms of the plains, but by the teeming cities like Indianapolis, Springfield, Columbus, and Chicago. In relation to this progressive conception of the American South and West, Canada appears as an anomaly, reflecting some American values and potentials, but retaining enough historical and geographical distinctiveness to resist assimilation with the United States. "Manitoba," Warner observes, "is Western in its spirit and its sympathies. Before the building of the Canadian Pacific its communication was with Minnesota. Its interests now lie largely with its southern neighbours" (p. 438). In spite of the "free independent spirit" of Manitoba, however, which reminds Warner of the social atmosphere of "one of our own western territories" (p. 437), he finds very little sympathy among Canadians, either easterners or westerners, for the idea of union with the United States.

> Put squarely to a popular vote, it would make little show in the returns. Among the minor causes of reluctance to a union are distrust of the Government of the United States, coupled with the undoubted belief that Canada has the better government;

dislike of our quadrennial elections; the want of a system of civil service, with all the turmoil of our constant official overturning; dislike of our sensational and irresponsible journalism, tending so often to recklessness; and dislike also, very likely, of the very assertive spirit which has made us so rapidly subdue our continental possessions. (p. 483)

At various stages throughout his "Comments on Canada," Warner recurs to another feature of the northern country that perhaps provides the most comprehensive explanation for the country's resistance to Americanization. "Canada," he observes at one point, "is really two countries, separated from each other by the vast rocky wilderness between the lakes and James Bay" (pp. 409-10). The northwest, he reports further, presents "a condition of soil, climate, and political development as different from eastern Canada as Montana is from New England" (pp. 483-84), and only the tenuous link of the Canadian Pacific Railway holds the two parts of the country together. Canada, in brief, is much more fragmented than the United States, with distinct geographical and social divisions between east and west, between French and English (which Warner touches on briefly in his concluding chapter), between the old, declining settlements of the Atlantic provinces and the new flourishing communities of the prairies and the Pacific. Thus the country seems to be particularly lacking in the capacity for unity, the capacity that is the special strength of the United States, where east, west, north, and south continuously grow together in a common purpose and towards a common set of ideals.

But if Canada is unable or unwilling to participate in the American republic, Warner is quite prepared to acknowledge the independent validity of the northern country's social, political, and economic achievements. "The railway development," he observes in closing, "has brought together the widely separated provinces, and... has produced a sort of unity which no Act of Parliament could ever create." In addition, it has brought Canada closer to Europe, has strengthened the British Empire, and has thereby reinforced the probability that Canada will remain "for a long time on her present line of development in a British connection" (pp. 483-84).

Another sympathetic American commentator on western Canada was the prolific New York journalist Julian Ralph (1853-1903), who was a disciple of Theodore Roosevelt in the pursuit of the strenuous life and in a zeal for muck-raking. The author of several novels and short stories of social reform as well as dozens of travel articles for *Harper's*, Ralph undertook, in 1890 and 1891, to report on the American and Canadian west for the magazine. Accompanied by his friend Frederic Remington, who illustrated the articles, he traversed and described the landscape and society from Winnipeg to Victoria, then headed south and east to conduct a similar literary survey from Washington to Minnesota. The first series of articles was collected as *On Canada's Frontier* (1892); the second series became a parallel volume on the United States, *Our Great West* (1893).

Like Warner, Ralph focuses especially on the burgeoning urbanization and industrialization of the American West: the essays collected in *Our Great West* have such titles as "The New Growth of St. Louis," "Wyoming: Another Pennsylvania," and "Western Modes of City Management." In Canada, however, he discovers what appears to be a much more primitive stage of development and, as the title of his Canada volume suggests, he emphasizes such subjects as homesteading in Manitoba, Indian life and customs, the activities of the Hudson's Bay Company, and the rugged plainsmen and construction gangs of the prairies and British Columbia. This is not to suggest, however, that Ralph is a romantic who deplores modern civilization and idealizes primitivism and adventure. There is a curious ambivalence in his attitude to the frontier, an ambivalence that is, in fact, evident in the whole "strenuous-life" tradition extending in American literature from Francis Parkman's *The Oregon Trail* (1849) to the outdoor sports and exploration narratives of Theodore Roosevelt and his disciples. On the one hand, Ralph approves of the taming of the west and the gradual spread of an urban civilization, which as he repeatedly implies, will prevail in Canada as it has prevailed in the United States. On the other hand he is eager to experience and describe an exotic way of life whose imminent passing is to some extent regrettable.

> Our wild life in this country is, happily, gone. The frontiersman is more difficult to find than the frontier, the cowboy has become a laborer almost like any other, our Indians are as the animals in our parks, and there is little of our country that is not threaded by railroads or wagon-ways. But in new or western Canada this is not so. A vast extent of it north of the Canadian Pacific Railway ... has been explored only as to its waterways, its valleys, or its open plains, and where it has been traversed much of it remains as Nature and her near of kin, the red men, had it of old. (p. 139)[21]

But these primeval conditions on the Canadian frontier, as interesting as they may be, are antagonistic to what Ralph takes to be the inevitable course of human history. The allegedly static cultures of aboriginal peoples must give place to the dynamic energy of settlers of European stock, just as the individual homesteader and the small farm must in turn be eclipsed by empire-building corporations, industrial complexes, and urban communities. For Ralph, as for Warner, the westward march of empire is a march of progress and material development.

As a disciple of the muck-raking Roosevelt, Ralph is not insensitive to the moral ambiguities of progress. His sympathies are particularly aroused by the North American Indian, who is given a great deal of attention in *On Canada's Frontier*. Although Ralph obviously believes, with the majority of his white contemporaries, that the Indian is doomed to disappear, he cannot approve of the methods by which bureaucracies on both sides of the border seem determined to hasten the process. "The policy of the Canadian government," he observes, for instance, "has been to make treaties with the dangerous tribes and to let the peaceful ones starve" (p. 16).

In contrast to his criticism of irresponsible government bureaucracy, however, is his approval of corporate efficiency. "The [Indians] do not need to starve in Canada," he continues; "they trust to the Hudson Bay Company for food and care, and not in vain" (p. 210). The Company is the subject of recurring laudatory references and a long chapter in *On Canada's Frontier*. The relative tranquility of Canada's Indian affairs Ralph attributes to "the just policy of the Hudson Bay men toward the Indians" (p. 210). "In the northern wilds of Canada are districts peopled by beggars who have been in such pitiful stress for food and covering that the Hudson Bay Company has kept them alive with advances of provisions and blankets winter after winter" (p. 237). The Company, in brief, is a model of the corporate self-reliance and initiative which, according to Ralph, will overcome the limitations of a primitive environment and realize Canada's full potential in the modern world.

There seems to be little conscious artifice in the structure of *On Canada's Frontier*, but it is worth noting that the first few essays are about Indians and settlers on the prairies, while the two concluding pieces are about railroad building and the founding of cities in British Columbia. Thus the book provides a loose paradigm of Canada's development from primitive frontier to complex nation, with concluding intimations of the rise of an urbanized and industrialized society such as that depicted in the succeeding book, *Our Great West*. Soon after publishing these two volumes of western travel, Ralph turned to writing two works of muck-raking fiction, *People We Pass: Stories of Life Among the Masses* (1896), and *An Angel in a Web* (1899), which expose the industrial and commercial corruption of the older, eastern regions of the United States. Thus his literary output of the 1890s succinctly records one possible perception of the history and geography of the New World north of Mexico, moving from the new frontier of Canada through the burgeoning urban civilization of the western United States, to the decaying cities of the oldest settlements of English-speaking America. As has been suggested, however, Ralph's images of Canada and the United States are not quite so simplistic as this general outline implies. In spite of his criticism of social evils, he is committed to the notion of progress and the spread of modern civilization; and although he is obviously gratified that a supposedly unspoiled frontier, where Americans like himself can pursue the strenuous life, has survived into his lifetime, he is conscious of the many negative aspects of primitivism, and quite content that the Canadian frontier should eventually go the way of its counterpart in the United States.

By the mid-1890s, however, the dominant American attitude towards the Canadian west was moving closer to W. H. H. Murray's boosterism than to the nostalgic admiration of Warner or Ralph. With the advent of Wilfrid Laurier's Liberal government at Ottawa in 1896, and the implementation of an aggressive policy of encouragement to foreign investors and settlers, the way was cleared for the American "invasion" of the Canadian west. The image of invasion was an especially popular cliché among the many American journalists and popular writers who were enlisted by private land promoters and by the Canadian Department of the Interior to publicize the northern prairies in the United States.

The first priorities of these promotional writers were to dispel American ignorance, indifference, or hostility towards Canada, and to emphasize the geographical unity of the western plains and the ethnic homogeneity of the English-speaking North American people. A writer in *The Cosmopolitan* in 1894 referred to "the number of [American] tourists one sees in Canada provided with heavy clothing, sweltering in a temperature of one hundred degrees in the shade," but by 1903 another writer was prepared to claim that promotional efforts had "changed the Western farmer's conception of the Canadian Northwest, which he formerly looked on as akin to Siberia."[22]

Yet while these publicists reassured prospective immigrants of the geographical continuity between the American and Canadian middle wests, they did not want to suggest that the regions were identical. Like Charles Dudley Warner and Julian Ralph, they represented the northern prairie as comparable to the American plains as they were twenty-five to fifty years earlier, before the disappearance of free land and the rise of cities. Thus an article called "The Great Plains of Canada" emphasized the "vastness and solitude and silence" of Manitoba, while other writers dwelt on the economic potential of the region. Western Canada offered "millions of acres of good wheat land waiting for occupation by the surplus population of the world"; "a vast country with abundance of the very best grain-growing, cattle raising [land]"; and agricultural resources "sufficient, if developed, to support a population of 200,000,000."[23]

Most of these writers emphasized, as W. H. H. Murray did, the infinite potential of the Canadian prairies, and many of them shared his belief in continental unity. "[T]he enterprising 'Yankee,' as the people from the United States are called in Canada... cross[es] a boundary line which is largely imaginary..."; "Americans and Canadians are so much alike that they fraternize wonderfully well in this new country—much better, in fact, than English and Canadians"; "The Canadians are Americans—they can't help themselves."[24] Other writers, however, draw back from annexationist statements—perhaps for fear of offending their magazines' Canadian readers, or perhaps for the more important reason that their primary intended audience is the dissatisfied American farmer, who would not want to find in Canada a mere continuation of the economic and political conditions he has found unsatisfactory. "It is not Canada's destiny to become annexed to the United States," wrote popular novelist James Oliver Curwood in 1905, just beginning his literary career as a contributor to magazines: "... Four out of five of the Americans, while not overjoyed at being subjects of a king, would vote against annexation to the United States."[25] The ideal conception of western Canada seems to be that of a new yet familiar nation, like the United States but not of it, sharing the virtues derived from the Jeffersonian ideal of a nation of yeoman farmers, while avoiding many of the modern republic's economic and political errors.

These hopeful visions of western Canada as an alternative America, however, were expounded mainly by publicists or literary hacks whose interest in Canada was rather mercenary and superficial. Charles Dudley Warner and Julian Ralph saw the region in more imaginative terms, but perhaps the most memorable literary vision of western Canada in the late nineteenth century was Hamlin Garland's narrative of travel through the interior of British Columbia, *The Trail of the Goldseekers* (1899). Garland, a journalist and writer of fiction particularly known for his realistic stories of the American middle west collected as *Main-Travelled Roads* (1891), set out in the summer of 1898 on a trek through northern

British Columbia towards the Klondike gold fields. Early in *The Trail of the Goldseekers* he explained his reasons for undertaking this expedition:

> I believed that I was about to see and take part in a most picturesque and impressive movement across the wilderness. I believed it to be the last great march of the kind which could ever come in America, so rapidly were the wild places being settled up. I wished, therefore, to take part in this tramp of the goldseekers, to be one of them, and record their deeds. I wished to return to the wilderness also, to forget books and theories of art and social problems, and come again face to face with the great free spaces of woods and skies and streams. I was not a goldseeker, but a nature hunter, and I was eager to enter this, the wildest region yet remaining in Northern America. (p. 8)[26]

Like Julian Ralph, Garland sees the disappearance of the "wild places" as inevitable and to some extent desirable, since he believes that the world of books, theories of art, and social problems represents a higher stage of existence. In comparison to more empirical or materialistic observers like Ralph, Warner, and Murray, however, the sensitive and imaginative Garland is inclined to see the wilderness in terms that recall early-nineteenth-century romanticism or transcendentalism. His expedition into the northern forest is, in effect, an attempt to rediscover elements in nature corresponding to the mysterious and primeval elements in his own being, rather like Henry Thoreau's similar quests in the woods of Massachusetts and Maine. But also like Thoreau, Garland finds the quest ambivalent: the British Columbia interior, like the interior of the self, is at once fascinating and threatening, familiar and strange. Throughout *The Trail of the Goldseekers*, imagery of death and desolation reflects the intimidating effects of the landscape. The Selkirks are "desolate, death-haunted, pushing their white domes into the blue sky in savage grandeur" (p. 12). In the valley of Lac La Hache "we passed lakes surrounded by ghostly dead trees, which looked as though the water had poisoned them" (p. 24). The valley of the Skeena is "empty of life" (p. 153). And in a final summary of the whole expedition, Garland says "the trail was a disappointment to me, not because it was long and crossed mountains, but because it ran through a barren, monotonous, silent, gloomy, and rainy country" (p. 180). Nature at times seems monstrous or demonic: at one point the travellers are forced to take to the scanty refuge of their tents, where they listen in horror to the screams of their horses being eaten alive by swarms of mosquitoes. Finally, Garland is defeated by this implacable wilderness. After completing an exhausting march from Creston to Telegraph Creek on the Stikine River, he abandons the attempt to reach the Klondike and takes a steamer out to the coast and back down to Seattle.

Yet even as he admits his inability to adapt himself to this primitive wilderness, he acknowledges the fascination it holds for him. "As the time came when I must return to the south and to the tame, the settled, the quiet, I experienced a profound feeling of regret, of longing for the wild and lonely" (p. 191). Throughout the expedition, moreover, even as the strange and hostile elements of nature assail him, Garland is continually discovering intimations of something familiar, even comforting. As in many of Henry Thoreau's travel narratives, the search for the self becomes inextricable with the search for America, particularly a simple, primitive, and mythically idyllic image of America. All along the route towards the gold fields he is reminded of the American frontier, especially of his own "middle-border" region as it was in his own youth or a generation earlier. His first sight of the Canadian prairies is "like Dakota as I saw it in 1881" (p. 11); the village of Ashcroft is compared to "an ordinary cow-town in the Western States" and "the hills which rose near resembled those of Montana or Colorado" (p. 13). Soda Creek is "not unlike a small Missouri River town" (p. 27); the Cariboo mining district calls up "visions of the hot sands, and the sun-lit buttes and valleys of Arizona and Montana" (p. 34). "I shall not soon forget," he says of one stage of his expedition, "the shining vistas through which we rode that day.... It was like going back to the prairies of Indiana, Illinois, and Iowa, as they were sixty years ago" (p. 60).

Not surprisingly, in the light of these comparisons and related descriptive and narrative details in *The Trail of the Goldseekers*, Garland expresses no interest in the political or sociological structures of western Canada. Unlike Warner or Ralph, he is indifferent to the question of whether the Canadian West is being subdued more efficiently than the American, and he shares none of Murray's belief in Manifest Destiny. The Canadian West, like the American, is for Garland a myth and a symbol, or perhaps more precisely a poetic image of various interacting and at times conflicting elements in man's nature as he confronts the New World.

CONCLUSION

Hamlin Garland, writing in 1899 about his experiences on the northwestern edge of the continent, provides an appropriate climax to the story of nineteenth-century American literary interest in Canada. If the nineteenth century is seen as a homogeneous segment in the social and cultural history of the United States, beginning with the exuberant optimism of the post-revolutionary period and ending with the recognition of the end of the great western frontier adventure, then Garland's low-keyed and nostalgic narrative reflects the sense of regret at the end of an era that must have been felt by many of his countrymen. The nature and significance of the so-called "closing" of the American frontier (to use the metaphor propagated in 1893 by the American historian Frederick Jackson Turner) is a complex and continuously debated controversy; but on the emotional and imaginative levels reflected in creative literature, there are, in the last decades of the nineteenth century, unmistakable intimations of a decline or deceleration towards some kind of conclusion.

To the American imagination, the Klondike gold rush was the seal and symbol of that conclusion: "the last great march," as Garland expressed it, into the vanishing "wild places" of the continent. Garland, of course, was not the principal literary chronicler of the Klondike. Jack London, writing in the first decade of the twentieth century, created the most memorable image of the last frontier, in almost a dozen volumes of fiction, beginning with the short-story collection *The Son of the Wolf* (1900) and climaxed by *The Call of the Wild* (1903). For London, as for Garland, the fact that the frontier was located in Canada did not detract from the essentially American significance of the gold rush. There are occasional references to Mounties, French-Canadians, and the authority of the British Crown in *The Call of the Wild* and the other Klondike works, but these elements are little more than incidental local colour. Ultimately, London's North is a super-national entity, an anonymous setting for the conflict between man and nature and for the "survival of the fittest" doctrine the author learned from his reading of Herbert Spencer. Yet at the same time, this setting and theme are inescapably American, by virtue of the fact that the frontier and the man-nature conflict are so deeply entrenched in United States experience. London's exposition of the setting and theme, furthermore, relates to the United States in that the cold and brutal North is set in opposition to a specifically located image of a warm and civilized southland, which is the author's native California. In *The Call of the Wild*, the human hero is destroyed by the North, and the canine protagonist is reclaimed by his primitive surroundings; but in *White Fang* (1906), the process is reversed: the wild dog is tamed in the sunny domesticity of California.

Thus London's image of Canada is directly related to the nineteenth-century American literary tradition, in which Canada appears mainly as an alternative or contrast to the values represented by the United States. For London, these values are predominantly natural and psychological: the North is a brutal land, where the more refined and virtuous elements in human nature are subdued in the savage struggle for survival. In the works of other writers, the values are predominantly social and political: Canadian attitudes or experience related to freedom and communal organization are compared to those of the United States. Sometimes, as in the Loyalist or the fugitive-slave traditions, the comparison is to the advantage of Canada; more often, the advantage is on the American side, as the authors discover, in the supposed defects of Canadian landscape and society, a justification of their own country. In its most complex form, in the histories of Francis Parkman, for instance, or in Thoreau's "A Yankee in Canada," the comparison tends towards ambivalence. The triumph of Anglo-American liberalism over French despotism was inevitable yet regrettable; the superiority of New England energy over French-Canadian inertia may be demonstrated in terms of results but not in terms of customs and attitudes.

Indeed, it could be argued that ambivalence and uncertainty constitute the most pervasive American literary reaction to Canada. Jack London's indecisive attitudes towards the doctrinal poles of socialism and Spencerian individualism have been frequently noted by his commentators; and his Klondike novels and stories repeatedly demonstrate his imaginative attraction to the grim northern landscape even as he asserts its fatal influence and the wisdom of withdrawal towards the warmth and community of the South. A similar ambivalent tendency can be identified in almost all American writing about Canada, even in that which appears most confident about the superiority of United States values.

The primitive allure of the North as opposed to the rational appeal of the South occurs again and again in American writing. In a similar way, many travellers, novelists, and other writers contrast the simplicity of Canadian—particularly French-Canadian—culture to the complexity of American, and often imply a wistful attraction to this simplicity, even as they acknowledge the historical inevitability of the technological and social development of the United States. On the ideological level, the encounter with Canadian political and social structures often reminds American observers of the intellectual elusiveness of such concepts as "liberty" and "progress," even though they may remain emotionally or rhetorically committed to the American assertion of such concepts. And as the late-nineteenth- and early-twentieth-century writers like Garland and London illustrate, the ambivalence of American attitudes to Canada is related to the sense of decline, disillusionment, and possible failure evident in the recognition of the end of the great American frontier experience.

This, perhaps, is one reason Canada is a relatively infrequent concern in the imaginative literature of the United States. Americans, eager to defend and keep vital their hard-won political and social beliefs, turn with reluctance to a national entity that appears to call these beliefs into question. It is not simply that Americans would prefer to avoid the contemplation of alternatives, for they do face, willingly enough, the comparison between their country and Europe. But Canada seems to present to them a particularly disconcerting comparison, in its superficial similarities to the United States and in its close geographical and historical ties, both of which seem at odds with a perverse determination to continue on a course different in certain essential details from that of the United States. Thus Canada repeatedly appears to nineteenth-century Americans as a reminder of alternatives, some of which seem wrong, but many of which too often present disturbing possibilities of United States error and failure. Perhaps this is why, in the twentieth century, Americans seem even less interested in Canada than they did in the nineteenth, and their interest is frequently directed towards denying the distinctions between the two countries. *The Americanization of Canada* (1902), by the American political scientist Samuel E. Moffett, is an attempt to support this denial with statistics. The novels of Jack London's most popular and prolific successor, James Oliver Curwood, are only nominally set in Canada; the northern wilderness of *The Danger Trail* (1910), *The Valley of Silent Men* (1920), and his many other adventure novels is not significantly differentiated from the stereotyped American "wild west." Willa Cather's historical novel of New France, *Shadows on the Rock* (1931), involves thinly disguised versions of landscapes and characters based on the author's native American middle west; and Wallace Stegner's *Wolf Willow* (1962) uses autobiographical reminiscence and fiction set in Saskatchewan to expound the author's personal and historical perceptions of midwestern America. Canadians perversely insist on "referring to us as 'the Americans,'" said Edmund Wilson in 1965, "as if Canadians were not Americans, too."[1] And although Wilson's *O Canada* discusses at length the local idiosyncrasies of French-Canadian politics and culture, it is clear that he considers the northern country as merely an extension of the "America" that is simultaneously both a nation and a continent.

In the nineteenth century, however, a significant number of American writers recognized the many distinctions between the two countries. This recognition, recorded in novels, poems, travel narratives, histories, and other types of literary work, reveals the authors' bemusement not only with Canada, but with the idea of the New World as a whole. As American literature everywhere indicates, the articulation of uncertainty or inconclusiveness is a significant form of assertion, even of discovery and revelation. Many of the classic works of American literature, such as *The Scarlet Letter* or *Moby-Dick*, use the ambiguities and infinite suggestiveness of objects and situations to explore the labyrinthine structure of experience. In a similar way, those authors, such as James Fenimore Cooper or Walt Whitman, who take as their focus a comprehensive vision of the North American landscape are struck by the sense of infinitude, potential meaning, and elusiveness that landscape conveys. In a sense, it might be argued, all American literature is about the geographical expanse of the New World: certainly nineteenth-century American writing is pervaded with images that suggest the infinitude and consequent ambiguity inherent in the exploratory encounter with the continent. From this perspective, the image of Canada is an essential element in the formative development of the literature of the United States. Like the western frontier, like the eastern urban experience, like the encounter with Europe or with other geographical and cultural entities such as South America or the Orient, Canada is an unavoidable element in the American imagination. Indeed, as has been suggested, by virtue of proximity if by nothing else, Canada is perhaps a particularly important element in the developing American imagination. The northern country inspired, admittedly, much that was ephemeral in American writing; but it occasionally touched the imaginations of important writers, such as Thoreau, Parkman, Howells, and Whitman. And even on the ephemeral level—in the historical novels, the amateur travel narratives, the literature of tourism—the American image of Canada, seen as a synthesis of settings, characterizations, and themes, constitutes a significant part of the imaginative response to the New World.

NOTES

NOTES TO INTRODUCTION

¹ Howells, *Their Wedding Journey*, ed. John K. Reeves (Bloomington: Indiana Univ. Press, 1968), p. 158.

² Warner, *Baddeck, and That Sort of Thing* (Boston: Osgood, 1874), p. 29.

³ Warner, *Studies in the South and West, with Comments on Canada* (New York: Harper, 1890), p. 438.

⁴ Garland, *The Trail of the Goldseekers: A Record of Travel in Prose and Verse* (New York: Macmillan, 1899), p. 8.

⁵ Craig, *The United States and Canada* (Cambridge: Harvard Univ. Press, 1968), p. 9.

NOTES TO CHAPTER I

¹ There is an excellent literary and historical analysis of the captivity-narrative tradition, with excerpts from representative works, in Alden T. Vaughn and Edward W. Clark, eds., *Puritans among the Indians: Accounts of Captivity and Redemption 1676-1724* (Cambridge, Mass.: Belknap, 1981).

² Williams, "The Redeemed Captive," in *Puritans among the Indians*, p. 182; Gyles, "Memoirs of Odd Adventures," in *Puritans*, pp. 128-130. Vaughn and Clark offer an interesting discussion of the captive's emotional reconciliation to his captors in "Cups of Common Calamity: Puritan Captivity Narratives as Literature and History," in *Puritans*, pp. 11-12.

³ John Maylem, *Gallic Perfidy: A Poem* (Boston: Benjamin Mecum, 1758), n. pag.;

Robert Stobo, *Memoirs of Major Robert Stobo, of the Virginia Regiment* (Pittsburgh: Davidson, 1854), p. 20.

[4] *March to Quebec: Journals of the Members of Arnold's Expedition*, ed. Kenneth Roberts (Garden City, N.Y.: Doubleday, 1947), p. 346.

[5] *March to Quebec*, pp. 364, 557.

[6] Hugh Henry Brackenridge, *The Death of General Montgomery in the Storming of the City of Quebec* (Philadelphia: Bell, 1777), p. 15.

[7] J. Hector St. John de Crèvecoeur, *Sketches of Eighteenth-Century America: More "Letters from an American Farmer,"* ed. H. L. Bourdin, R. H. Gabriel, and S. T. Williams (New Haven: Yale Univ. Press, 1925), pp. 172, 174.

[8] [John Cousens Ogden], *A Tour through Upper and Lower Canada. By a Citizen of the United States. Containing a View of the Present State of Religion, Learning, Commerce, Agriculture, Colonization, Customs and Manners, among the English, French, and Indian Settlements* (Litchfield, Conn.: n.p., 1799), pp. 15, 18, 22.

[9] Ogden, p. 51.

[10] Joseph Stansbury, "To Cordelia," in *The Evolution of Canadian Literature in English: Beginnings to 1867*, ed. Mary Jane Edwards (Toronto: Holt, Rinehart and Winston, 1973), p. 5.

[11] William S. Bartlet, ed., *The Frontier Missionary: A Memoir of the Life of Jacob Bailey, A.M.* (Boston: Ide and Dutton, 1853), p. 154.

[12] Benjamin Mortimer, "To Fairfield (Moraviantown) in Upper Canada, 1798," in *Thirty Thousand Miles with John Heckewelder*, ed. Paul A. W. Wallace (Pittsburgh: Univ. Pittsburgh Press, 1958), p. 353.

[13] Mortimer, p. 365.

[14] Mortimer, p. 365.

[15] John Heckewelder, "Journal with the Commissioners to the Indian Treaty," in *Thirty Thousand Miles with John Heckewelder*, p. 304.

[16] Timothy Bigelow, *Journal of a Tour to Niagara Falls in the Year 1805* (Boston: Wilson, 1876), p. 103.

[17] [William Jenks], *Memoir of the Northern Kingdom, Written A.D. 1872, by the Late Rev. Williamson Jahnsenykes, Ll.D., and Hon. Member of the Royal American Board of Literature. In Six Letters to his Son. Now First Published, Quebec, A.D. 1901* [Boston: n.p., 1808], p. 46.

[18] *Journal of an American Prisoner at Fort Malden and Quebec in the War of 1812* (Quebec: Frank Carrel, 1909), pp. 24, 28.

[19] "Journal of William K. Beall, July-August, 1812," *American Historical Review*, July 1912, pp. 784, 787.

[20] [Jacob Bigelow], *The Wars of the Gulls: An Historical Romance* (New York: The Dramatic Repository, 1812), pp. 4-5.

[21] Richard Emmons, *The Fredoniad: or, Independence Preserved, An Epick Poem on the Late War of 1812* (Boston: Emmons, 1827), p. 68.

NOTES TO CHAPTER II

[1] All quotations from this work refer to Joseph Sansom, *Travels in Lower Canada, with the Author's Recollections of the Soil, and Aspect; the Morals, Habits, and Religious Institutions, of that Country* (London: Phillips, 1820).

[2] [J. de Wallenstein], "Lower Canada," *The North American Review*, July 1828, p. 12.

[3] Philip Stansbury, *A Pedestrian Tour of Two Thousand Three Hundred Miles in North America. To the Lakes,—the Canadas,—and the New-England States. Performed in the Autumn of 1821* (New York: Myers and Smith, 1822), pp. 159-60.

[4] Moses Guest, *Poems on Several Occasions. To which Are Annexed Extracts from a Journal Kept by the Author While He Followed the Sea, and during a Journey from New Brunswick, in New Jersey, to Montreal and Quebec* (Cincinnati: Looker and Reynolds, 1823), p. 141.

[5] [Theodore Dwight], *The Northern Traveller, and Northern Tour: with the Routes to the Springs, Niagara, and Quebec, and the Coal Mines of Pennsylvania; also the Tour of New England*, rev. ed. (New York: Harper, 1831), p. 214.

[6] The popularity of *Awful Disclosures* is discussed in Frank Luther Mott, *Golden Multitudes: The Story of Best Sellers in the United States* (New York: Macmillan, 1947), pp. 245-46.

[7] Washington Irving, *Astoria, or Anecdotes of an Enterprise beyond the Rocky Mountains*, 1836 ed., intro. W. H. Goetzman (Philadelphia: Lippincott, 1961), I, 187.

[8] Irving, *The Adventures of Captain Bonneville, U.S.A., in the Rocky Mountains and the Far West*, ed. E. W. Todd (Norman: Univ. Oklahoma Press, 1961), p. 19.

[9] Edgar Allan Poe, "The Journal of Julius Rodman," *Complete Works of Edgar Allan Poe* (1902; rpt. New York: AMS, 1965), IV, 25.

[10] Francis Parkman, *The Oregon Trail: Sketches of Prairie and Rocky Mountain Life*, vol. XVI of *Francis Parkman's Works*, Frontenac Ed. (New York: Scribner's, 1915), p. 16.

[11] Parkman, pp. 17-18.

[12] Parkman, p. 17.

[13] All quotations from this work refer to [William Tappan Thompson], *Major Jones's Sketches of Travel: Comprising the Scenes, Incidents, and Adventures, in His Tour from Georgia to Canada* (Philadelphia: Peterson, 1848).

[14] All quotations from Dana's journal refer to vol. 2 of *The Journal of Richard Henry Dana, Jr.*, ed. Robert F. Lucid (Cambridge, Mass.: Belknap, 1968).

NOTES TO CHAPTER III

[1] H. S. Canby, in *Thoreau* (Boston: Houghton Mifflin, 1939), p. 370, dismissed it

as "relatively simple... factual and direct"; Walter Harding, in his *Thoreau Handbook* (New York: New York State Univ. Press, 1959), p. 57, pronounced the work "one of Thoreau's least inspired 'Excursions'"; John A. Christie in *Thoreau as World Traveler* (New York: Columbia Univ. Press), p. 100, attributes some potential significance to "A Yankee", but concludes his brief discussion with the unsupported declaration that the work lacks "the immediacy of Thoreau's keen observation and involvement that gave vitality to his later accounts of Maine and Cape Cod." One of the few modern critics who finds much artistic and intellectual substance in the work, although he, too, gives it brief attention, is Sherman Paul in *The Shores of America: Thoreau's Inward Exploration* (1958; rpt. Urbana: Univ. of Illinois Press, 1972), pp. 369-78.

[2] Thoreau, *A Week on the Concord and Merrimack Rivers*, ed. Carl F. Hovde *et al.* (Princeton: Princeton Univ. Press, 1980), p. 218.

[3] *The Journal of Henry David Thoreau* (1906; rpt. New York: Dover, 1962), I, 365.

[4] Thoreau, *Walden*, ed. J. Lyndon Shanley (Princeton: Princeton Univ. Press, 1971), pp. 145, 158.

[5] All quotations from this work refer to "A Yankee in Canada," in *Excursions*, Vol. IX of *The Writings of Henry David Thoreau* (Boston: Houghton Mifflin, 1893).

NOTES TO CHAPTER IV

[1] R. W. B. Lewis, *The American Adam* (Chicago: Univ. of Chicago Press, 1955), p. 159.

[2] George Bancroft, *History of the United States of America from the Discovery of the Continent* (1885; rpt. Port Washington, N.Y.: Kennikat, 1967), II, 426.

[3] Bancroft, p. 434.

[4] Bancroft, p. 433.

[5] Manning Hawthorne and H. W. L. Dana, *The Origin and Development of Longfellow's "Evangeline"* (Portland, Me.: Anthoensen, 1947), p. 12.

[6] Henry Wadsworth Longfellow, *Evangeline* (Toronto: McClelland and Stewart, 1962), pp. 13-14.

NOTES TO CHAPTER V

[1] James Fenimore Cooper, *The Last of the Mohicans* (New York: New American Library, 1962), p. 180.

[2] Cooper, p. 212.

[3] Alfred B. Street, *Frontenac: A Poem* (London: Bentley, 1849), Canto V, stanza iv.

[4] Fiedler, *Love and Death in the American Novel*, rev. ed. (New York: Dell, 1966), pp. 205-09.

[5] J. L. E. W. Shecut, *Ish-noo-Ju-Lut-Sche; or The Eagle of the Mohawks* (New York: Price, 1841), I, 184.

[6] Bradbury, *Lucelle: or The Young Iroquois! A Tale of the Indian Wars* (Boston: Williams, 1845), p. 28.

[7] Parkman, Preface to *The Romance of Dollard* by Mary Hartwell Catherwood (New York: Century, 1889), p. 2.

NOTES TO CHAPTER VI

[1] Parkman to Abbé Ferland (professor of history at l'Université Laval), 10 Sept. 1856, *The Letters of Francis Parkman*, ed. Wilbur R. Jacobs (Norman: Univ. of Oklahoma Press, 1960), I, 119.

[2] Parkman, "The Works of James Fenimore Cooper," *Francis Parkman: Representative Selections*, ed. Wilbur L. Schramm (New York: American Book Company, 1938), pp. 202-17.

[3] Parkman, in an autobiographical letter to Martin Brimmer, *Representative Selections*, pp. 13-14.

[4] Thoreau, "A Yankee in Canada," p. 84.

[5] William R. Taylor, "Francis Parkman," *Pastmasters: Some Essays on American Historians*, ed. Marcus Cunliffe and Robin W. Winks (New York: Harper & Row, 1969), p. 4. Taylor cites a few historians who have expressed this view.

[6] Wilbur L. Schramm, for instance, defends Parkman's treatment of these subjects in his Introduction to *Representative Selections*, p. cv.

[7] For several good illustrations of Parkman's adaptation of source materials, see Taylor, "Francis Parkman," and Richard C. Vitzthum, *The American Compromise: Theme and Method in the Histories of Bancroft, Parkman, and Adams* (Norman: Univ. of Oklahoma Press, 1974), pp. 126-43.

[8] All quotations from *France and England in North America* refer to *Francis Parkman's Works*, Frontenac Edition, 16 vols. (New York: Scribner's, 1915).

[9] For a full discussion of these and related ideas in nineteenth-century American historiography, see David Levin, *History as Romantic Art: Bancroft, Prescott, Motley, and Parkman* (Stanford: Stanford Univ. Press, 1959), especially chapter two.

[10] *The Letters of Francis Parkman*, II, 82.

[11] Parkman, autobiographical letter to Martin Brimmer, *Representative Selections*, p. 14

[12] This association between Parkman's image of nature and his reservations about liberalism is developed by Richard C. Vitzthum in *The American Compromise*,

p. 91; but Vitzthum does not explore fully the ambiguities inherent in Parkman's treatment of the subject.

[13] Taylor, "Francis Parkman," p. 34.

NOTES TO CHAPTER VII

[1] O. L. Holley, ed., *The Picturesque Tourist; Being a Guide through the Northern and Eastern States and Canada: Giving an Accurate Description of Cities and Villages, Celebrated Places of Resort, etc.* (New York: Disturnell, 1844), p. 219.

[2] [Jesse Walker], *Queenston: A Tale of the Niagara Frontier* (Buffalo: Steele's Press, 1845), pp. 110-11.

[3] *The Journals and Miscellaneous Notebooks of Ralph Waldo Emerson*, ed. William H. Gilman and J. E. Parsons (Cambridge, Mass.: Belknap, 1970), XIII, 395.

[4] *Letters and Journals of Thomas Wentworth Higginson, 1846-1906*, ed. Mary Thacher Higginson (1921; rpt. New York: Da Capo, 1969), p. 95.

[5] The most comprehensive history of the border skirmishes involving American interventionists in 1838 is Edwin C. Guillet, *The Lives and Times of the Patriots: An Account of the Rebellion in Upper Canada, 1837-1838, and the Patriot Agitation in the United States, 1837-1842* (1938; rpt. Toronto: Ontario Publishing, 1963). See also Oscar A. Kinchen, *The Rise and Fall of the Patriot Hunters* (New York: Bookman, 1956). As Guillet notes, almost all the interventionists who wrote of their penal-colony experiences misspelled Van Diemen's Land.

[6] Linus W. Miller, *Notes of an Exile to Van Dieman's Land...* (1846; rpt. New York: Johnson, 1968), pp. 2, 7.

[7] E. A. Theller, *Canada in 1837-38, Showing, by Historical Facts, the Causes of the Late Attempted Revolution and of its Failure* (Philadelphia: Anners, 1841), p. 110.

[8] Robert Marsh, *Seven Years of My Life, or Narrative of a Patriot Exile* (Buffalo: Faxon & Stevens, 1848), pp. 138-39.

[9] William Gates, *Recollections of Life in Van Dieman's Land*, ed. George Mackaness (1850; rpt. Sydney, Australia: D. S. Ford, 1961), I, 13.

[10] Gates, I, 14-15.

[11] Marsh, p. iii.

[12] *Narrative of the Adventures and Sufferings of Captain Daniel D. Heustis...* (Boston: Wilder, 1847), p. 29.

[13] [Thomas Jefferson Sutherland], *Loose Leaves from the Portfolio of a Late Patriot Prisoner in Canada* (New York: Colyer, 1840), pp. 7, 19.

[14] Samuel Snow, *Exile's Return: or, Narrative of Samuel Snow, Who was Banished to Van Dieman's Land, for Participating in the Patriot War in Upper Canada in 1838* (Cleveland: Smead & Cowles, 1846), p. 3.

[15] Heustis, *Narrative*, p. 167.

[16] Jedediah Hunt, Jr., *An Adventure on a Frozen Lake: A Tale of the Canadian Rebellion of 1837-38* (Cincinnati: Franklin, 1853), p. 38.

[17] See Lyle H. Wright, *American Fiction 1851-1875: A Contribution towards a Bibliography* (San Marino, Calif.: Huntington, 1965), p. 268.

[18] [George S. Raymond], *The Empress of the Isles, or, The Lake Bravo. A Romance of the Canadian Struggle in 1837* (New York: Stringer and Townsend, 1853), pp. 55, 68.

[19] For a brief survey of Myers's life and career, see Albert Johannsen, *The House of Beadle and Adams and its Dime and Nickel Novels* (Norman: Univ. Oklahoma Press, 1950), II, 213-14.

[20] See Guillet, pp. 138-39 and 285, for an account of the battle and its aftermath, based on a synthesis of sources. There is a possibility that Myers was one of the American "patriots" involved in the battle. One nineteenth-century account of the battle includes a list of prisoners, with the names "Peter Meyer," who was released without trial, and "Sebastian Meyer," sentenced to be hanged and subsequently pardoned. If "Meyer" is a mistake for "Myers," and if these two were brothers, they could have provided the inspiration for the fictional Vrail brothers. See F. B. Hough, *A History of St. Lawrence and Franklin Counties, New York, from the Earliest Period to the Present Time* (Albany: Little, 1853), chapter 10.

[21] Harriet Beecher Stowe, *Uncle Tom's Cabin; or, Life Among the Lowly* (Boston: Jewett, 1852), II, 238.

[22] Stowe, I, 221.

[23] Stowe, *Dred: A Tale of the Great Dismal Swamp* (Boston: Phillips, Sampson, 1856), p. 574.

[24] There were many fugitive-slave narratives published in the United States before the Civil War, but relatively few of them were concerned, to any substantial extent, with Canada. A representative selection is in Robin Winks, ed., *Four Fugitive Slave Narratives* (Reading, Mass.: Addison-Wesley, 1969). Winks's *The Blacks in Canada: A History* (Montreal: McGill-Queen's Univ. Press, 1971) gives a comprehensive view of the fugitive experience, and extensive information on published and unpublished sources.

[25] *The Life of Josiah Henson, Formerly a Slave, Now an Inhabitant of Canada, as Narrated by Himself* (1849; rpt. Dresden, Ont.: Uncle Tom's Cabin & Museum, n.d.), pp. 54-55.

[26] Henson, p. 63.

[27] Samuel Ringold Ward, *Autobiography of a Fugitive Negro: His Anti-Slavery Labours in the United States, Canada, & England* (1855; rpt. New York: Arno, 1968), pp. 150, 153, 218.

[28] Benjamin Drew, *A North-Side View of Slavery. The Refugee: or, The Narratives of Fugitive Slaves in Canada, Related by Themselves, with an Account of the

History and Conditions of the Colored Population of Canada (Boston: Jewett, 1856), p. 39.

NOTES TO CHAPTER VIII

[1] Thoreau, "A Yankee in Canada," *Excursions*, Vol. IX of *The Writings of Henry David Thoreau* (Boston: Houghton Mifflin, 1893), p. 52.

[2] Owen Duffy, *Walter Warren, or, The Adventurer of the Northern Wilds* (New York: Stringer and Townsend, 1854), p. 5.

[3] [John B. Coppinger], *The Renegade: A Tale of Real Life* (New York: Sherman, 1855), p. 4.

[4] William Cullen Bryant, *Letters of a Traveller; or, Notes on Things Seen in Europe and America* (New York: Putnam, 1850), p. 248.

[5] Bryant, p. 283.

[6] Charles Lanman, *Adventures in the Wilds of the United States and British Provinces* (Philadelphia: Moore, 1856), I, 327, 265.

[7] Lanman, p. 275.

[8] Frederick Swartwout Cozzens, *Acadia; or, A Month with the Bluenoses* (New York: Derby & Jackson, 1859), pp. 40-41, 44-45.

[9] Cozzens, pp. 90, 183.

[10] John Mullaly, *A Trip to Newfoundland: its Scenery and Fisheries; with an Account of the Laying of the Submarine Telegraph Cable* (New York: Strong, 1855), p. 46.

[11] Louis L. Noble, *After Icebergs with a Painter: A Summer Voyage to Labrador and around Newfoundland* (New York: Appleton, 1861), p. 74.

[12] Charles H. Foster, "A Study of David A. Wasson," *Beyond Concord: Selected Writings of David Atwood Wasson* (Bloomington: Indiana Univ. Press, 1965), p. 3.

[13] David A. Wasson, "Ice and Esquimaux," chapter 1: "Off!", *The Atlantic Monthly*, Dec. 1864, p. 728.

[14] Wasson, "Ice and Esquimaux," chapter 4: "Autochthones," *The Atlantic Monthly*, April, 1865, p. 438.

[15] *The Poems of Robert Lowell* (Boston: Dutton, 1864), p. 72.

[16] Robert Traill Spence Lowell, *The New Priest in Conception Bay* (Toronto: McClelland and Stewart, 1974), pp. 6-7.

[17] Harold Blodgett, "Robert Traill Spence Lowell," *New England Quarterly*, Dec. 1943, p. 578.

NOTES TO CHAPTER IX

[1] Mark Twain, *The Innocents Abroad, or, The New Pilgrim's Progress* (1859; rpt. Hartford: American, 1890), p. 27.

[2] [Charles F. Browne], *Artemus Ward: His Travels* (New York: Carleton, 1865), pp. 41, 44, 46-47.

[3] Charles Dudley Warner, *Baddeck, and That Sort of Thing* (Boston: Osgood, 1874), p. 168.

[4] See editors' comments in *Mark Twain's Notebooks & Journals, Vol. II (1877-1883)*, ed. Frederick Anderson, Lin Salamo, and Bernard L. Stein (Berkeley: Univ. California Press, 1975), pp. 403-14. See also [A. G. Sedgwick], "Mark Twain's Visit to Canada," *The Nation*, 5 Jan. 1882, pp. 7-8.

[5] *Mark Twain's Notebooks*, II, 409, 410, 414.

[6] All quotations from Godkin's article refer to E. L. Godkin, "French Canada," *The Nation*, 13 Aug., 1868, pp. 128-29; 20 Aug., 1868, pp. 146-48.

[7] Henry James, "Francis Parkman: *The Jesuits in North America*," *Literary Reviews and Essays on American, English, and French Literature*, ed. Albert Mordell (New York: Twayne, 1957), p. 222.

[8] All quotations from James's article refer to Henry James, "Quebec," in *Portraits of Places* (Boston: Osgood, 1884).

[9] All quotations from Howells' novel refer to *Their Wedding Journey*, ed. John K. Reeves (Bloomington: Indiana Univ. Press, 1968).

[10] Howells, *Criticism and Fiction*, ed. Clara M. Kirk and Rudolf Kirk (New York: New York Univ. Press, 1959), p. 62.

[11] All quotations from this novel refer to *A Chance Acquaintance*, ed. Jonathan Thomas, David J. Nordloh, and Ronald Gottesman (Bloomington: Indiana Univ. Press, 1971).

[12] Howells, *The Quality of Mercy*, ed. James P. Elliott and David J. Nordloh (Bloomington: Indiana Univ. Press, 1979), pp. 183-84.

[13] Howells, "Editor's Easy Chair," *Harper's Monthly Magazine*, Jan., 1907, pp. 318, 319, 320.

NOTES TO CHAPTER X

[1] Edmund Wilson, *O Canada: An American's Notes on Canadian Culture* (New York: Noonday, 1966), p. 36.

[2] See Warder H. Cadbury, Introduction to William H. H. Murray, *Adventures in the Wilderness*, ed. William K. Verner (Syracuse: Adirondack Museum/Syracuse Univ. Press, 1970), pp. 40-41.

³ John Burroughs, "The Halcyon in Canada," in *Locusts and Wild Honey*, Vol. IV of *The Writings of John Burroughs* (Boston: Houghton Mifflin, 1907), pp. 218-19, 226, 227-28.

⁴ Henry Van Dyke, "Au Large," in *Little Rivers: A Book of Essays in Profitable Idleness* (New York: Scribner's, 1895), p. 229.

⁵ Van Dyke, "A Brave Heart," in *The Ruling Passion: Tales of Nature and Human Nature* (New York: Scribner's, 1901), p. 95.

⁶ "Octave Thanet" [Alice French], "The Ogre of Ha Ha Bay," in *Knitters in the Sun* (Boston: Houghton Mifflin, 1877), p. 11.

⁷ Robert Grant, *Jack in the Bush; or A Summer on a Salmon River* (Boston: Jordan, Marsh, 1888), p. 25.

⁸ S. Weir Mitchell, *When All the Woods Are Green* (1894; rpt. New York: Century, 1905), p. 334.

⁹ Mitchell, p. 211.

¹⁰ Florence Wilkinson [Evans], *The Lady of the Flag-Flowers* (Chicago: Stone, 1899), p. 55.

¹¹ Wilkinson, p. 76.

NOTES TO CHAPTER XI

¹ See Wilbur R. Jacobs, *The Letters of Francis Parkman* (Norman: Univ. of Oklahoma Press, 1960), II, 190 (note), for a summary of Farnham's life and career.

² Farnham, "The Canadian Habitant," *Harper's New Monthly Magazine*, Aug. 1883, p. 381.

³ "Canadian Voyageurs on the Saguenay," *Harper's*, March 1888, p. 549; "Quebec," *Harper's*, Feb. 1888, p. 357.

⁴ "Quebec," p. 357.

⁵ "Labrador," *Harper's*, Oct. 1885, p. 651.

⁶ "A Winter in Canada," *Harper's*, Feb. 1884, p. 394.

⁷ "The Canadian Habitant," pp. 378, 379, 384, 387, 384.

⁸ "Canadian Voyageurs on the Saguenay," p. 541.

⁹ All quotations from the Diary refer to *Daybooks and Notebooks, Vol. III: Diary in Canada, Notebooks, Index*, ed. William White (New York: New York Univ. Press, 1978).

¹⁰ See Matthiessen, *American Renaissance: Art and Expression in the Age of Emerson and Whitman* (London: Oxford, 1941), pp. 596-625.

¹¹ Brasher, *Whitman as Editor of the Brooklyn Daily Eagle* (Detroit: Wayne State Univ. Press, 1970), pp. 85-95.

¹² Whitman, *Specimen Days: Prose Works 1892*, ed. Floyd Stovall (New York: New York Univ. Press. 1963), I, 241.

NOTES TO CHAPTER XII

[1] John Hovey Robinson, *Pathaway; or Nick Whiffles, the Old Trapper of the Nor'West*. Beadle's Dime Library, I, No. 13 (1878), 3. This edition, with its slightly different sub-title, is evidently the same novel as that published in 1859.

[2] Joseph E. Badger, *The Lone Chief; or, The Trappers of the Saskatchewan. A Tale of the Long Trail*. Beadle's Pocket Novels, No. 145 (New York: Beadle & Adams [1873]), p. 9.

[3] W. J. Hamilton, *Mountain Gid, the Free Ranger; or The Bandit's Daughter*. Beadle's New Dime Novels, No. 103 (New York: Beadle & Adams [1878]), p. 49.

[4] Robinson, *Pathaway*, p. 8.

[5] Edward L. Wheeler, *Deadwood Dick Jr.'s Desperate Strait; or, The Demon Doctor of Dixon's Deposit. A Romance of the North Border Line*. Beadle's Half Dime Library, No. 758 (2 Feb. 1892), p. 2.

[6] Wheeler, *Canada Chet, the Counterfeiter Chief; or, Old Anaconda in Sitting Bull's Camp. A Tale of Two Boys' Adventures*. Beadle's Half Dime Library, 4, No. 92 (29 April 1879), 15.

[7] Robinson, *Pathaway*, p. 27.

[8] Hamilton, *Mountain Gid*, p. 36.

[9] For a summary of these early travel experiences, see Irene M. Spry, "Early Visitors to the Canadian Prairies," *Images of the Plains: The Role of Human Nature in Settlement*, ed. Brian W. Blouet and Merlin P. Lawson (Lincoln: Univ. of Nebraska Press, 1975), p. 171. Spry's article includes a survey of the many British accounts of travel in the Canadian West.

[10] Manton Marble, "To Red River and Beyond," *Harper's New Monthly Magazine*, Feb. 1861, p. 310.

[11] Randolph B. Marcy, "Rupert's Land and Its People," *Harper's New Monthly Magazine*, July 1870, p. 290.

[12] Henry Van Dyke, "The Red River of the North," *Harper's New Monthly Magazine*, May 1880, p. 815.

[13] Charles C. Coffin, *The Seat of Empire* (Boston: Osgood, 1871), p. 61.

[14] For a detailed discussion of American responses, see Donald F. Warner, "Drang Nach Norden: The United States and the Riel Rebellion," *The Mississippi Valley Historical Review*, March 1953, pp. 693-712.

[15] See James B. Hedges, *The Building of the Canadian West: The Land and Colonization Policies of the Canadian Pacific Railway* (New York: Macmillan, 1939), p. 94; and Harold Martin Troper, *Only Farmers Need Apply: Official Canadian Encouragement of Immigration from the United States, 1896-1911* (Toronto: Griffin, 1972), p. 5.

[16] Murray's life and career are summarized in Warder H. Cadbury's Introduction to

Adventures in the Wilderness, ed. William K. Verner (Syracuse: Adirondack Museum/Syracuse Univ. Press, 1970).

[17] Murray, *Continental Unity: An Address... Delivered in Music Hall, Boston... Dec. 13, 1888*, 2nd ed. (Boston: Calkins, 1888), pp. 1, 6, 7.

[18] All quotations from this work refer to W. H. H. Murray, *Daylight Land* (Boston: Cupples & Hurd, 1888).

[19] A. K. Weinberg, *Manifest Destiny: A Study of Nationalist Expansionism in American History* (1935; rpt. Chicago: Quadrangle Books, 1963), pp. 244-45.

[20] All quotations from this work refer to Charles Dudley Warner, *Studies in the South and West, with Comments on Canada* (New York: Harper, 1890).

[21] All quotations from this work refer to Julian Ralph, *On Canada's Frontier* (New York: Harper, 1892).

[22] Lee Meriwether, "The Great British Northwest Territory," *The Cosmopolitan*, Nov. 1894, p. 15; [C. W. Hager], "'Americanization' of Western Canada," *The Nation*, 2 July 1903, p. 6.

[23] C. A. Kenaston, "The Great Plains of Canada," *The Century*, August 1892, p. 565; Sydney C. D. Roper, "The Wheat Lands of Canada," *Appleton's Popular Science Monthly*, Oct. 1899, p. 777; Cy Warman, "Migration to the Canadian Northwest," *American Monthly Review of Reviews*, Sept. 1902, p. 296; Frederick A. Ogg, "Vast Undeveloped Regions," *The World's Work*, Oct. 1906, p. 8079.

[24] Warman, p. 296; Theodore M. Knappen, "Western Canada in 1904," *American Monthly Review of Reviews*, Nov. 1904, pp. 581-82; Theodore M. Knappen, "Winning the Canadian West," *The World's Work*, Sept. 1905, p. 6598.

[25] Curwood, "The Effect of the American Invasion," *The World's Work*, Sept. 1905, pp. 6607, 6611.

[26] All quotations from this work refer to Hamlin Garland, *The Trail of the Goldseekers* (New York: Macmillan, 1899).

NOTE TO CONCLUSION

[1] Edmund Wilson, *O Canada: An American's Notes on Canadian Culture* (New York: Noonday, 1965), p. 35.

LIST OF WORKS CITED

Primary Sources

Arnold, Benedict, et al. *March to Quebec: Journals of the Members of Arnold's Expedition.* Ed. Kenneth Roberts. Garden City, N.Y.: Doubleday, 1947.

[Bacon, Delia Salter.] *Tales of the Puritans.* New Haven: Maltby, 1831.

Badger, Joseph E. *Death Trailer, The Scourge of the Plains Crees.* Beadle's New Dime Novels, New Series, No. 104. New York: Beadle & Adams [1873].

———. *The Lone Chief; or, The Trappers of the Saskatchewan. A Tale of the Long Trail.* Beadle's Pocket Novels, No. 145. New York: Beadle & Adams [1873].

Bancroft, George. *History of the United States of America from the Discovery of the Continent.* Rev. Ed. 6 Vols. 1885; rpt. Port Washington: Kennikat Press, 1967.

Barker, Benjamin. *Cecilia; or, The White Nun of the Wilderness: A Romance of Love and Intrigue.* Boston: Gleason's, 1845.

Bartlet, William S. *The Frontier Missionary: a Memoir of the Life of the Rev. Jacob Bailey, A.M. Missionary at Pownalborough, Maine; Cornwallis and Annapolis, N.S.* Boston: Ide and Dutton, 1853.

Beall, William K. "Journal of William K. Beall, July-August, 1812." *American Historical Review*, July 1912, pp. 783-808.

[Bigelow, Jacob.] *The Wars of the Gulls; an Historical Romance.* New York: The Dramatic Repository, Shakespeare Gallery, 1812.

Bigelow, Timothy. *Journal of a Tour to Niagara Falls in the Year 1805.* Boston: Wilson, 1876.

[Bourne, George.] *Lorette. The History of Louise, Daughter of a Canadian Nun: Exhibiting the Interior of Female Convents.* New York: Mercein, 1833.

———. *The Picture of Quebec.* New York: Bourne, 1830.

Brackenridge, Hugh Henry. *The Death of General Montgomery in the Storming of the City of Quebec. A Tragedy.* Philadelphia: Robert Bell, 1777.

[Bradbury, Osgood.] *Lucelle, or the Young Iroquois! A Tale of the Indian Wars.* Boston: Williams, 1845.

[Browne, Charles F.] *Artemus Ward: His Travels.* New York: Carleton, 1865.

Bryant, William Cullen. *Letters of a Traveller; or, Notes on Things Seen in Europe and America.* 2nd ed. New York: Putnam, 1850.

Cather, Willa. *Shadows on the Rock.* 1931; rpt. New York: Vintage, 1971.

Catherwood, Mary Hartwell. *The Chase of Saint-Castin and Other Stories of the French in the New World.* Boston: Houghton Mifflin, 1894.

———. *The Romance of Dollard.* New York: Century, 1889.

———. *The Lady of Fort St. John.* Boston: Houghton Mifflin, 1892.

———. *The Story of Tonty.* Chicago: McClurg, 1890.

[Cheney, Harriet Vaughan.] *The Rivals of Acadia; an Old Story of the New World.* Boston: Wells and Lilley, 1827.

[Clarke, C. Dunning.] *Despard, The Spy; or, The Fall of Montreal.* Beadle's Dime Novels, No. 172. New York: Beadle, 1869.

———. *Graybeard, The Sorcerer. Or, The Recluse of Mount Royale.* Beadle's New Dime Novels, No. 174. New York: Beadle & Adams, 1874.

———. *The Silent Slayer; or, The Maid of Montreal.* Beadle's Dime Novels, No. 171. New York: Beadle, 1869.

[Clemens, Samuel E.] *Mark Twain's Notebooks & Journals, Vol. II 1877-1883.* Ed. Frederick Anderson *et al.* Berkeley: Univ. of California Press, 1975.

Cockings, George. *The Conquest of Canada: or, The Siege of Quebec. An Historical Tragedy of Five Acts.* Albany: Robertson, 1773.

———. *War; an Heroic Poem, from the Taking of Minorca, by the French; to the Reduction of the Havannah, by the Earle of Albemarle, Sir George Pocock, Ec. The Second Edition, to the Raising of the Siege of Quebec: with Large Amendments, and Additions.* Boston: S. Adams, 1762.

Coffin, Charles Carleton. *The Seat of Empire.* Boston: Osgood, 1871.

Cooper, James Fenimore. *The Last of the Mohicans.* New York: New American Library, 1962.

[Coppinger, John B.] *The Renegade: A Tale of Real Life.* New York: Sherman, 1855.

Cozzens, Frederick S. *Acadia; or, A Month with the Bluenoses.* New York: Derby and Jackson, 1859.

Crèvecoeur, J. Hector St. Jean. *Sketches of Eighteenth-Century America: More "Letters of an American Farmer."* Ed. H. L. Bourdin *et al.* New Haven: Yale Univ. Press, 1925.

Curwood, James Oliver. *The Country Beyond.* New York: McKinlay, Stone & Mackenzie, 1922.

———. "The Effect of the American Invasion." *The World's Work*, Sept. 1905, pp. 6607-13.
———. *God's Country—And the Woman*. Garden City, N.Y.: Doubleday, Page, 1921.
———. *The Valley of Silent Men: A Story of the River Country*. Toronto: Copp Clark, 1923.
Dana, Richard Henry, Jr. *The Journal of Richard Henry Dana, Jr.* Ed. Robert F. Lucid. 3 vols. Cambridge, Mass.: Belknap, 1968.
[de Wallenstein, J.] "Lower Canada." *The North American Review*, July, 1828, pp. 1-30.
Drew, Benjamin. *A North-Side View of Slavery. The Refugee: or, The Narratives of Fugitive Slaves in Canada. Related by Themselves, with an Account of the History and Condition of the Colored Population of Canada*. 1856; rpt. New York: Negro Universities Press, 1968.
Duffey, Owen. *Walter Warren; or, The Adventurer of the Northern Wilds*. New York: Stringer & Townsend, [1854].
[Dwight, Theodore.] *Awful Disclosures of Maria Monk, as Exhibited in a Narrative of her Sufferings, during a Residence of Five Years as a Novice, and Two Years as a Black Nun, in the Hotel Dieu Nunnery at Montreal*. London: the Booksellers, [n.d.].
[———.] *The Northern Traveller, and Northern Tour: with the Routes to the Springs, Niagara, and Quebec, and the Coal Mines of Pennsylvania; also the Tour of New-England*. Rev. ed. New York: Harper, 1831.
Emerson, Ralph Waldo. *The Journals and Miscellaneous Notebooks of Ralph Waldo Emerson*. 16 vols. Ed. William H. Gilman and J. E. Parsons. Cambridge, Mass.: Belknap, 1970.
Emmons, Richard. *The Fredoniad: or, Independence Preserved. An Epick Poem on the Late War of 1812*. 4 vols. Boston: Emmons, 1827.
[Evans], Florence Wilkinson. *The Lady of the Flag-Flowers*. Chicago: Stone, 1899.
Fairchild, G. M., ed. *Journal of an American Prisoner of Fort Malden and Quebec in the War of 1812*. Quebec: Carrel, 1909.
Farnham, Charles Haight. "The Gibraltar of America." *The Century*, Oct. 1882, pp. 840-50.
———. "The Canadian Habitant." *Harper's New Monthly Magazine*, Aug. 1883, pp. 375-92.
———. "A Winter in Canada." *Harper's New Monthly Magazine*, Feb. 1884, pp. 392-408.
———. "Labrador." *Harper's New Monthly Magazine*, Sept. 1885, pp. 489-502; Oct. 1885, pp. 651-66.
———. "Cape Breton Folk." *Harper's New Monthly Magazine*, March 1886, pp. 607-25.

———. "Quebec." *Harper's New Monthly Magazine*, Feb. 1888, pp. 356-73.
———. "Canadian Voyageurs on the Saguenay." *Harper's New Monthly Magazine*, March 1888, pp. 536-56.
———. "The Montagnais." *Harper's New Monthly Magazine*, Aug. 1888, pp. 379-94.
———. "The Lower St. Lawrence." *Harper's New Monthly Magazine*, Nov. 1888, pp. 814-25.
———. "Montreal." *Harper's New Monthly Magazine*, June 1889, pp. 83-98.
"Fidfaddy, Frederick Augustus." *The Adventures of Uncle Sam, in Search after His Lost Honor. By Frederick Augustus Fidfaddy, Esq., Member of the Legion of Honor, Scratch-etary to Uncle Sam, and Privy Counsellor to Himself*. Middletown, Conn.: Seth Richards, 1816.
[French, Alice.] "The Ogre of Ha Ha Bay." In *Knitters in the Sun*, by "Octave Thanet." Boston: Houghton Mifflin, 1887.
Garland, Hamlin. *The Trail of the Goldseekers: A Record of Travel in Prose and Verse*. New York: Macmillan, 1899.
Gates, William. *Recollections of Life in Van Dieman's Land*. 2 vols. Ed. George Mackaness. 1850; rpt. Sydney, Australia: Ford, 1961.
[Godkin, E. L.] "French Canada." *The Nation*, 13 Aug., 1868, pp. 128-29; 20 Aug., 1868, pp. 146-48.
Grant, Robert. *Jack in the Bush; or A Summer on a Salmon River*. Boston: Jordan, Marsh, 1888.
Guest, Moses. *Poems on Several Occasions. To which are Annexed Extracts from a Journal Kept by the Author while he Followed the Sea, and during a Journey from New Brunswick, in New-Jersey, to Montreal and Quebec*. Cincinnati: Looker & Reynolds, 1823.
Gyles, John. "Memoirs of Odd Adventures, Strange Deliverances, &c., in the Captivity of John Gyles, Esq." In *Puritans among the Indians: Accounts of Captivity and Redemption, 1676-1724*. Ed. Alden T. Vaughn and Edward W. Clark. Cambridge, Mass.: Belknap, 1981.
[Hager, C. W.] "'Americanization' of Western Canada." *The Nation*, 2 July 1903, pp. 6-7.
Hall, Charles Winslow. *Twice Taken: An Historical Romance of the Maritime British Provinces*. 1867; rpt. Boston: Lee and Shepard, 1899.
Hamilton, William J. *Mountain Gid, the Free Ranger; or, The Bandit's Daughter*. Beadle's New Dime Novels, No. 103. New York: Beadle and Adams, [1878].
Heckewelder, John. "Journal with the Commissioners to the Indian Treaty." In *Thirty Thousand Miles with John Heckewelder*, ed. Paul. A. W. Wallace. Pittsburgh: Univ. Pittsburgh Press, 1958.
Henson, Josiah. *The Life of Josiah Henson, Formerly a Slave, Now an Inhabitant of Canada, as Narrated by Himself*. 1849; rpt. Dresden, Ont.: Uncle Tom's Cabin & Museum, n.d.

Heustis, Daniel D. *Narrative of the Adventures and Sufferings of Captain Daniel D. Heustis, and His Companions, in Canada and Van Dieman's Land, during a Long Captivity; with Travels in California and Voyages at Sea.* Boston: Wilder, 1847.

Higginson, Thomas Wentworth. *Letters and Journals of Thomas Wentworth Higginson, 1846-1906.* Ed. Mary Thacher Higginson. 1921; rpt. New York: Da Capo Press, 1969.

Holley, O. L., ed. *The Picturesque Tourist; Being a Guide through the Northern and Eastern States and Canada: Giving an Accurate Description of Cities and Villages, Celebrated Places of Resort, etc.* New York: Disturnell, 1844.

Hough, Emerson. *The Sowing: A "Yankee's" View of England's Duty to Herself and to Canada.* Winnipeg: Vanderhoof-Gunn, 1909.

How, Nehemiah. *A Narrative of the Captivity of Nehemiah How in 1745-1747.* Cleveland: Burrows Brothers, 1904.

Howells, William Dean. *A Chance Acquaintance.* Vol. VI of *A Selected Edition of W. D. Howells.* Ed. Jonathan Thomas, David J. Nordloh, and Ronald Gottesman. Bloomington: Indiana Univ. Press, 1971.

[Howells, William Dean.] "Editor's Easy Chair." *Harper's Monthly,* Jan. 1907, pp. 317-20.

Howells, William Dean. *The Quality of Mercy.* Vol. XVIII of *A Selected Edition of W. D. Howells.* Ed. James P. Elliott and David J. Nordloh. Bloomington: Indiana Univ. Press, 1979.

———. *Their Wedding Journey.* Vol. V of *A Selected Edition of W. D. Howells.* Ed. John K. Reeves. Bloomington: Indiana Univ. Press, 1968.

Hoyt, Janet Chase. "Babes in the Wood: Through Maine to Canada in a Birch-Bark Canoe." *Scribner's Monthly,* Aug. 1877, pp. 488-501.

Hunt, Jedediah. *An Adventure on a Frozen Lake: A Tale of the Canadian Rebellion of 1837-8.* Cincinnati: Ben Franklin Book and Job Office, 1853.

Irving, Washington. *The Adventures of Captain Bonneville, U.S.A. in the Rocky Mountains and the Far West.* Ed. Edgeley W. Todd. Norman: Univ. of Oklahoma Press, 1961.

———. *Astoria, or Anecdotes of an Enterprise beyond the Rocky Mountains.* Intro. by William H. Goetzmann. 2 vols. Philadelphia: Lippincott, 1961.

James, Henry. "Francis Parkman: The Jesuits in North America." In *Literary Reviews and Essays on American, English, and French Literature.* Ed. Albert Mordell. New York: Twayne, 1957.

———. "Quebec." In *Portraits of Places.* Boston: Osgood, 1884.

[Jenks, William.] *Memoir of the Northern Kingdom, Written A.D. 1872, By the Late Rev. Williamson Jahnsenykes, Ll.D., and Hon. Member of the Royal American Board of Literature. In Six Letters to His Son. Now First Published, Quebec, A.D. 1901.* [Boston: n.p., 1808].

Jones, James A. *Haverhill; or, Memoirs of an Officer in the Army of Wolfe*. 2 vols. New York: Harper, 1831.

[Jones, Justin.] *Jessie Manton, or The Novice of Sacre-Coeur. A Tale of the Canadian Invasion*. Boston: Jones, 1848.

Kenaston, C. A. "The Great Plains of Canada." *The Century*, Aug. 1892, pp. 565-80.

Knappen, Theodore M. "Western Canada in 1904." *American Monthly Review of Reviews*, Nov. 1904, pp. 578-85.

———. "Winning the Canadian West." *The World's Work*, Sept. 1905, pp. 6596-6606.

Lanman, Charles. *Adventures in the Wilds of the United States and British American Provinces*. 2 vols. Philadelphia: Moore, 1856.

London, Jack. *The Call of the Wild*. New York: Macmillan, 1903.

———. *The Son of the Wolf: Tales of the Far North*. New York: Grosset & Dunlap, 1900.

———. *White Fang*. New York: Macmillan, 1906.

Longfellow, Henry Wadsworth. *Evangeline*. Toronto: McClelland and Stewart, 1962.

Lowell, Robert Traill Spence. *The New Priest in Conception Bay*. Toronto: McClelland and Stewart, 1974.

———. *The Poems of Robert Lowell*. Boston: Dutton, 1864.

———. "A Raft That No Man Made." *Atlantic Monthly*, March 1862, pp. 365-72.

Marble, Manton. "To Red River and Beyond." *Harper's New Monthly Magazine*, Aug. 1860, pp. 289-311; Oct. 1860, pp. 581-606; Feb. 1861, pp. 306-22.

Marcy, Randolph Barnes. "Rupert's Land and Its People." *Harper's New Monthly Magazine*, July 1860, pp. 286-92.

Marsh, Robert. *Seven Years of My Life, or, Narrative of a Patriot Exile. Who Together with Eighty-two American Citizens Were Illegally Tried for Rebellion in Upper Canada in 1838, and Transported to Van Dieman's Land, Comprising a True Account of Our Outrageous Treatment during Ten Months Imprisonment in Upper Canada, and Four Months of Horrible Suffering in a Transport Ship on the Ocean. With a True But Appalling History of Our Cruel and Unmerciful Treatment during Five Years of Unmitigated Suffering on that Detestable Prison Island. Showing, Also, the Cruelty and Barbarity of the British Government to Its Prisoners Generally in That Penal Colony, with a Concise Account of the Island, its Inhabitants, Productions, &c., &c.* Buffalo: Faxon & Stevens, 1848.

Maylem, John. *Gallic Perfidy: A Poem*. Boston: Mecom, 1758.

McSherry, James. *Père Jean, or, The Jesuit Missionary: A Tale of the North American Indians*. Baltimore: J. Murphy, 1847.

Meriwether, Lee. "The Great British Northwest Territory." *The Cosmopolitan*, Nov. 1894, pp. 15-26.

Miller, Linus W. *Notes of an Exile to Van Dieman's Land: Comprising Incidents of* the Canadian Rebellion in *1838, Trial of the Author in Canada, and Subsequent Appearance before Her Majesty's Court of Queen's Bench, in London, Imprisonment in England, and Transportation to Van Dieman's Land.* 1846; rpt. New York: Johnson, 1968.

Mitchell, S. Weir. *When All the Woods Are Green.* 1894; rpt. New York: Century, 1905.

Moffett, Samuel E. *The Americanization of Canada.* Ed. Allan Smith. Toronto: Univ. of Toronto Press, 1972.

Mortimer, Benjamin. "To Fairfield (Moraviantown) in Upper Canada, 1798." In *Thirty Thousand Miles with John Heckewelder.* Ed. Paul A. W. Wallace. Pittsburgh: Univ. of Pittsburgh Press, 1958.

Mullaly, John. *A Trip to Newfoundland: Its Scenery and Fisheries; with an Account of the Laying of the Submarine Telegraph Cable.* New York: Strong, 1855.

Murray, W. H. H. *Continental Unity: An Address... Delivered in Music Hall, Boston... Dec. 13, 1888.* 2nd ed. Boston: Calkins, 1888.

———. *Daylight Land.* Boston: Cupples & Hurd, 1888.

———. *Mamelons and Ungava: A Legend of the Saguenay.* Boston: De Wolfe, Fiske, 1890.

Myers, Peter Hamilton. *The Prisoner of the Border: A Tale of 1838.* New York: Derby & Jackson, 1857.

Noah, Mordecai. "She Would Be a Soldier; or, The Plains of Chippewa." In *Dramas from the American Theatre, 1762-1909.* Ed. Richard Moody. Cleveland: World, 1966.

Noble, Louis L. *After Icebergs with a Painter: A Summer Voyage to Labrador and around Newfoundland.* New York: Appleton, 1861.

Norton, Charles L., and John Habberton. *Canoeing in Kanuckia, or Haps and Mishaps Afloat and Ashore of the Statesman, the Editor, the Artist, and the Scribbler.* New York: Putnam's, 1878.

[Ogden, John Cousens.] *A Tour through Upper and Lower Canada. By a Citizen of the United States. Containing a View of the Present State of Religion, Learning, Commerce, Agriculture, Colonization, Customs and Manners, among the English, French, and Indian Settlements.* Litchfield, Conn.: n.p., 1799.

Ogg, Frederick A. "Vast Undeveloped Regions." *The World's Work,* Oct. 1906, pp. 8078-82.

Parkman, Francis. *France and England in North America.* Vols. I to XII of *Francis Parkman's Works,* Frontenac ed. New York: Scribner's, 1915.

———. *The Oregon Trail: Sketches of Prairie and Rocky Mountain Life.* Vol. XVI of *Francis Parkman's Works,* Frontenac ed. New York: Scribner's, 1915.

Pierce, George W. "Two Weeks' Sport on the Coulonge River." *The Atlantic Monthly,* Sept. 1873, pp. 267-84.

Poe, Edgar Allan. "The Journal of Julius Rodman." Vol. IV of *The Complete Works of Edgar Allan Poe*. Ed. James A. Harrison. 1902; rpt. New York: AMS, 1965.

Ralph, Julian. *On Canada's Frontier: Sketches of History, Sport, and Adventure and of the Indians, Missionaries, Fur-Traders, and Newer Settlers of Western Canada*. New York: Harper, 1892.

[Raymond, George S.] *The Empress of the Isles, or The Lake Bravo. A Romance of the Canadian Struggle in 1837*. New York: Stringer and Townsend, 1853.

Robinson, John Hovey. *Pathaway; or Nick Whiffles, the Old Trapper of the Nor'-West*. Beadle's Dime Library, 1, No. 13, 1878.

Roper, Sydney C. D. "The Wheat Lands of Canada." *Appleton's Popular Science Monthly*, Oct. 1899, pp. 766-77.

Sansom, Joseph. *Sketches of Lower Canada, Historical and Descriptive; with the Author's Recollections of the Soil, and Aspect; the Morals, Habits, and Religious Institutions, of That Isolated Country; during a Tour to Quebec, in the Month of July, 1817*. New York: Kirk & Mercein, 1817.

[Shecut, John Lewis Edward Whitredge.] *Ish-Noo-Ju-Lut-Sche; or, The Eagle of the Mohawks: A Tale of the Seventeenth Century*. 2 vols. New York: Price, 1841.

[———.] *The Scout, or The Fast of St. Nicholas: A Tale of the Seventeenth Century*. New York: Stickney, 1844.

Shrimpton, Charles. *The Black Phantom; or, Woman's Endurance. A Narrative Connected with the Early History of Canada and the American Revolution*. New York: Miller, 1867.

Silliman, Benjamin. *Remarks, Made on a Short Tour, between Hartford and Quebec, in the Autumn of 1819*. New Haven: Converse, 1820.

Snow, Samuel. *Exile's Return: or, Narrative of Samuel Snow, Who Was Banished to Van Dieman's Land, for Participating in the Patriot War in Upper Canada in 1838*. Cleveland: Smead & Cowles, 1846.

Stansbury, Joseph. "To Cordelia." In *The Evolution of Canadian Literature in English: Beginnings to 1867*. Ed. Mary Jane Edwards. Toronto: Holt, Rinehart and Winston, 1973, pp. 5-6.

Stansbury, Philip. *A Pedestrian Tour of Two Thousand Three Hundred Miles in North America. To the Lakes,—the Canadas,—and the New-England States. Performed in the Autumn of 1821*. New York: Myers and Smith, 1822.

Stephens, Ann S. *Ahmo's Plot; or, The Governor's Indian Child*. Beadle's Dime Novels, No. 56. New York: Beadle, 1863.

———. *The Indian Queen*. Beadle's Dime Novels, New Series, No. 186. New York: Beadle, 1864.

———. *Mahaska, The Indian Princess*. Beadle's Dime Novels, No. 63. New York: Beadle, 1863.

Stobo, Robert. *Memoirs of Major Robert Stobo, of the Virginia Regiment*. Pittsburgh: Davidson, 1854.

Stowe, Harriet Beecher. *Dred: A Tale of the Great Dismal Swamp*. Boston: Phillips, Sampson, 1856.

———. *Uncle Tom's Cabin, or Life Among the Lowly*. 2 vols. Boston: Jewett, 1852.

Street, Alfred B. *Frontenac: A Poem*. London: Bentley, 1849.

[Sutherland, Thomas Jefferson.] *Loose Leaves from the Portfolio of a Late Patriot Prisoner in Canada*. New York: Colyer, 1840.

Theller, E. A. *Canada in 1837-38, Showing, by Historical Facts, the Causes of the Late Attempted Revolution and of its Failure; the Present Condition of the People, and Their Future Prospects, Together with the Personal Adventures of the Author, and Others Who Were Connected with the Revolution*. 2 vols. Philadelphia: Anners, 1841.

[Thompson, William Tappan.] *Major Jones's Sketches of Travel: Comprising the Scenes, Incidents, and Adventures, in his Tour from Georgia to Canada*. Philadelphia: Peterson, 1848.

Thoreau, Henry David. *The Journal of Henry David Thoreau*. 1906; rpt. New York: Dover, 1962.

———. *Walden; or, Life in the Woods*. Ed. J. Lyndon Shanley. Princeton: Princeton Univ. Press, 1971.

———. *A Week on the Concord and Merrimack Rivers*. Ed. Carl Hovde et al. Princeton: Princeton Univ. Press, 1980.

———. "A Yankee in Canada." In *Excursions*. Vol. IX of *The Writings of Henry David Thoreau*. Boston: Houghton Mifflin, 1893.

Van Dyke, Henry. *Little Rivers: A Book of Essays in Profitable Idleness*. New York: Scribner's, 1895.

———. "The Red River of the North." *Harper's New Monthly Magazine*, May, 1880, pp. 801-17.

———. *The Ruling Passion: Tales of Nature and Human Nature*. New York: Scribner's, 1901.

———. *The Unknown Quantity: A Book of Romance and Some Half-Told Tales*. New York: Scribner's, 1912.

[Walker, Jesse.] *Fort Niagara; A Tale of the Niagara Frontier*. Buffalo: Steele's, 1845.

[———.] *Queenston; A Tale of the Niagara Frontier*. Buffalo: Steele's, 1845.

Ward, Charles C. "Moose-Hunting." *Scribner's Monthly*, Feb. 1878, pp. 449-65.

Ward, Samuel Ringold. *Autobiography of a Fugitive Negro: His Anti-Slavery Labours in the United States, Canada, & England*. 1855; rpt. New York: Arno, 1968.

Warman, Cy. "Migration to the Canadian Northwest." *American Monthly Review of Reviews*, Sept. 1902, pp. 293-96.

Warner, Charles Dudley. *Baddeck, and That Sort of Thing*. Boston: Osgood, 1874.

———. *Studies in the South and West, with Comments on Canada*. New York: Harper, 1890.

Wasson, David Atwood. "Ice and Esquimaux." *The Atlantic Monthly*, Dec. 1864, 728-34; Jan. 1865, 39-51; Feb. 1865, 201-12; April 1865, 437-48; May 1865, 564-72.

Wheeler, Edward L. *Canada Chet, the Counterfeiter Chief; or, Old Anaconda in Sitting Bull's Camp. A Tale of Two Boys' Adventures*. Beadle's Half Dime Library, 4, No. 92, 29 April 1879.

———. *Deadwood Dick Jr.'s Desperate Strait; or, The Demon Doctor of Dixon's Deposit. A Romance of the North Border Line*. Beadle's Half Dime Library, No. 758, 2 Feb. 1892.

Whitman, Walt. *Diary in Canada, Notebooks, Index*. Vol. III of *Daybooks and Notebooks. The Collected Writings of Walt Whitman*. Ed. William White. New York: New York Univ. Press, 1978.

———. *Specimen Days*. Vol. 1 of *Prose Works 1892*. Ed. Floyd Stovall. *The Collected Writings of Walt Whitman*. New York: New York Univ. Press, 1963.

Wilkinson, A. G. "Notes on Salmon Fishing." *Scribner's Monthly*, Oct. 1876, pp. 769-96.

Williams, Mrs. Catherine A. *The Neutral French: or The Acadians of Nova Scotia*. 2 vols. in one. Providence: the Author, 1841.

Williams, John. "The Redeemed Captive Returning to Zion, or, The Captivity and Deliverance of Rev. John Williams of Deerfield." In *Puritans Among the Indians: Accounts of Captivity and Redemption 1676-1724*. Ed. Alden T. Vaughn and Edward W. Clark. Cambridge, Mass.: Belknap, 1981.

Wilson, Edmund. *O Canada: An American's Notes on Canadian Culture*. New York: Noonday, 1966.

Woodworth, Samuel. *The Champions of Freedom; or, The Mysterious Chief*. 2 vols. New York: Baldwin, 1816.

Secondary Sources

Blodgett, Harold. "Robert Traill Spence Lowell." *New England Quarterly*, Dec. 1943, pp. 578-91.

Brasher, Thomas L. *Whitman as Editor of the Brooklyn Daily Eagle*. Detroit: Wayne State Univ. Press, 1970.

Cadbury, Warder H. "Introduction." *Adventures in the Wilderness* by W. H. H. Murray. Ed. William K. Verner. Syracuse: Adirondack Museum/Syracuse Univ. Press, 1970.

Canby, Henry Seidel. *Thoreau*. Boston: Houghton Mifflin, 1939.

Christie, John A. *Thoreau as World Traveler*. New York: Columbia Univ. Press, 1965.

[Clemens, Samuel L.] *The Innocents Abroad; or, The New Pilgrim's Progress*. 1859; rpt. Hartford: American, 1890.

Craig, Gerald M. *The United States and Canada.* Cambridge, Mass.: Harvard Univ. Press, 1968.

Fiedler, Leslie. *Love and Death in the American Novel.* Rev. ed. New York: Dell, 1966.

Foster, Charles H. "A Study of David Atwood Wasson." *Beyond Concord: Selected Writings of David Atwood Wasson.* Ed. Charles H. Foster. Bloomington: Indiana Univ. Press, 1965.

Gauthier, Joseph-Delphis. *Le Canada français et le roman américain (1826-1948).* Paris: Tolra, 1948.

Guillet, Edwin C. *The Lives and Times of the Patriots: An Account of the Rebellion in Upper Canada, 1837-38, and the Patriot Agitation in the United States, 1837-1842.* 1938; rpt. Toronto: Ontario Publishing, 1963.

Harding, Walter. *A Thoreau Handbook.* New York: New York Univ. Press, 1959.

Hawthorne, Manning, and H. W. L. Dana. *The Origin and Development of Longfellow's "Evangeline".* Portland, Me.: Anthoensen, 1947.

Hedges, James B. *The Building of the Canadian West: The Land and Colonization Policies of the Canadian Pacific Railway.* New York: Macmillan, 1939.

Hough, Franklin B. *A History of St. Lawrence and Franklin Counties, New York, from the Earliest Period to the Present Time.* Albany: Little, 1853.

Howells, William Dean. *Criticism and Fiction, and Other Essays.* Ed. Clara M. Kirk and Rudolf Kirk. New York: New York Univ. Press, 1959.

Johannsen, Albert. *The House of Beadle and Adams and Its Dime and Nickel Novels.* 2 vols. Norman: Univ. of Oklahoma Press, 1950.

Jones, Howard Mumford. *O Strange New World: American Culture: The Formative Years.* New York: Viking, 1964.

Kinchen, Oscar A. *The Rise and Fall of the Patriot Hunters.* New York: Bookman, 1956.

Levin, David. *History as Romantic Art: Bancroft, Prescott, Motley and Parkman.* Stanford: Stanford Univ. Press, 1959.

Lewis, R. W. B. *The American Adam: Innocence, Tragedy and Tradition in the Nineteenth Century.* Chicago: Univ. of Chicago Press, 1955.

Marx, Leo. *The Machine in the Garden: Technology and the Pastoral Ideal in America.* New York: Oxford, 1964.

Matthiessen, F. O. *American Renaissance: Art and Expression in the Age of Emerson and Whitman.* London: Oxford Univ. Press, 1941.

Mott, Frank Luther. *Golden Multitudes: The Story of Best Sellers in the United States.* New York: Macmillan, 1947.

Murray, William H. H. *Adventures in the Wilderness.* Ed William K. Verner. Syracuse: The Adirondack Museum/Syracuse University Press, 1970.

Parkman, Francis. *The Letters of Francis Parkman.* Ed. Wilbur R. Jacobs. 2 vols. Norman: Univ. of Oklahoma Press, 1960.

Paul, Sherman. *The Shores of America: Thoreau's Inward Exploration.* Urbana: Univ. of Illinois Press, 1958.

Schramm, Wilbur L. "Introduction." *Francis Parkman: Representative Selections.* Ed. Wilbur L. Schramm. New York: American Book, 1938.

Smith, Henry Nash. *Virgin Land: The American West as Symbol and Myth.* 1950; rpt. New York: Vintage, 1970.

Spry, Irene M. "Early Visitors to the Canadian Prairies." In *Images of the Plains: The Role of Human Nature in Settlement.* Ed. Brian W. Blouet and Merlin P. Lawson. Lincoln: Univ. of Nebraska Press, 1975.

Taylor, William R. "Francis Parkman." *Pastmasters: Some Essays on American Historians.* Ed. Marcus Cunliffe and Robin W. Winks. New York: Harper & Row, 1969, pp. 1-38.

Troper, Harold Martin. *Only Farmers Need Apply: Official Canadian Encouragement of Immigration from the United States, 1896-1911.* Toronto: Griffin, 1972.

Vitzthum, Richard C. *The American Compromise: Theme and Method in the Histories of Bancroft, Parkman, and Adams.* Norman: Univ. of Oklahoma Press, 1974.

Warner, Donald F. "Drang Nach Norden: The United States and the Riel Rebellion." *The Mississippi Valley Historical Review*, March 1953, pp. 693-712.

Weinberg, A. K. *Manifest Destiny: A Study of Nationalist Expansionism in American History.* 1935; rpt. Chicago: Quadrangle, 1963.

Winks, Robin. *The Blacks in Canada: A History.* Montreal: McGill-Queen's Univ. Press, 1971.

Wright, Lyle H. *American Fiction 1851-1875: A Contribution towards a Bibliography.* San Marino, Calif.: Huntington, 1965.

INDEX

Acadia; or, A Month with the Bluenoses 88-90
Acadian expulsion, the 41-46
Adventure on a Frozen Lake, An 75, 79
Adventures in the Wilderness 114, 135
Adventures in the Wilds 87-88, 114
Adventures of Captain Bonneville, The 26
Adventures of Uncle Sam 19
After Icebergs with a Painter 90-91
Ahmo's Plot 50, 51
American Adam, The 2
American revolution 11-14
Americanization of Canada, The 7, 149
Angel in a Web, An 143
Artemus Ward: His Travels 97
Astoria 25-26
Aunay (Aulnay), Charles d' 50, 69
Autobiography of a Fugitive Negro 83
Awful Disclosures of Maria Monk 24

"Babes in the Wood" 116
Bacon, Delia Salter 50
Baddeck, and That Sort of Thing 3, 97-98
Badger, Joseph E. 131, 132
Bailey, Jacob 16
Bancroft, George 41-44, 57
Barker, Benjamin 25
Beall, William K. 19

"Beauport Loup-Garou, The"   55
Bigelow, Jacob   19
Bigelow, Timothy   17
Bourne, George   24
Brackenridge, Hugh Henry   13
Bradbury, Osgood   53
Brant, Joseph   17
Brasher, Thomas L.   127
Browne, Charles F. ("Artemus Ward")   97
Bryant, William Cullen   87
Bucke, Richard Maurice   125
Burroughs, John   114-15

Call of the Wild, The   147-48
Canada Chet   132-33
Canada français et le roman américain, Le   2
Canada in 1837-38   75, 77
"Canadian Habitant, The"   122
"Canadian Voyageurs on the Saguenay"   122
Canoeing in Kanuckia   116
Cape Cod   33
Captivity narratives   9-10
Cartier, Jacques   66
Casgrain, Abbé   61
"Castine"   50
Cather, Willa   150
Catherwood, Mary Hartwell   54-56, 58, 62
Cecilia; or, The White Nun of the Wilderness   25
Champions of Freedom, The   19
Champlain, Samuel de   62
Chance Acquaintance, A   104, 109-10
Chase of Saint-Castin, The   54
Cheney, Harriet Vaughan   50
"Civil Disobedience"   38
Clarke, C. Dunning (W. J. Hamilton)   53
Clemens, Samuel E. ("Mark Twain")   97, 98, 136
"Clewline, Charley" (George S. Raymond)   79
Cockings, George   10-11, 13
Coffin, Charles C.   134-35
"Comments on Canada"   7, 138-40
Conquest of Canada, The   10-11
Cooper, James Fenimore   47-49, 53-54, 58, 80
Coppinger, John B.   86
Count Frontenac and New France under Louis XIV   59-60

Covered Wagon, The   7
Cozzens, Frederick S.   88-90
Craig, Gerald M.   8
Crèvecoeur, Hector St. Jean de   14
Criticism and Fiction   104
Curwood, James Oliver   132, 144, 149-50

Dana, Richard Henry   1, 30-31
Danger Trail, The   150
Daulac (Dollard), Adam   63
Daylight Land   7, 135-37
Deadwood Dick Jr.'s Desperate Strait   132
Death of General Montgomery, The   13
Death Trailer   131, 132
Democracy in America   12
Despard, the Spy   53
"Diary in Canada"   125-29
Discovery of the Great West, The   59
Dred   82
Drew, Benjamin   84
Duffey, Owen   85
Dwight, Theodore   24

"Editor's Easy Chair"   111-12
Eliot, Samuel A.   83
Emerson, Ralph Waldo   4, 74
Emmons, Richard   20
Empress of the Isles, The   79-80
"En Passant"   103
Evangeline   1, 41, 44-46, 85, 88
Evans, Florence Wilkinson   120
Exile's Return: or, Narrative of Samuel Snow   75, 78
Farnham, Charles Haight   121-24
"Fidfaddy, Frederick Augustus"   19
Fiedler, Leslie   51
Fort Niagara   73
France and England in North America   1, 57-71, 99
Fredoniad, The   20
French, Alice ("Octave Thanet")   117
"French Canada" (E. L. Godkin)   99-101
Frontenac: A Poem   50, 51
Frontenac, governor of New France   50-51, 65

Gallic Perfidy   10

Garland, Hamlin   7, 144-47
Gates, William   75, 77
Gauthier, Joseph-Delphis   2
"Gibraltar of America, The"   121
Gilded Age, The   139
"Glimpses of Summer Travel"   103
Godkin, E. L.   99-101
Grant, Robert   117
Graybeard, the Sorcerer   53
"Great Plains of Canada, The"   144
Gyles, John   10

Habberton, John   116
"Halcyon in Canada, The"   114-15
Half-Century of Conflict, A   60, 65
Hall, Charles W.   53
Hamilton, W. J. (C. Dunning Clarke)   53, 131, 133
Haverhill   52
Heckewelder, John   16-17
Hedges, James B.   135
Henry, Alexander   33-34
Henry, John Joseph   12
Henson, Josiah   82-83
Heustis, Daniel D.   75, 78-79
Higginson, Thomas Wentworth   74
History of the United States   41, 42-44, 57
Hough, Emerson   7
Howells, William Dean   1, 99, 103-12
Hoyt, Janet Chase   116
Hunt, Jedediah   75, 79

"Ice and Esquimaux"   91-92, 114
Indian Queen, The   50
Innocents Abroad, The   97, 136
Irving, Washington   25-26
Ish-Noo-Ju-Lut-Sche   52
Jack in the Bush   117-18
"Jahnsenykes, Williamson" (William Jenks)   18
James, Henry   99, 101-03, 126
Jenks, William ("Williamson Jahnsenykes")   18
Jessie Manton, or The Novice of Sacre-Coeur   25
Jesuits in North America, The   59, 63-64, 66, 68
Jones, Howard Mumford   2
Jones, James A.   52

Jones, Justin   25
Journal of an American Prisoner   19
"Journal of Julius Rodman, The"   26-27

Klondike Gold Rush   144-49
Knitters in the Sun, The   117

La Salle and the Discovery of the Great West   59, 67, 69-70
La Tour, Charles de   50, 69
"Labrador" (Farnham)   122
Lady of Fort St. John, The   54, 55, 56
Lady of the Flag-Flowers, The   120
Lanman, Charles   87-88, 114
Last of the Mohicans, The   48-49, 53
Leaves of Grass   127, 128
Letters of a Traveller   87
Lewis, R. W. B.   2, 40
Life of Josiah Henson   82-83
Literary Friends and Acquaintance   103
Little Rivers   116
Locusts and Wild Honey   114
London, Jack   147-49
Lone Chief, The   131, 132
Longfellow, Henry Wadsworth   1, 3, 41, 44-46, 85, 88
Loose Leaves from the Portfolio of a Late Patriot Prisoner   75, 78
Lorette. The History of Louise   24
Love and Death in the American Novel   51
Lowell, Robert Traill Spence   93-95
"Lower St. Lawrence, The"   122
Loyalist writers   14-16
Lucelle, or The Young Iroquois!   53

Machine in the Garden, The   2
McSherry, James   53-54
Mahaska   50
Main-Travelled Roads   144
Maine Woods, The   33, 92
Major Jones's Sketches of Travel   1, 3, 28-30
Marble, Manton   134
Marcy, Randolph B.   134
Maria Monk and the Nunnery of the Hotel Dieu   25
Marsh, Robert   75, 77-78
Marx, Leo   2
Matthiessen, F. O.   126

Maylem, John   10
Memoir of the Northern Kingdom   18
Memoirs of Odd Adventures   9-10
Miller, Linus W.   75, 76-77
Mitchell, S. Weir   117, 118-19
Modern Instance, A   109
Moffett, Samuel E.   7, 149
"Montagnais, The"   122
Montcalm and Wolfe   60, 61
Montcalm, Marquis de   48-49
"Montreal" (Farnham)   121
"Moose-Hunting"   116
Mortimer, Benjamin   16-17
Mountain Gid, the Free Ranger   131
Mullaly, John   90
Murray, W. H. H.   7, 114, 135-37
Myers, P. Hamilton   80-81

Narrative of the Adventures and Sufferings   75
Narrative of the Captivity of Nehemiah How, The   10
"Nature"   4
Neutral French, The   41-42
New Priest in Conception Bay, The   93-95
"Newfoundland" (poem by R. T. S. Lowell)   93
Noah, Mordecai   19-20
Noble, Louis L.   90
North American Review, The   23
Northern Traveller, The   23
North-Side View of Slavery, A   84
Norton, Charles L.   116
Notes of an Exile to Van Dieman's Land   75, 76-77
"Notes on Salmon Fishing"   115

O Canada   150
O Strange New World   2
Ogden, John Cousens   14-15, 31
"Ogre of Ha Ha Bay, The"   117
Old Regime in Canada, The   59, 63, 64, 65, 66, 67, 69
On Canada's Frontier   7, 141-42
Oregon Trail, The   27-28
Our Great West   141, 142

Parkman, Francis   1, 3, 11, 27-28, 39, 54-71, 85, 99, 101, 106, 121
Pathaway   131-32, 133

Pathfinder, The 48
People We Pass 143
Père Jean 53-54
Picture of Quebec, The 24
Picturesque Tourist, The 73
Pierce, George W. 115
Pioneers of France in the New World 59, 60, 62, 66
Poe, Edgar Allan 26-27
Portraits of Places 101
Prisoner of the Border, The 80-81

Quality of Mercy, The 110-11
"Quebec" (Farnham) 121
"Quebec" (James) 101-03
Queenston 73-74

"Raft That No Man Made, A" 94-95
Ralph, Julian 7, 140-43
Ramsey, Alexander 134
Raymond, George S. ("Charley Clewline") 79
Rebellion of 1837-38 75-81
Recollections of Life in Van Dieman's Land 75, 77
Redeemed Captive Returning to Zion, The 9
Remington, Frederic 141
Renegade, The 86-87
Reynolds, James 19
Riel rebellions 135
Rivals of Acadia, The 50
Robinson, John Hovey 131, 133
Romance of Dollard, The 54-56, 58, 62
Roosevelt, Theodore 114
Ruling Passion, The 116

Saint-Castin, Baron 64-65
Sansom, Joseph 21-23
Scout, The 52
Seat of Empire, The 135
Seven Years of My Life 75, 77-78
Shadows on the Rock 150
She Would Be a Soldier 20
Shecut, J. L. E. W. 52-53
Silent Slayer, The 53
Sketches of Lower Canada 21
Smith, Henry Nash 2

Snow, Samuel   75, 78
Son of the Wolf, The   147
"Song of Myself"   125, 127
Sowing, The   7
Stansbury, Joseph   15
Stansbury, Philip   23
Stegner, Wallace   150
Stephens, Ann   50-51
Stobo, Robert   10
Stocking, Abner   12
Stone, William Leete   25
Story of Tonty, The   54-56
Stowe, Harriet Beecher   81-82
Street, Alfred B.   50-51
Studies in the South and West, with Comments on Canada   137
Sutherland, Thomas Jefferson   75, 78

Tales of the Puritans   50
Taylor, William R.   70
"Thanet, Octave" (Alice French)   117
Their Wedding Journey   1, 104-09, 111
Theller, E. A.   75, 77
Therien, Alek   34-35
Thompson, William Tappan   1, 28-30
Thoreau, Henry   1, 32-40, 57, 58, 66, 85, 91-92, 99, 122, 126
"To Cordelia"   15
"To Red River and Beyond"   134
Tocqueville, Alexis de   12
Tour through Upper and Lower Canada, A   14-15
Trail of the Goldseekers, The   7, 144-46
Travels and Adventures in Canada and the Indian Territories   34
Travels in Lower Canada   21-23
Trip to Newfoundland, A   90
Turner, Frederick Jackson   147
Twain, Mark (Clemens, Samuel E.)   97, 98, 136
Twice Taken   53
"Two Weeks' Sport on the Coulonge River"   115
Two Years before the Mast   30

Uncle Tom's Cabin   81-82
Unknown Quantity, The   116

Valley of Silent Men, The   150
Van Dyke, Henry   116-17, 134

Virgin Land 2

Walden 34, 35, 92
Walker, Jesse 73
Walter Warren 85-86
War; an Heroic Poem 10-11
War of 1812 18-20
"Ward, Artemus" (Charles F. Browne) 97
Ward, Charles C. 116
Ward, Samuel 83
Warner, Charles Dudley 3, 7, 97-98, 137-40
Wars of the Gulls, The 19
Wasson, David A. 91-92, 114
Week on the Concord and Merrimack Rivers, A 33-34
Weinberg, A. K. 137
Wheeler, Edward L. 132-33
When All the Woods Are Green 117, 118-19
White Fang 148
Whitman, Walt 124-30
Wilkinson, A. G. 115
Williams, Catherine 41
Williams, John 9, 10
Wilson, Edmund 113, 150
"Winter in Canada, A" 121
Wolf Willow 150
Woodworth, Samuel 19

"Yankee in Canada, A" 1, 32-40, 99

185